"The Jim Crow Museum was founded by the intrepic
David Pilgrim with the mission to display in unflinch
scaffolding of the Jim Crow system. By encountering its astonishing array
of tangible objects, from the stereotypical to the horrifying to the searingly
symbolic, those coming of age as students and visitors today learn to
recognize what was while remaining vigilant about the residues that remain.
Undergirding Pilgrim's effort is his powerful belief that we, as a society, heal
better when we stare down the evils that have walked among us, together. The
Jim Crow Museum at Ferris State University is one of the most important
contributions to the study of American history that I have ever experienced."
—Henry Louis Gates Jr., Alphonse Fletcher University Professor, Harvard University

"This was a horrific time in our history, but it needs to be taught
and seen and heard. This is very well done, very well done."
—Malaak Shabazz, daughter of Malcolm X and Betty Shabazz on the Jim Crow Museum

"The museum's contents are only a small part of the damaging effects of the
Jim Crow laws that were found all across America, including bright and
sunny California. This history is not only an important part of understanding
where America was but, in an age of states making it harder and harder
for citizens to vote, it is relevant to note that we have been here before."
—Henry Rollins, host of the History Channel's *10 Things You Don't Know About*

"In its compelling reimagination of the museum experience, the
Jim Crow Museum of Racist Memorabilia leverages the potential
of museums to effect positive social change in a troubled world. By
creating a forum for the safe exchange of ideas, Jim Crow transforms
its campus and the world it inhabits, one visit at a time. Through its
collections, exhibitions, and public programs, Jim Crow both sets and
exceeds a gold standard for the next generation of museums."
—Bradley L. Taylor, associate director, Museum Studies Program, University of Michigan

"There has not been any time in the history of African Americans that we
have not faced full frontal attack and been depicted in negative, stereotypical
fashion. One would hope that after almost four hundred years there would
be a decrease in these painful characterizations. Unfortunately these demons
are not only still evident but may even be worse. Pilgrim's book is a well-
researched, comprehensive, and ever-present documentation of where we've
been and where we still are. All of America needs to confront these injustices
in order to put them where they belong, in the past, not the present."
—Philip J. Merrill, CEO and founder of Nanny Jack & Co.

"This is a horrifying but important book that should be widely read to gain an accurate view of the long history of racism in the U.S."
—Barbara H. Chasin, *Socialism and Democracy*, on *Understanding Jim Crow*

"For decades the author has been on a Pilgrimage to bring out from our dank closets the racial skeletons of our past. His is a crucial mission, because he forces us to realize that race relations grew worse in the first several decades of the twentieth century—something many Americans never knew or now want to suppress. This book allows us to see, even feel the racism of just a generation or two ago—and Pilgrim shows that elements of it continue, even today. See it! Read it! Feel it! Then help us all transcend it!"
—James W. Loewen, author of *Lies My Teacher Told Me* on *Understanding Jim Crow*

"To justify the exclusion of and violence toward African Americans after the Civil War, pop culture churned out objects, images, songs, and stories designed to reinforce widespread beliefs about white supremacy and black inferiority. Pilgrim has pulled together examples of such so-called black memorabilia, and he clearly explains the meaning and purpose behind them."
—Lisa Hix, *Collectors Weekly*, on *Understanding Jim Crow*

"This heavily illustrated book is a memoir of the author's decades-long drive to collect racist books, illustrations, and knickknacks in order to help Americans confront, understand, and move past racism."
—Jan Gardner, *Boston Globe*, on *Understanding Jim Crow*

"*Understanding Jim Crow* contains examples of racist memorabilia. . . . However, it is Pilgrim's thoughtful and passionately told story that makes the book more than just another, albeit unique, history of U.S. racism."
—Bill Berkowitz, truth-out.org, on *Understanding Jim Crow*

"An amazing, wonderful, and important book whose objects and images may offend some readers. Highly recommended for all public and academic levels/libraries."
—F.W. Gleach, *CHOICE*, on *Understanding Jim Crow*

Watermelons, Nooses, and Straight Razors

Stories from the Jim Crow Museum

David Pilgrim

Watermelons, Nooses, and Straight Razors: Stories from the Jim Crow Museum
David Pilgrim
Copyright © 2018 PM Press
All rights reserved. No part of this book may be transmitted by any means without permission
in writing from the publisher.

ISBN: 978-1-62963-437-1

LCCN: 2017942911

Cover by John Yates/Stealworks
Interior design by briandesign

10 9 8 7 6 5 4 3 2 1

PM Press
PO Box 23912
Oakland, CA 94623
www.pmpress.org

Printed in the USA by the Employee Owners of Thomson-Shore in Dexter, Michigan.
www.thomsonshore.com

Contents

Dedication

Watermelons, Nooses, and Straight Razors: Stories from the Jim Crow Museum is dedicated to my children: Haley Grace, Gabrielle Lynne, and Eustace Jamison. I write what I write because I want them to live in a better America—and I believe a better America is possible.

Acknowledgments

A good colleague is silver, a good friend is gold. Both are precious. The colleagues who helped me with this book are also friends. Fran Rosen provided valuable editorial assistance. Franklin Hughes, who reminds me of J.A. Rogers, offered important critiques and direction. Lisa Kemmis helped locate images for the book. Patty Terryn worked with me to prepare the iterations of the manuscript that were sent to PM Press.

I owe the greatest debt to Margaret Elizabeth, my wife, partner, and ally. We held each other and cried tears of joy and hope when Barack Obama was sworn in as the forty-fourth president of the United States. Eight years later we cried again, different tears. Any good that I do is done with her encouragement and help.

Studying the Past in Search of Present-Day Healing

In 1983, I graduated from college with a history degree. My desire to study the past sprang from my belief that it held critical lessons for the future. The department teemed with passionate professors. The library shelves groaned with research books and periodicals. The curriculum offered more than I could squeeze into my course load. At the time I would have told you the department lacked nothing. Yet in 2017 I am appalled by the limitations of the education I received.

This is not to point fingers at my college, which, like most colleges and universities in the United States, takes its cues from a broader U.S. culture rife with an intentional and unintentional denial that allows for one-sided history telling and vigorous mythmaking. Though I learned about Christopher Columbus and the European context of his pursuits, I did not learn about his history of atrocities toward his own men or the impact of his "discovery" on indigenous peoples. Though we explored the concept of bias in interpreting and recording history, never was I asked to consider whose perspectives might be missing altogether. Also notable to me now is the absence of heart that permeated my education. A simple question such as "What would it feel like to have ships full of foreigners invading your hometown?" would have created a human connection that might have driven me to seek a range of perspective while reflecting on my own.

Reading *Watermelons, Nooses, and Straight Razors* offers a prime example of how crucial the telling of unglossed history can be. It is precisely the kind of material my high-class education lacked. Not only do the stories contained in this book add dimension to my understanding of the black experience past and present, they advance my understanding of the white experience that shaped and continues to shape dominant United States culture and beliefs. As I absorbed what I didn't know that I didn't know, new questions arose, questions that have opened both my mind and my heart.

As you read the pages ahead, I wonder if you, like me, will unearth questions about the present-day impacts of unacknowledged actions that can only be labeled as terrorism? Will you ask yourself what it means to be human? And what it takes to be dehumanized? Will you wonder about the ongoing psychological and material costs of the stereotypes of the black brute pulsing through the dominant U.S. narrative? Will you question what gets filed away in the heart and mind when glimpsing a black lawn jockey? Or consider how many times you've used a word that retraumatizes someone in your midst? Will you wonder about your own capacity to otherize a fellow human being? In the end, will you lay the book down and mourn for our broken human family, divided and torn through the legacy of white supremacy? And will you then wonder: Where do we go from here?

Of all the issues and questions *Watermelons, Nooses, and Straight Razors* has raised for me, the most nagging is: What drives some human beings to find satiation in cruelty and torture? It's one thing to ingest a false myth that shapes a belief that black men pose a danger to society. It's something else entirely to pack that belief with a supersonic charge of hatred and contempt, one so fierce that it justifies skinning, raping, bone crushing, flogging, dismembering, burning, and lynching. How might understanding the human capacity to otherize and persecute equip us to manage such urges and instead cultivate empathy in our common humanity?

Far from a recording of an isolated past, Pilgrim's book offers connections to present day racial issues and images. Reading about Jim Crow–era profiteering from the abduction and containment of black men reminds me of the ongoing perpetration that exists today in the form of mass incarceration. Learning more about the pack-like behavior entangled in Jim Crow community lynchings conjures images of baton-wielding police swarming a defenseless black man curled on the ground. The random selection of which black man might become fodder for ruthless treatment shakes me with the state of perpetual fear it necessarily creates. Justifying brutal and inhumane practices with a false narrative that "good" white citizens must be protected against the "bad" black man remains central to U.S. racial lore. Repeatedly I felt the hypocrisy of the uninterrupted U.S. narrative about who is savage and who is civilized.

In addition to finding myself unable to divide the past from the present, I found myself unable to separate the damage done to victims and their communities from the sickness propagated in perpetrators and their communities. Each spirit-crushing, life-ending act of terror lives on the damaged souls of perpetrators. That many individuals of the Jim Crow era may no longer be alive does not diminish, in my mind, the toxic energy of our shared dehumanized past. One aspect of the suppression of real and detailed Jim Crow history is that it allows stereotypes and artifacts to take on lives of their own, perpetuating ideas that distort who people really are, thereby keeping us from authentically relating across racial lines. Another aspect of the suppression of real and detailed Jim Crow history is an utter inability to move toward the kind of healing necessary to live up to the democratic ideals the *United* States espouses. Reading *Watermelons, Nooses, and Straight Razors* reminded me that four hundred years into the "American Experiment," signs of injustice are all around us, yet they have become so normalized that they are seen as artifacts of an American past not the markers of an open wound in search of a salve.

Instead, amid cultural denial, it is mostly extreme racial flare-ups that grab national attention, and even then are too easily written off as isolated events as opposed to predictable symptoms of an unacknowledged, unhealed past. In 2015, Dylann Roof repeated the American racial tradition of swallowing whole the myth of the black brute and using violence to discharge the fear and rage it stoked in him. After falling for a barrage of online photos of white people purportedly killed by black people, Roof stepped into the Emanuel AME Church in Charleston, South Carolina, and assumed the historical role of randomly targeting and killing black Americans—nine to be exact—worshipers who'd welcomed Roof into their evening prayer circle.

For white people, the Charleston massacre may have appeared to be an isolated act of violence, a lone wolf incident. For black communities, however, it served as a traumatizing reminder of an uninterrupted pattern of white propaganda followed by violence toward black bodies. Just as one hundred years earlier D.W. Griffith's film *The Birth of a Nation* stoked and promoted white fear of black men through false images, a website Dylann Roof stumbled upon stoked and promoted the same uninterrupted narrative. The promulgation of racial fear based on false characterization is as much an American tradition as baseball. The stories within *Watermelons, Nooses, and Straight Razors* bring me closer to understanding the roots of America's fear-based, antiblack mythology.

An idea that has long intrigued me is that all human emotion can be traced back to love or fear, those being the two fundamental emotions from which all others stem. Isn't fear the emotion that breeds and continues to perpetuate racial hatred and mistrust? The degree of American divisiveness we are witnessing today is not just born of an inherent us vs. them tribalism; it's a predictable outgrowth of a planted fear of other, of missing history, of fabricated history, of missing voices, and of a lack of emotional stamina to dig deep and root out the individual and collective woundedness that all of that has spawned.

Though *Watermelons, Nooses, and Straight Razors* might suggest a collection of isolated artifacts, in fact it offers insight to an epic tragedy born of white supremacist philosophy and reproduced by good people unaware of hushed history. Mother Teresa once said, "We have forgotten that we belong to each other." I'd add that we have forgotten that we were taught to hate and fear one another. We have forgotten that a requirement of fearing and hating another human being is a denial of one's own capacity for compassion and empathy. We have forgotten that in the stew of hate-based emotions, there is no room for love of self or other. Instead we get a stomach-churning pit to be filled with contempt for self and other. Some may feel that raising a history as grisly as that of Jim Crow is a dangerous exposure. I believe it is far more dangerous not to bring this chapter of U.S. history in to the light of day. For people young and old, of all races and ethnicities, understanding the world we've inherited is essential to creating the world we envision for our descendants.

Debby Irving
author of *Waking Up White, and Finding Myself in the Story of Race*

First Words

> **"You'd better tell**
> **Your story fast/**
> **And if you lie**
> **It will come to pass."**
> —Stevie Wonder[1]

Cleotis Threadgill was a good man—a decent, hardworking man. Though he did not say it to others, he believed that hard work was a way—in fact, the best way—to honor God. Cleotis preferred to work on the Alabama State Docks, but those jobs were not always available, so most days he did odd jobs for white people: mowing lawns, painting, roofing, hauling trash, tearing down and rebuilding sheds, and gathering pecans. The jobs did not pay much. And, truth be told, though he had never complained, he resented being paid a few dollars for work that should have earned him more. Thirty-plus years of menial labor had earned him precious little except his daily meals and a jalopy that sat in the dirt road in front of his small house. Cleotis wanted more, and it was the desire for more that prompted him to talk in a way that got black men killed in the early 1950s in the Deep South.

Cleotis had for several days gathered buckets of pecans for Sam Ryan, the white owner of an orchard that supplied local businesses. It was sweaty, back-straining work. At the end of each day the pecans were weighed and the pickers were paid. Cleotis usually gathered more pecans than the other workers and, therefore, was paid more. One day all the workers received the same amount, the paltry sum of three dollars.

Cleotis knew that it made sense—Jim Crow sense—to say nothing, take the money, and walk away. But on that day, standing in an Alabama pecan orchard, he complained. "I picked more than the others." Sam ignored him. Cleotis looked the white man in the eyes and said, "I think I earned more than this." Sam said, "You got what you deserve," then he threw the money to the ground. "It seems like you calling me a liar, nigger." Cleotis did not respond. He stooped, picked up the three bills, and left.

That night Cleotis told his friends about the argument. They encouraged him to leave the city until the white man cooled down. Cleotis didn't understand why he should have to run away—he had, after all, only asked for a fair wage. He had not hit the white man or even threatened to hit him. His friends persisted. Cleotis packed clothes into the old car. As he was pulling away he passed a car of white men, including Sam. They recognized him and gave chase, all the while shouting taunts, "We're gonna get you, nigger!" and "Get that black son of a bitch!" They chased him for several miles, until Cleotis's car stopped. He leapt from the heap and ran through a wooded area. The men stopped their car and gave chase on foot. A man runs fast when he is running for his life. After twenty minutes or so the white men gave up. They had meant to beat him, to stomp him, to cut him, to hang his dead body from a tree, but he had gotten away. The white men were so angry they lynched Cleotis's car.

The story about Cleotis Threadgill was told to me—well, told in my presence—by old black men who sat on the porch that surrounded a neighborhood store. The story scared me. I was only eight or nine years old, too young to recognize it as an apocryphal tale, a fictional anecdote that we might today call an urban legend. I didn't know many white people. None lived in the section of Prichard, Alabama, where we lived. I believed that the story was true, and I wondered what the white men in the car might do to me.

Today I understand that the story of Cleotis Threadgill was a way for those men to make sense of and talk about the horrific crime of lynching. Born and raised during the Jim Crow period, they knew that lynchings had occurred and were still possible in the 1960s when they told the story. They may have known the story of Elton Mitchell of Earle, Arkansas, who in 1918 refused to work on a white-owned farm without pay. The prominent white citizens of the city cut him into pieces with butcher knives and hung what was left from a tree.[2]

Maybe they had heard of the Reverend T.A. Allen, who was lynched in 1935, in Hernando, Mississippi, for trying to start a sharecroppers' union for exploited black workers like the fictional Cleotis Threadgill.[3] Maybe they knew the story of Jesse Thornton, who was beaten and shot to death in 1940 for failing to say "Mister" when he referred to a white man. It is

This is a single-sheet greeting card, no publisher or date.

2

GREETINGS

MASSAS' IN DE COLD COLD GROUND

156

3

The Jim Crow Museum staff continues to buy racist objects. This photograph was taken at the National Black Memorabilia, Fine Art & Craft Show in Gaithersburg, Maryland, in 2014.

likely that they knew about Emmett Louis Till, the fourteen-year-old boy who was beaten, had his eyes gouged out, and was shot through the head after he was falsely accused of flirting with and grabbing a white woman.[4] And I believe they knew the story of the nine African American teenagers known as the Scottsboro Boys, who were falsely accused of raping two white women in 1931.

While doing the research for this book, I came to understand Prichard's long ugly racial history, a history that included lynchings. In 1906, Jim Robinson and Will Thompson, two African Americans accused of raping white women, were taken from a sheriff by men wearing masks. A large, heavily armed mob watched as the two men were hanged. One newspaper ran the headline "A Quiet Lynching," because the bodies of Robinson and Thompson were not riddled with bullets. That same newspaper argued that the lynching was a public service because had the suspects received a trial the white populations of Prichard and Mobile would have rioted.[5] A year later, Mose Dossett, another African American male, was accused of attempting to rape an elderly white woman. He too was lynched from the same oak tree that had held the swaying bodies of Robinson and Thompson—a tree near my neighborhood. We do not know if they were innocent or guilty. None of the black men received a trial, and none of their lynchers were ever arrested.

In January 1968, the white citizens of Prichard, with the aid of the John Birch Society, violently opposed the desegregation of the local public schools. A speeding carful of whites shot down two African American pedestrians in separate incidents. Jerry Pogue, a Southern Christian Leadership Conference leader, was one of many black people who marched in support of the proposed desegregation. He carried a large American flag. A white man took the flag from Pogue and stabbed him in the head with the metal eagle on the flagstaff. Groups of whites clubbed black people who marched in support of desegregation. Later that year the body of a black man, E.C. Deloach, was found hanging head down from the roof of an abandoned school in the section of Prichard where we lived. The mayor, V.O. Capps, said, "As far as we know, there are no racial overtones."[6] This was near the time that the old men told me the story of Cleotis Threadgill.

The stories we tell express a great deal about their subjects—and about ourselves. The Cleotis Threadgill story revealed a kind of matter-of-fact scorn toward and distrust of white people. This hostility was, in part, a defensive response to years of being mistreated by white people, especially whites with money and influence; but it was also a product of living in a segregated half-world shaped by everyday poverty. Many of the white people who shared our city—though not our neighborhoods—were pitiable, with a level of poverty that Americans often associated with Third World countries. These were the other men in the car with Sam Ryan. Yes, they were white in a nation that favored white people, but they were poorly educated and paid starvation wages. Many were dirty and smelled of dock work. They did not have the power and privilege of middle-class, "respectable" whites, so they were summarily dismissed as "trash." They were stereotyped as "Wretched Others"—nasty, lazy, ignorant. And this sentiment was shared by middle-class whites and poor blacks. The same men who told the Cleotis Threadgill story also said of poor whites, "They are pathetic. If you can't make it as a white man then you really are shit." Those black men hated all white people: those with money and those who did the bidding of the ones who had money.

The stories we are told as children may become central to our sense of self. The Cleotis Threadgill story was instructive, a warning to a young boy to be alert, vigilant, careful in dealings with white people. Cleotis was a highly memorable character, and even after I came to understand that he was fictional, I understood that he was a symbol of real hurt suffered by real people. The story helped me to construct my identity as a black person coming of age in the last years of Jim Crow.

In 2003, I had the opportunity to "debate" Christopher Bing, an awarding-winning illustrator. Bing had recently reintroduced the children's book *Little Black Sambo*.[7] The story, a onetime favorite of children in this country, was written by Helen Bannerman, an English woman living in India at the dawning of the twentieth century. She wrote the story to amuse her two little girls. The tale, set in India, is about a boy named Little Black Sambo who lives with his mother, Black Mumbo, and his father, Black Jumbo. His mother made the boy a beautiful red coat and a pair of handsome trousers. His father bought him a green umbrella and a pair of purple shoes. Little Black Sambo struts through the jungle. He has several encounters with tigers. Each time he surrenders a piece of his clothing or an accessory in exchange for not being eaten. The tigers turn on each other in a jealous rage. They take off the clothing and begin to claw one another. They end in a circle, each tiger's tail in the mouth of another tiger. They spin, faster and faster, until they disappear into a clump of butter. Black Jumbo, coming home from work, happens upon the butter and takes it to Black Mumbo. She uses the butter to help make more than a hundred pancakes. Little Black Sambo gets his clothes back and his family enjoys a feast.

Bannerman's *Little Black Sambo* was first published in 1899, quickly found an audience, and was reprinted in the United States the next year. She did not copyright her work, so American publishers were free to do with the story what they pleased—and it pleased them to substitute grotesquely caricatured black characters in place of Bannerman's caricatured Indian family. And, of course, some of the American versions of *Little Black Sambo* replaced the original text with supposed Negro dialect. The books were immensely popular for several decades. In the 1940s and 1950s, the NAACP waged a campaign to remove the book from this country's classrooms, but by that time the image of Little Black Sambo was a well-established piece of darky iconography promoted with board games, printed cartoons, musical records, toys, public murals, and movie cartoons. The term "Sambo" did not originate with the book, but *Little Black Sambo* helped to popularize it as a racial slur akin to "darky," "coon," or "pickanniny" directed at black people, especially males with dark skin.

Bing and I were interviewed on the National Public Radio program *All Things Considered* in 2003. He explained his nostalgic connection with the book. As a child he sat, listening intently, admiringly, as his grandfather read the story. He imagined himself as Little Black Sambo, a clever little boy who outwitted ferocious tigers. During the interview he said, "The book to me means love." He published his version of *Little Black Sambo* hoping to introduce a new generation of children of all races to the little black boy whom he admired. He dedicated the book to his

Sheet music, words by John Queen, music by Hughie Cannon, 1901.

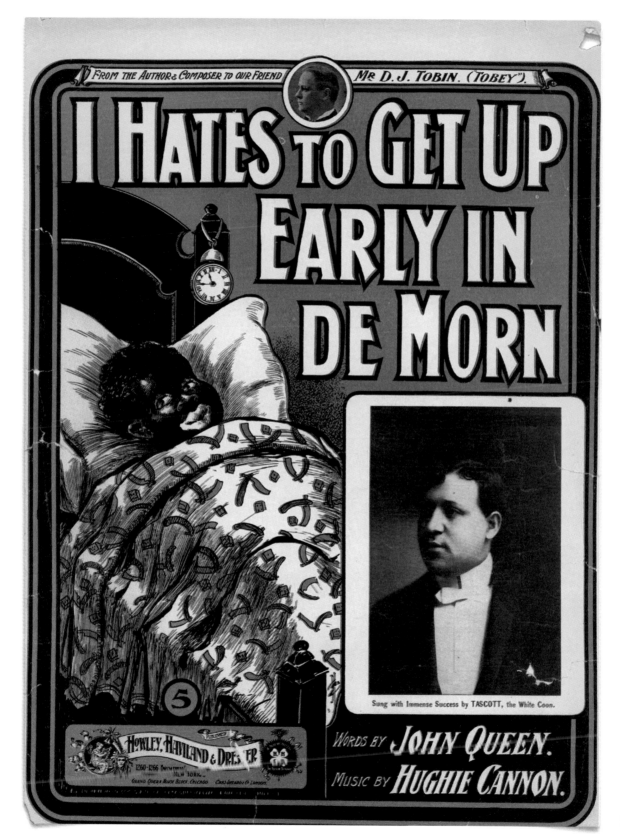

grandfather. Bing explained that his version does not include the crude drawings done by Bannerman or the nasty caricatures found in later pirated editions: ink black skin, red or pink lips, wild darting eyes, and matted or wild hair. Bing's *Little Black Sambo* is an attractive black child, yet the text remains nearly precisely as Bannerman wrote it, including the names of the characters.

Little Black Sambo helped engender the bonding of Bing and his grandfather, but for African American children it was another instance of them being told that they were ugly and different. I told Melissa Block, the show's host, that we should tell new stories instead of trying to sanitize old racist ones for a new generation. I have no illusion that I persuaded Bing (or Block) to see the book through my eyes, nor did he convince me that the story of Little Black Sambo—even a "cleaned up" version—could divorce itself from its history. Bing had the power and privilege to retell *Little Black Sambo* and to tell new stories about the importance of this story for his life.

All groups tell stories, but some groups have the power to impose their stories on others, to label others, stigmatize others, paint others as undesirables, and to have these social labels presented as scientific fact, God's will, or wholesome entertainment. This power differential was evident in 1915 with the release of D.W. Griffith's epic silent film *The Birth of a Nation*. Drawing upon Thomas Dixon's novel *The Clansman*,[8] Griffith set out to, in his words, "tell the truth about the war between the states."[9] Griffith's truth was that during Reconstruction ignorant and bestial black men, aided by evil white Northerners, subjugated the white South. These savage blacks, drunk with ambition and power, were not content to lord over white people; they desired sexual relations with virginal white women. The black brutes were stymied and ultimately defeated by the Ku Klux Klan, which helped reestablish white supremacy in the South. This was Griffith's truth, his story. Before beginning the film, he lamented that usually "only the winning side in the war ever gets to tell the story."[10] Richard Wormser, a contemporary screenwriter, criticized Griffith's story:

> The film presented a distorted portrait of the South after the Civil War, glorifying the Ku Klux Klan and denigrating blacks. It falsified the period of Reconstruction by presenting blacks as dominating Southern whites (almost all of whom are noble in the film) and sexually forcing themselves upon white women. The Klan was portrayed as the South's savior from this alleged tyranny. Not only was this portrayal untrue, it was the opposite of what actually happened. During Reconstruction, whites dominated blacks and

assaulted black women. The Klan was primarily a white terrorist organization that carried out hundreds of murders.[11]

The Birth of a Nation was this nation's first blockbuster film. Filmgoers, most of whom were white, paid the then-pricey sum of $2 a ticket. Viewing the film was an event, an adventure. Within two years the film had grossed $60 million, an unheard-of sum at that time. Some of the film's success may be attributed to its groundbreaking camerawork, including tracking shots, night photography, and close-ups, but its success was also due to the white audiences' knowledge and acceptance of an overarching racial narrative: white people are immutably superior to black people in all ways that matter; efforts to treat black people as equals are doomed to failure and may damage society; and two races sharing the same country will lead to repeated conflict.

There was a private showing of *The Birth of a Nation* in the White House. President Woodrow Wilson, a friend of Thomas Dixon, was a Southerner and a supporter of Jim Crow segregation. On February 18, 1915, the president, his family, cabinet officers, and their wives watched the film. There is some dispute about how Wilson responded to the film. Twenty-two years later, a magazine writer claimed that the president said of the film: "It is like writing history with lightning. And my only regret is that it is all so terribly true."[12] This quote is widely credited to Wilson, but there is disagreement regarding whether he uttered those words. One Wilson biographer claims that the last person alive who attended the White House screening recalled that the president paid scant attention to the film and left without saying a word.[13] Griffith often insinuated that President Wilson had endorsed the film.

Wilson may not have used the "writing history with lightning" line, but it is clear that many white viewers saw *The Birth of a Nation* as a historically accurate account—more objective documentary than fictional story—and were incensed, lashing out angrily at their black neighbors. In Lafayette, Indiana, a white man murdered a black teenager after viewing the film. Another white man, William Joseph Simmons, used *The Birth of a Nation* as a tool to restart the Ku Klux Klan, which had been dormant since the 1870s. Within a decade the organization had several million members. As recently as the 1970s, Klan organizations were using the film to recruit members.

When we watch movies or read novels we know that they are stories; we identify the characters, follow the plot, and anticipate the conclusion. But there are other stories that are not so easily identified—sometimes they masquerade as objective, race-neutral truth. For example, the subjugation of Africans and their descendants in the United States, beginning

US FO' AND NO MO'.

COPYRIGHTED, 1897, AND
PUBLISHED BY KNAFFL & BRO.,
KNOXVILLE, TENN

This postcard was originally distributed in 1897.

10

with the enslavement of black people and continuing with Jim Crow racial persecution of black people, was supported by the stories told by scientists. These stories, sometimes tightly woven, sometimes loosely organized, taught Americans to "know" that black people are inferior and a threat to white people.

In 1851, Samuel A. Cartwright, a physician, claimed to have discovered a new disease that afflicted enslaved black people: "drapetomania." In "Diseases and Peculiarities of the Negro Race," Cartwright claimed that the previously unknown mental illness had the "diagnostic symptom" of "absconding from service." In other words, black people who fled from slavery were mentally ill. In his words:

DRAPETOMANIA, OR THE DISEASE CAUSING NEGROES TO RUN AWAY.
It is unknown to our medical authorities, although its diagnostic symptom, the absconding from service, is well known to our planters and overseers . . .

In noticing a disease not heretofore classed among the long list of maladies that man is subject to, it was necessary to have a new term to express it. The cause in the most of cases, that induces the negro to run away from service, is as much a disease of the mind as any other species of mental alienation, and much more curable, as a general rule. With the advantages of proper medical advice, strictly followed, this troublesome practice that many negroes have of running away, can be almost entirely prevented, although the slaves be located on the borders of a free state, within a stone's throw of the abolitionists.[14]

Cartwright was a scientist and a slavery defender. It was common in the 1850s for slavery advocates to claim that blacks benefited from being enslaved. For Cartwright and other slavery defenders, any enslaved black person who tried to escape must be mentally defective. Cartwright not only recommended the "whipping the devil out of them" treatment, he also suggested amputating the toes of runaway slaves. A *New York Times* article written in 1855 referred to drapetomania as a "veritable disease," and added that slaves who escaped were "poor weak-mind colored people" who are flogged severely "for their own good of course."[15]

Cartwright described another mental disorder, "dysaethesia aethiopica," to explain the apparent lack of work ethic exhibited by many slaves. The diagnosable symptoms included disobedience, insolence, and refusing to work—and physical lesions. What treatment did Cartwright suggest? "Put the patient to some hard kind of work in the open air and sunshine," under the watchful eye of a white man. Cartwright traveled the nation telling the story of mentally ill black people trying to flee slavery and the efforts of mentally balanced enslavers to stop them.

The goal of the scientific racist was, and remains, the defense of a racial hierarchy. Cartwright was, unfortunately, not the last scholar to use science, or more correctly, pseudoscience, to rationalize or justify the subordination of Africans and Americans of African descent. In the nineteenth and twentieth centuries many white scientists—craniologists, phrenologists, evolutionists, geneticists, and others—argued that dark-skinned people were inherently, hence immutably, intellectually, morally, socially, and culturally inferior to light-skinned people. American and European scientists have long histories of using scientific stories to rationalize and support racial hierarchies, with white people at the top lording over people of color.

Central to the stories told by proslavery scientists, and later by prosegregation scientists, is the narrative that innately superior white people are in a cultural war with inferior black people. This overarching cultural narrative was supported by race-based stories shared from behind university lecterns and church pulpits, and seconded by politicians, newspaper editors, business leaders, novelists, playwrights, and later the producers of radio shows, films, and television shows. The black men who taught me about Cleotis Threadgill did not have the power to share their stories in this country's cinemas. They did not own newspapers, magazines, or radio stations. They were not respected scholars who could publish their stories in reputable academic journals. They were poor black men who could only share their stories with one another, their neighbors, and me.

Black people know that not all stories are true, and that the stories about them are too often shaped by and around racial caricatures and stereotypes. The Jim Crow Museum has the nation's largest collection of publicly accessible racist objects. These everyday objects—books, plates, games, detergent boxes, and more—are used as teaching aids to help visitors gain a deeper understanding of race, race relations, and racism in the United States. The museum's holdings, more than twelve thousand objects and growing weekly, give insight into the racial stories that guided how white people saw and interacted with black people, and how white people saw themselves. These stories also had a more practical, instrumental purpose: they legitimized the oppression of black people by white people, including the use of violence.

The racial stories that mocked black people and labeled them as inferiors had the expected consequence of creating a sense of inferiority in some black people. How else to explain young black boys in the 1940s imitating the slow, subservient, shuffling gait and unintelligible mumbling of Stepin Fetchit, the quintessential cinematic coon? What stories had been heard and lived by the black children who then thought black dolls were ugly and bad—and those who hold those beliefs today? And what about the black people who not only call other blacks "niggers," but who believe that some black people are, indeed, niggers? If every major societal institution tells a people they are ugly and bad, some of the defamed people will internalize those messages, and some, maybe most, of the labeling group will believe they are superior in all ways that matter.

On November 7, 2015, more than ninety thousand people crammed into Bryant-Denny Stadium to watch the host team, the Alabama Crimson Tide, defeat the Louisiana State University (LSU) Tigers, 30–16. The game was important for the looming football playoffs: the Tigers entered the game ranked second in the nation and the Crimson Tide ranked fourth. The game also featured two of the leading candidates for the Heisman Trophy: Leonard Fournette, from LSU, and Alabama's Derrick Henry, both running backs, both African Americans. The game was, of course, shown on national television.

My daughter Gabrielle Lynne was one of the spectators. It was her first time attending a big-time college football game, and few games

are as major as clashes between traditional football powers from the Southeastern Conference. She was in town for a couple of days as a guest of several white coeds who attend the University of Alabama. Gabrielle later told me that she was stunned at how important the game was to those students and others. One of them told her that she was so nervous about the game that she could not sleep the night before.

Gabrielle also told me that while in Tuscaloosa she heard comments about black people that disappointed and angered her. One of the girls mentioned that there are sororities that do not allow black students to become members. Gabrielle wondered aloud how it was that white students could fill a stadium to root for a football team heavily populated with African Americans and then return to campus to discriminate against black students. One of the white coeds said of the black athletes, "They are here for our entertainment."

That statement uses the language of division and separation: "they" and "our." They are outsiders; the university is ours. She did not say, "We find it entertaining to watch football." Her statement was unequivocal and unapologetic: black athletes are here for the enjoyment of white students, to provide pleasure to the real, legitimate owners of the institution.

Anti-Obama shirt, 2012.

13

The blacks on the field are seen as intellectual inferiors who are tolerated because they are superior athletes. In the United States athletes have been admired, sometimes gloried, and black people have been degraded, sometimes demonized. Viewing black athletes as entertainment gives the white students a way to cheer for black people at a specified time, without challenging (or even contributing to) everyday patterns of racism.

A society that elevates race to a master status—a social position that trumps most aspects of our identity—will create racist stories to justify the lifting of one race above others. These stories will be so pervasive and omnipresent that they will be intimately linked to the day-to-day functioning of the society. This is an example of racial hegemony. Some stories will be easily identified; others will be hidden as science, sermons, songs, or other vehicles of expression. There will be good guys, bad guys, and tension between them. The racial hierarchy is supported by a grand, all-inclusive narrative: whites are superior to blacks, and conflict between the groups is inevitable. This overarching narrative is expressed through and supported by numerous smaller, more targeted stories that employ caricatures and stereotypes.

Caricatures and Stereotypes

All racial groups have been caricatured in the United States, but none have been caricatured as often or in as many ways as Africans and African Americans. Although there is no consensus about the number of antiblack caricatures or their conceptualization, there is agreement that certain ones exist: the lazy and cowardly Sambo, the angry Sapphire, the impoverished pickaninny, the pitiable tragic mulatto, the loyal and contented mammy and Tom, the menacing coon, brute, and Nat, and the hypersexual Jezebel and buck. These caricatures are shorthand ways of saying that black people are others, specifically, Lesser Others.

With racial caricatures, traits that are argued to exist within a racial group are highlighted, then exaggerated, until the traits are seen as absurd, bizarre, or fantastically ugly. The exaggerated trait may be physical—skin color, body size and shape—or it may be a prop—raggedy clothes, a razor, or a watermelon. The Sambo caricature, for example, portrays black men as dark-skinned and ugly, with bald heads or unkempt hair. In some instances he has a simian-like appearance. Sambo wears raggedy clothes signifying poverty and lack of ambition. His physical appearance suggests that he is one of society's failures. This is the Sambo that "stars" in many stories about black people.

The exaggerated traits upon which racial caricatures are built also include behaviors. Sambo not only looks a certain way, he acts a certain way. He lounges under a tree, sleeping or eating a watermelon.

He personifies laziness. He wants to be fed but does not want to work, so he occasionally steals. He is a coward, fleeing when there is danger. Sambo runs from the white man who is angry about him stealing chickens. When he sees a ghost he is so petrified that he turns (temporarily) white. Sambo's approach to life suggests that he is not a man but a buffoonish child, a deviant brat. One could argue that the Smokey character in the film *Friday* (1995) is a Sambo caricature.[16]

Visual representations of antiblack caricatures take many forms. There are sketches, drawings, and portraits that ludicrously and harshly exaggerate the imagined peculiarities or defects of black people. These representations focus, primarily but not exclusively, on physical appearance. This is demonstrated by examining the mammy caricature, drawn or painted as a physically ugly servant. With her fat sides, rolling gait, and shining black skin, she is depicted as the antithesis of American beauty. Her flowing apron, extended bloomers, and kerchiefed head mark her as a servant. One postcard, illustrated by Richard F. Outcault (the inventor of the modern comic strip), shows three black women and a child. All four characters have dark skin and blood-red lips. One of the women is portrayed as a mammy. She has a red kerchief hiding her hair. She wears a shawl, apron, and dress. The text at the bottom of the postcard reads "DARKYTOWN DAMES." Outcault's postcard was first produced in 1892. In the century to follow there would be thousands of different mammy images produced on postcards, trade cards, posters, sheets of music, calendars, board games, detergent boxes, and card games.

The visual debasement of black women as mammies is not confined to images that appear on paper. She is recreated on countless ceramic figurines, candles, aprons, dustpans, memo pads, pothangers, and Halloween masks. There are several versions of mammy mechanical banks. These objects function as racial propaganda. For example, there is a stuffed cushion with printed fabric that bears the image of a mammy. The words "DO YOU'S WANT ANY HELP?" are printed on her apron. The attached mailing tag has these words, a sort of ode to servitude:

High Class Help Furnished, City or Country
Our Servants are Guaranteed
    To remain where sent.
    To answer truthfully or remain silent.
    To not break dishes.
    To be content with small wages.
N B. Any servant not satisfactory can be returned to us at our expense.
If I don't make a good servant, use me for a pincushion.

During the Jim Crow period, mammy—a smiling, overweight, loyal servant—was the most popularly disseminated representation of black women on everyday objects.

Mammy, as a visual representation, was displayed on minstrel stages, where white men (and later some black performers) wore blackface makeup and "mammy attire" and spoke in presumed Negro dialect. In 1890, not long after the popularity of professional minstrel shows had begun to wane, the R.T. Davis Milling Company hired Nancy Green as a "spokesperson" for Aunt Jemima pancake mix. Her job was to pretend to be Aunt Jemima. She told stories about how she had cooked pancakes for her "master." As Aunt Jemima, she operated a pancake-cooking display at the World's Fair held in Chicago in 1893, appearing beside the "world's largest flour barrel." Afterward, the company centered its marketing strategy on Aunt Jemima, and she became the prototypical commercial mammy representation.

Some of the most well-known visual representations of mammy occurred in film. *Coontown Suffragettes* (1914) tells the story of a group of brash black washerwomen who try to keep their lazy husbands home and away from saloons.[17] In *The Birth of a Nation*, Mammy (a white woman dressed in blackface) refuses to leave her white family throughout the Civil War and defends them against the "Reconstruction Negroes." *Gone with the Wind* (1939), a film that romanticizes and glorifies slavery, has a loyal mammy servant.[18] In *Imitation of Life* (1934), the mammy loves her white boss so much she gives her the secret to the family pancakes, and the millions of dollars in profits that come with the recipe, then begs her boss to not send her away.[19]

Not all representations of mammy (and other racial caricatures) are visual, some are audio representations. One prominent example involves Beulah, a supporting character on the *Fibber McGee and Molly* radio show in 1944. One critic referred to that character as a "chuckling Aunt Jemima handkerchief-head not all that far removed from a minstrel show, with her introductory cry, 'Somebody bawl fo' Beulah.'"[20] In 1945, the Beulah character was given her own radio show, *The Marlin Hurt and Beulah Show* (later *The Beulah Show*), a situation comedy that aired on CBS Radio from 1945 to 1954.[21] In her radio show, Beulah, still employed as a housekeeper and cook for a white family, acts less like a buffoon, but she remained a domestic servant in keeping with mammy portrayals. White listeners to *The Beulah Show* did not see the mammy, but they heard and imagined mammy, and they imagined the differences between themselves and black people.

Representations of racial caricatures, in this case, mammy, are found in conversations, in lectures, and especially in jokes. The following story told in the 1920s reveals a great deal about perceptions of mammy and her relation to her white "family."

> A young girl in the South, who had been brought up from the time she was a little baby by her Negro Mammy, got married and went away with her husband on her wedding trip. After a two weeks' absence she returned and the old Mammy made up her mind the next morning she was going to fix dat Chile the kind of a breakfast she liked. So, piling up a tray with all the appetizing things she could think of, that her darling liked, she went up and knocked at the door but was told she didn't want anything and neither did her husband. Somewhat disappointed, she said to herself, well, for lunch she would spread herself and she did. Going up with the tray she received the same answer as before. Not discouraged, she made up her mind to try it once more, and in the evening she fixes up a tray with creamed chicken, corn pone, and all the other dishes that her young mistress loved and took them up, and kicking at the door, the young woman opens, and says, Oh, Mammy, you all know what I like.
>
> Yaas, Missy, youh Mammy, she all know what you like, but Honey, you is got to eat.[22]

Mammy is a racial caricature, not a racial stereotype. They are interrelated, but caricatures and stereotypes are not the same. Racial

caricatures are grotesque portraits, either literal or metaphorical. Racial stereotypes are oversimplified generalized beliefs about the members of a race. Racial stereotypes are the ideas and claims attached to and used to define and describe racial caricatures. The mammy caricature, for example, is supported by the racial stereotype that black people are ugly. Racial caricatures do not exist without racial stereotypes.

Racial stereotypes can be applied to multiple racial caricatures. For example, the stereotype that black people are obsessively fond of watermelons can be applied to most antiblack caricatures. Indeed, there are countless visual representations of mammies, Toms, Sambos, and pickanninies eating watermelons together. Also, the contention that black people are not intelligent is often applied to multiple antiblack caricatures. Some racial caricatures of black people are visually indistinguishable from one another; for instance, portrayals of the Sambo and the coon may use the same imagery of a black man. It is important to understand the context of the image. At the risk of an oversimplification, using the above example, a Sambo and a coon image may look identical, and they may both have a watermelon or a chicken, but, of the two, only the coon has a razor for fighting.

Racial caricatures and the stereotypes that undergird them are based on overgeneralizations, but this does not mean that they are not real. They are real in their consequences. They become justifications for discrimination and other forms of mistreatment. The depiction of black men as Sambos became a rationalization for denying them admission to colleges—"They are too lazy and dumb to do college work." The portrayal of black men as brutes was a defense for lynchings—"They must be lynched to protect the virtue of white women."

I am a sociologist trained to observe and examine group behavior and the thinking beneath it, but you do not have to be a sociologist to notice patterns in the artifacts in the Jim Crow Museum. Visitors to the museum note that the artifacts portray black people as physically ugly, dirty, dumb, and dangerous. They express surprise at the sheer volume of antiblack artifacts. Even elderly visitors who lived during the Jim Crow period are astonished to see thousands of everyday objects that portray black people in unfavorable ways. If you can think of a run-of-the-mill object—postcard, toy, ashtray, poster, drinking glass, clock, and so forth—it is likely that a racist version of that object was created, and some version of it is in the museum. Visitors notice that the belittlement and denigration of black people is accomplished through racial caricatures.

There is a hallway that leads to the Jim Crow Museum. On one side there are several showcases, the first is a display with African artifacts. These objects afford us the opportunity to tell stories about the African

The person who sold this object used it as a dishcloth holder and said it had been in their family since the 1950s.

19

civilizations that thrived long before black people were enslaved in this country. The remaining showcases recount the journey of black people in this country from slavery to the election of President Barack Obama. We use these items to examine the "dominant" stories and to offer counter-stories about Reconstruction, de jure and de facto segregation, and the civil rights movement.

On the other side of the hallway are relatively large images of people doing the things that people do: walking, talking, laughing and singing, marching, studying, and playing. They are not one-dimensional caricatures; they are real people, wholly human. Most of the depicted people are black. They are in the hallway that leads to the museum as not-so-subtle reminders that the images of black people in the museum are racist caricatures, propagandistic stories used to support systems of oppression, most notably, slavery and the racial hierarchy commonly referred to as Jim Crow.

Goodbye Uncle Tom

Years ago, I wanted the students in my Images of Blacks in Popular Culture course to analyze some of the ways slavery in the United States had been depicted in films. We started with *Gone with the Wind*. The movie's main white characters are primarily portrayed as multidimensional, and in some instances as dignified and elegant. The white Southerners are noble defenders of traditional values. The blacks are one-dimensional caricatures—for example, the character Prissy is a pickaninny, Pork fits the Tom caricature, and Mammy, as indicated by the name, is a prototypical mammy caricature. Even though the movie is set in the South and much of the action occurs on and near a plantation, the issue of slavery is largely ignored.

Next, we watched *Roots: The Saga of an American Family*, the epic tale of Pulitzer Prize–winning author Alex Haley's ancestors, beginning with the capture of a free African (Kunta Kinte) and his enslavement and ending with a retailing of the personal journey of Alex Haley to discover his roots.[23] In January 1977, Americans sat transfixed and stunned watching the eight-part miniseries. For the first time many people realized that slavery was more than people working without pay. *Roots* showed enslaved black people being forcibly separated from their families and whipped and later generations of Haley's family struggling against poverty, ignorance (theirs and whites'), and Jim Crow racism. Most of my students had never seen *Roots*, but when it first aired on television it riveted the nation. The seven episodes that followed the opener earned the top spots in the ratings for their week. The final episode was the highest-rated single episode until 1983. *Roots* was a cultural

phenomenon prompting important national dialogues on slavery and race relations.

Roots gave Americans a glimpse into the horrors of slavery, but it was only a partial view. The miniseries was a docudrama, not a documentary. An accurate depiction of the African American experience, especially their enslavement, would be difficult to watch as entertainment. It would be obscene and pornographic in every sense of those words. Witnessing beatings, rapes, torture, and killings would make viewers turn away, run, and find ways to distance themselves and their world from what they know. The producers of *Roots* were daring to show as much as they did.

The final movie we watched was *Goodbye Uncle Tom* (*Addio Zio Tom* in Italian), a bizarre and repulsive portrayal of slavery in the United States.[24] Before watching the movie, we read reviews that described the abundance of sex and violence in the film. Many critics claimed that Gualtiero Jacopetti and Franco Prosperi, the movie's producers, delighted in the rape and torture of the black people, as evidenced by the way the camera lingered on black women being raped and the way black men were killed in slow motion. We discussed the genre of shockumentaries, including *Africa Addio* (1966), that depicted Africans as savages and included scenes

A student examines the Jim Crow case.

Uncle Tom and Little Eva.
Copyright, 1895, by Strohmeyer & Wyman.

of deplorable animal butchering and people killed onscreen.[25] We knew that these producers had reputations for being incendiary gore merchants with a fetish for debasing Africans.

I watched *Goodbye Uncle Tom* before showing it to my students. I tried to answer my students' questions about the film in an objective, matter-of-fact manner. Then I told them that anyone who did not want to watch the movie could watch *The Birth of a Nation*. Four students took that option. On the day that we watched *Goodbye Uncle Tom* three students had unexcused absences, several cried while watching, one almost vomited—most sat, sad and disgusted. I taught for another fifteen years, but I never again showed that movie.

The movie was made in 1971. Richard Nixon was president of the United States. The nation was dealing with the aftermath of the My Lai Massacre, the assassination of Martin Luther King Jr., scores of antiwar protests, the Kent State University and Jackson State University massacres, and many civil rights demonstrations. A revolt broke out at the maximum-security prison in Attica, New York. State police and the National Guard stormed the facility, killing forty-two people, ten of them hostages. The Black Power movement—which emphasized racial pride and the creation of black political and cultural institutions to nurture and promote black collective interests—was in full bloom in the United States. Black people were watching Melvin Van Peebles's *Sweet Sweetback's Baadasssss Song*, Gordon Parks's *Shaft*, a blaxploitation movie that featured blacks killing whites.[26]

LEFT: This is a trade card from 1881.
ABOVE: This is a stereograph card from 1895. Stereographs, also known as stereoviews, were popular in the nineteenth-century and used two nearly identical images seen through a handheld viewer to produce the illusion of three dimensions.

23

Jacopetti and Prosperi observed with great interest the general turmoil and racial conflicts in the United States. They believed that slavery meant that blacks and whites would always hate one another, and they decided to produce a movie to prove it. The simple, though far-fetched, approach of the film: identify some of the worst documented features of slavery and have modern-day interviewers (themselves) go back in time to observe and interview the people involved. The bulk of the film is an orgy of brutality against slaves portrayed in the most graphic

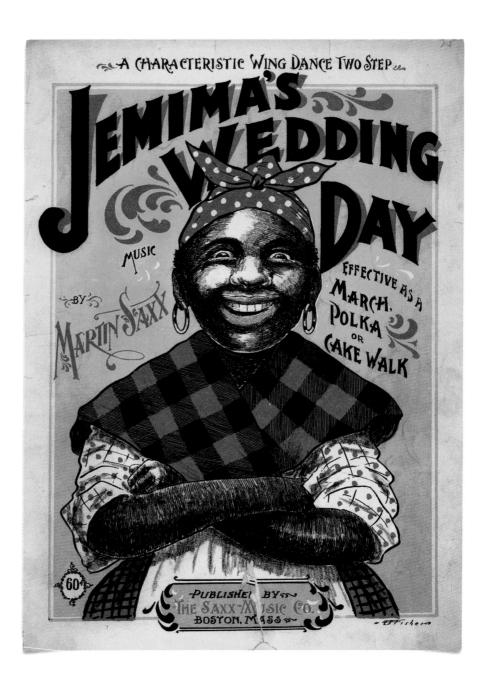

Sheet music, words by Jere O'Halloran, music by Martin Saxx, 1899.

ways imaginable, with the tormentors pausing long enough to rationalize their behavior to the (mostly) invisible interviewers.

The interviewers visit a slave ship discharging its cargo, several hundred diseased and malnourished Africans. The imagery is stomach-turning. The people who played the roles of slaves were, in real life, impoverished Haitians. Papa Doc Duvalier, the Haitian dictator, gave the filmmakers freedom to film on the island and access to as many extras as they wanted. In many of the film's scenes, especially the auction scenes, black people are naked or near naked. Why would the "actors" (they received no mention in the movie's credits) subject themselves to this treatment? Poverty is a harsh master. Maybe this explains why parents allowed their children to be presented in what can only be described as pornographic scenes. There are brothels populated by black women for white men and effeminate black boys for white men; the young boys are naked. Young girls are offered to old white men for sexual purposes, and in one instance a thirteen-year-old begs the interviewer to have sexual relations. There is a horrific rape scene where a virginal black woman is mated to a "black stud." This occurs on a breeding farm. Slaves are tortured for offenses, real and imagined. The viewer hears from a preacher who argues that slavery is a moral institution. White hunters of escaped slaves are interviewed. Blacks are handled like animals, especially at auctions where they are sold or won in raffles. At the auctions they are gaudily dressed, sometimes like minstrels, or they are naked. The language used to refer to blacks is dehumanizing, for example, calling a boy being auctioned "it." In one scene, a well-dressed white girl runs with a black boy, holding a chain around his neck. Whites are referred to as humans, while mixed-race blacks are called part-humans. Throughout the film it is clear that major portions of all of society's most important institutions: government, religion, education, science, criminal justice, politics, and family support the institution of slavery. This is, alas, historically accurate.

Goodbye Uncle Tom is a more truthful portrayal of the brutality and obscenity of slave life than was *Roots*. It is, however, ironic that a movie that explored the exploitation and degradation of black people was filmed in a way that exploited and degraded black people. In some ways *Goodbye Uncle Tom* was an X-rated movie set against the backdrop of slavery, with that "peculiar institution" serving as an excuse for sexual decadence and violent gore meted out against black bodies. Roger Ebert, the noted film critic, asserted:

> This is cruel exploitation. If it is tragic that the barbarism of slavery existed in this country, is it not also tragic—and enraging—that

for a few dollars the producers of this film were able to reenact that barbarism? Make no mistake. This movie itself humiliates its actors in the way the slaves were humiliated 200 years ago. A man without a hand is photographed shoving mash into his mouth from a trough. Very young girls are mocked in auction scenes. Pregnant women—women who are really pregnant—are corralled into a scene about the "breeding" of slaves. The fact that this film could find a booking in a legitimate motion-picture theater is depressing.[27]

Jacopetti and Prosperi told a painful truth about the brutal enslavement of black people, while debasing hundreds of blacks. In their story black people are caricatures: mammy, Tom, Sambo, Nat, Jezebel, buck, and pickaninnies. They believed that some black people were, indeed, "happy darkies." Despite being victimized, black people are frequently shown laughing and grinning, including one scene where a crowd of

The museum staff has been unable to obtain information on this image.

blacks laugh excitedly as a black man is castrated. The producers saw blacks as violent savages shackled by slavery. Once they were free of bondage their natural predilections for violence would manifest. This is apparent at the movie's conclusion, where a 1970s African American is reading William Styron's *The Confessions of Nat Turner* and fantasizing reenacting Turner's bloody massacre of whites.[28] *Goodbye Uncle Tom* is not the story of slavery, it is Jacopetti and Prosperi's story.

One Object, Many Stories

All objects tell stories. Racist objects tell stories about racial inferiority and racial superiority. Among the thousands of objects in the Jim Crow Museum are a dozen or so lawn jockeys—iron or cement statues of black men holding up one hand, sometimes carrying a lantern or a metal ring suitable for hitching a horse. For some African Americans lawn jockeys are a source of pride, but for many they are a symbol of slavery and Jim Crow segregation.

The story begins the icy night in December 1776 when General George Washington decided to cross the Delaware River to launch

The museum displays many versions of the lawn jockey, including an original one from the 1800s (tall figure with white shirt and blue pants at far right). The museum has no information on this image.

a surprise attack on the British forces at Trenton. Jocko Graves, a twelve-year-old African-American, sought to fight the Redcoats, but Washington deemed him too young and ordered him to look after the horses, asking Jocko to keep a lantern blazing along the Delaware so the company would know where to return after battle. Many hours later, Washington and his men returned to their horses that were tied up to Graves, who had frozen to death with the lantern still clenched in his fist. Washington was so moved by the young boy's devotion to the revolutionary cause he commissioned a statue of the "Faithful Groomsman" to stand in Graves's honor at the general's estate in Mount Vernon.[29]

The above account was offered by the River Road African American Museum in Louisiana to explain the origins of lawn jockeys, especially the Faithful Groomsman version. I have heard this story from several African Americans and it is frequently cited on internet sites. It is a heroic tale and, like many such tales, its historical accuracy is questionable. In a 1987 letter to the Enoch Pratt Free Library, Ellen McCallister Clark, a Mount Vernon librarian, concluded that the story is fictional.

The story is apocryphal; conveying a message about heroism among blacks during the Revolutionary War and General Washington's humanitarian concerns, but it is not based on an actual incident. Neither a person by the name of Jocko Graves, nor the account of any person freezing to death while holding Washington's horses has been found in any of the extensive records of the period. Likewise, the Mount Vernon estate was inventoried and described by a multitude of visitors over the years and there has never been any indication of anything resembling a "jockey" statue on the grounds. I have put the story in the category with the cherry tree and silver dollar, fictional tales that were designed to illustrate a particular point.[30]

Many of the heroic deeds performed by Africans and their American descendants are ignored in the history books that line this nation's shelves. This neglect was frequently intentional, designed to buttress the idea that black people were deficient in all important ways. The creation and acceptance of Jocko stories are ways for African Americans to say, "We were always brave, always worthy of inclusion, even admiration." It is a good story, a chest-puffer, but there is no evidence that the Jocko legend is true.

Most of the white people who have black lawn jockeys in their yards have never heard of Jocko Graves or the stories about him. These

Sheet music by H.A. Fischler, 1910.

black-faced, racially caricatured lawn ornaments were not purchased to celebrate the bravery of a little boy. So why are they in people's yards? Some people inherit them, as I have come to learn from many owners of black lawn jockeys. Others see the lawn jockeys as cute. (I must confess that when someone describes the black-faced objects as cute, I throw up both my hands.) Some people like schlock gardens that include traditional lawn warts: garden gnomes, concrete geese, pink flamingos, black lawn jockeys, and other aesthetically questionable objects. And, of course, there are always Americans who own controversial objects as a way of saying, "No one tells me what to do and what not to do." Personal liberty is, after all, one of this nation's core values.

There is another Jocko story that is almost as remarkable as the Revolutionary War creation account, but this one is more plausible.[31] Charles Blockson, a historian and collector of Underground Railroad artifacts, claims that from the late 1700s through the Civil War, lawn jockeys were used to warn escaped slaves of danger or to signal that a building was a safe house. A brightly colored ribbon or strip of fabric tied to the statue's arm or a lighted lantern affixed in its hands sent messages to runaway slaves—red meant danger and green, safety. One problem with this story is that runaway slaves often traveled at night and the darkness would have made it difficult to see different shades of cloth—but not necessarily impossible. Frankly, no system for escape was without problems for the runaway. If a slave had to get precariously close to a home to see the signal, well, that is what he or she had to do. And though it was not preferred, some runaway slaves traveled in daylight. Of course, a signal would have been easy to send by lighting a lantern and placing it in the hand of the lawn jockey so that light off might have meant that the house was full and had no more room for runaways. I do not doubt that a black-faced lawn ornament was used as a signal to black people escaping slavery. There had to be ways to send cryptic messages to runaways, and given that slavery lasted more than two hundred years, it is likely that it happened at least occasionally. Nevertheless, there is little evidence that this practice was widespread.

Are the white families that have black-faced lawn jockeys honoring the slaves who fled for their lives or the families that aided them? Probably not. The contemporary families who own and display lawn jockeys have most likely not heard the stories about lawn jockeys and the Underground Railroad. The black-faced servant with the stooped back is a reminder of the decades when blacks occupied the bottom rung on America's racial hierarchy—a time when blacks "knew their place." Some people find lawn jockeys nostalgic, reminiscent of the "good old days" of Jim Crow segregation. After World War II, white residents of

Sheet music, ragtime/blues song written by Shelton Brooks, 1913.

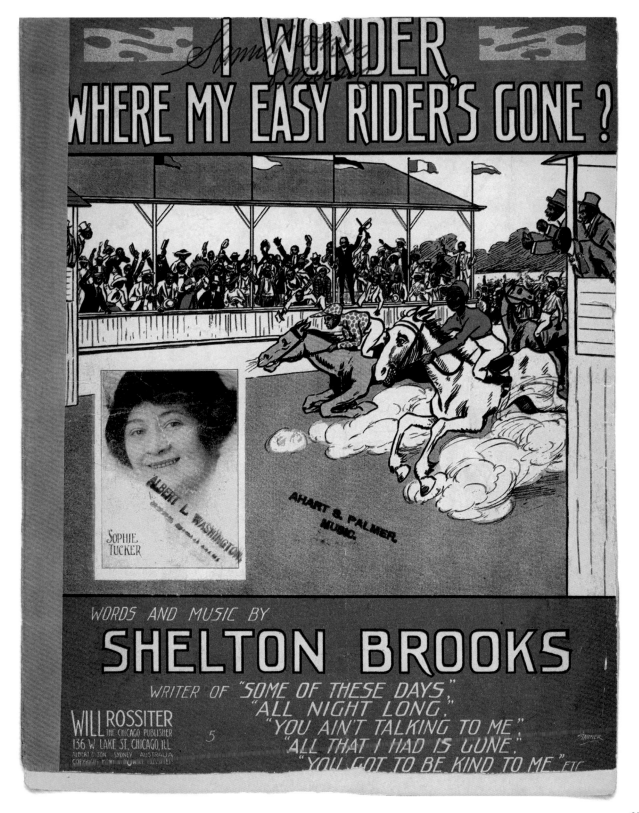

new housing developments, "perhaps to give themselves more of a sense of being a member of the privileged master class, began placing 'Jocko' on their lawns in great numbers," wrote Kenneth W. Goings in his book *Mammy and Uncle Mose*.[32] I can tell you that more than a half century later lawn jockeys are still seen by many African Americans as markers of white space, objects that send a message to black people: "You are not welcome here."

The early black-faced lawn ornaments were dressed in slave clothing (the groomsmen), but at some point in the 1800s, these figures were joined and eventually superseded by the Jocko (short and stocky) and Cavalier (slender and erect) statues wearing the garb of horse riders. The dressing of black-faced ornaments as jockeys does not answer the question of their source, but it might give hints to their longtime popularity. Blacks were often used to train horses and, not surprisingly, some became skillful riders. It is possible that black lawn jockeys became popular because of the preeminence of blacks as jockeys.

Horse racing was very popular in the 1800s, and at many races all or most of the jockeys were African Americans. After Emancipation, blacks continued to dominate major horse racing events. At the first race of the famed Kentucky Derby in 1875, thirteen of the fifteen riders were African Americans. Blacks rode the winners of fifteen of the first twenty-eight Kentucky Derby races.[33] The dominance of black jockeys ended just before World War I, when whites brought Jim Crow norms into horse racing. I am not arguing that black lawn jockeys came into existence because blacks dominated amateur and professional horse racing, but the popularity of the objects coincided with the dominance of black jockeys. This fact was not lost on the makers, distributors, and buyers of lawn jockeys.

For years I have tried to find the name of the company that first received a patent for the lawn jockey, and I have sought to identify the first designer of the Jocko version. Both searches failed. Of course, a greater aid to our understanding would be to find narratives written by slaves or newly freedmen that discuss the lawn jockeys. To my knowledge, however, no such narratives exist, but I hope that I am wrong.

To call an African American a lawn jockey is to insult him or her. When used by a black person against another black person, lawn jockey means Uncle Tom, a derogatory term with at least two distinct meanings. In the past it referred to the black servant, especially a cook, butler, or waiter, who was perceived to be weak, ignorant, too religious, and humiliatingly deferential to white people. This definition was common before the civil rights movement. Today, Uncle Tom is an in-group pejorative that is used against blacks whose views are considered selfish, conniving, too politically conservative, and detrimental to African Americans as a whole. Black conservatives like Supreme Court Justice Clarence Thomas, Ward Connerly, Herman Cain, Allen West, Michael Steele, and Ben Carson are sometimes called Uncle Toms and lawn jockeys. In 1996, *Emerge*, a liberal black magazine, devoted most of an issue to criticizing Thomas.[34] The magazine's cover displays a caricature of Justice Thomas as a lawn jockey, accompanied by these words: "Uncle Thomas: Lawn Jockey for the Far Right." Thomas is shown in spectacles, grinning widely, and dressed as the Cavalier version of a lawn jockey. Inside is a cartoon of a kneeling Thomas shining the shoes of Justice Antonin Scalia.

Today, lawn jockeys are frequently painted white or nearly white, particularly the Cavalier Spirit version. Lawn jockeys lost a lot of their popularity after the civil rights movement, but they have been making a comeback. Search the internet using the words "lawn jockey" and you will find dozens of companies and hundreds of individuals selling old and new versions of the statues. An internet search also reveals a foreign market for lawn jockeys. They are not cheap. There are, of course, also other black yard ornaments, including cement black-faced boys eating watermelons or fishing.

Driving from my home, I cannot go more than five minutes in any direction without seeing a waist-high, black lawn statue dressed in jockey's clothing, holding one hand in waiting for the reins of a horse, with blood-red lips, wild darting eyes, a large flat nose, and a stooped back. And each time I see the black statues I think: "The owners have a right to put what they want in their yards"; "I wish they would donate the lawn jockey to the Jim Crow Museum"; and, finally, I think that I would be uncomfortable in their yards or homes.

A Continuing Story

The Cleotis Threadgill story taught me about lynching, and it had another impact: it shaped in me a way of seeing stories. Stories are a way of making sense of our lives, the lives of others, and the social order, and this is true for both the oppressed and the oppressors. I came to see many expressions about race relations as stories—literally stories. Some have a beginning, a middle, and an end, others do not, but they all narrate (either implicitly or explicitly) an account of past events or anticipated acts. Many are invented fiction, including some that purport to be true, and even the ones that include objective facts still contain the elements of story. The stories I hear in everyday conversation often draw from or react to overarching racial narratives. These are stories that existed long before I was a child.

Many years have passed since I was a boy, but I am sometimes reminded of Cleotis Threadgill. In 1981, for example, when the body of

This is a photograph of Michael Donald, who was lynched by two Ku Klux Klan members in 1981.

Michael Donald, a young African American, was found hanging from a tree in Mobile, Alabama. He was killed by two Ku Klux Klan members who were angry that a different black man had been acquitted of killing a white police officer in Birmingham, Alabama. On June 7, 1998, in Jasper, Texas, three white supremacists beat James Byrd Jr., a black man, urinating on him, cutting his throat, and chaining him by his ankles to their pickup truck. He was dragged behind the truck along an asphalt road for more than a mile. Byrd's lynching by dragging resulted in the severing of his right arm and his decapitation. His body—more accurately his torso—was dumped in front of an African American church. The killers left the murder and went to a barbecue cookout. An autopsy concluded that Byrd was alive during most of his ordeal. How could I not be reminded of Cleotis Threadgill when I hear about a black man hanged from a tree or dragged behind a car until decapitated?

I was also reminded of Cleotis Threadgill in the weeks following the 2012 Republican National Convention. Actor and director Clint Eastwood gave a surprise nationally televised speech. His ad-libbed talk was delivered as a conversation with President Obama. Of course, the president was not on the stage, and Eastwood directed his comments toward an invisible Obama sitting in a chair on the stage. One can argue whether the actor's approach was silly or clever, but there is little doubt that it tapped into a historical narrative about lynching black people who displeased white people. How? Within a few days of Eastwood's appearance there were several highly publicized instances of white people "lynching" chairs in their yards. In Austin, Texas, a white man hung an empty folding chair from a tree branch in front of his house and later attached an American flag to the chair. When someone complained about the chair and the message it sent, he said, "I don't really give a damn whether it disturbs you or not. You can take [your concerns] and go straight to hell and take Obama with you. I don't give a [expletive]. If you don't like it, don't come down my street."[35]

The Eastwood story is unsettling, but it pales in comparison to the story of Walter Lamar Scott. He is not alive to tell his story, so I will tell it for him. On April 4, 2015, he was driving his twenty-year-old Mercedes Benz in North Charleston, South Carolina, a city of about a hundred thousand. Scott, a fifty-year-old African American, was headed to an auto parts store. On his way he was stopped by Michael T. Slager, a white police officer, for driving with a broken taillight. The officer approached Scott's car, spoke to him, and returned to his patrol car.

DARKYTOWN DAMES

Desperate people do desperate things. Scott owed more than $18,000 in child support and court fees. South Carolina is a state where men go to jail for not paying child support, and Scott had been arrested before for nonpayment, so he ran. Slager gave chase on foot; when he caught Scott, the two men briefly tussled. Slager fired his Taser, striking Scott. Again, Scott ran. Slager drew his handgun and fired eight times at the fleeing Scott. A coroner reported that Scott was struck a total of five times: three times in the back, once in the upper buttocks, and once on one of his ears, with one bullet entering his heart. "Shots fired and the subject is down, he took my Taser." Those were the words that Slager radioed to a dispatcher. In his report, the police officer said that he felt threatened and feared for his life.

Slager's account was later challenged by footage from a handheld phone shot by Feidin Santana, who was walking by and saw the encounter. Slager's story that he felt threatened was undermined by footage that shows him calmly aiming, as if at a firing range, and then shooting Scott in the back from distances of fifteen to thirty feet. Slager walks to Scott—who is face down, dead or dying—saying, "Hands behind your back." He handcuffs him. Then the police officer runs to the site of the initial confrontation and picks up a Taser. As he returns to the body, another police officer arrives. He is an African American. Slager discretely drops the Taser near the body. Police reports claimed that an officer performed CPR on Scott. He did not. Two other police officers arrive. Slager tells his story to one of them. Scott is pronounced dead at the scene.

This postcard was copyrighted in 1892. It was postmarked in Big Rapids, Michigan, which a century later would become the home of the Jim Crow Museum.

What if the encounter had not been recorded? It would have been easy for many Americans to accept the narrative of the heroic police officer who was obliged to use deadly force against a dangerous menace. That narrative neatly fits into stories told about big, burly black brutes who attack innocent white people. The footage, however, showed an execution, the cold-blooded murder of a scared black man by a white police officer. Slager was subsequently indicted for murder. How different would be our understanding of history had citizens carried handheld video recorders during the Jim Crow period? We would be telling different stories or telling old stories in different ways.

So much of what we do in the Jim Crow Museum is about telling stories. The fluid narrative of storytelling helps visitors tie historical facts together. They learn about what it was like to live as a black person—and a white person—under Jim Crow segregation. Moreover, they come to understand the many ways that violence and everyday caricatured objects were used to support the Jim Crow racial hierarchy. They also learn that African Americans were not passive victims of institutional and individual racism. The museum tells stories about black artists using their art to deconstruct racist imagery. We also engage visitors in stories about the achievements of African Americans, including many lesser-known individuals who do not show up in Black History Month poster sets. Many of today's youth know little about the civil rights movement. The museum helps them better understand the historical events associated with that movement. Yes, we tell many stories, but, equally important, we listen to the stories that our visitors tell.

This book examines several longstanding antiblack stories, each one intimately tied to the subjugation of black people in the United States. Each chapter includes stories related to a specific topic. While not definitive, each chapter can be viewed as an introduction. Where useful, photographs of objects from the museum are included—even though I understand that many are deeply offensive and serve as a ready excuse for some people to avoid the book. That is unfortunate. These images represent not only moments in time; they are evidence of the social injustice that Martin Luther King Jr. referred to as a "pus-filled boil." They are material evidence of the oppression of black people and they must be confronted directly. Each chapter concludes with a story from my journey that challenges the intent of the racial narratives. We begin with the most insulting of all stories—the narrative that black people are not really people.

CHAPTER TWO

Not Quite Human

> "The vast majority of people of their race are but two or three inches removed from gorillas: it will be a sheer impossibility, for a long, long while, to interest them in anything above pork-chops and bootleg gin."
>
> —H.L. Mencken[1]

On March 3, 1991, white Los Angeles police officers brutally beat Rodney King, a black motorist who had led them on a high-speed car chase. The beating was videotaped by a witness and frequently shown to the nation on the news. Laurence Powell, one of the officers, used his nightstick to repeatedly strike King. In messages on his in-car computer the night of the whipping, he boasted about beating King and referred to an unrelated domestic disturbance involving two black people as something straight from *Gorillas in the Mist*.[2] His comments surfaced in the trial to determine if the police officers had used excessive force against King.

When directed at people of African descent, the names of simians function as racial slurs. To call a black person a monkey or an ape is to insult their intelligence, temperament, physical appearance, social fit, even their humanness. And, of course, the slurring includes types of monkeys (baboons) and apes (chimpanzees, gorillas, and orangutans).

Associating a black person with a monkey or ape has a long history in this country. Thomas Jefferson, the third U.S. president and the primary author of the Declaration of Independence, wrote in *Notes on the State of Virginia* that black men preferred white women "as uniformly as is the preference of the Oran-utan [orangutan] for the black woman over those

"STILL HANGING ON."

COPYRIGHTED, 1905, AND
PUBLISHED BY KNAFFL & BRO., KNOXVILLE, TENN.

of his own species."[3] Jefferson's comments are today understood as the product of a mind deeply shaped by and committed to antiblack racism, but when he linked black people to orangutans in 1781, he reflected a belief held by many of his contemporaries. The narrative that black people are at best an inferior race—at worst, not quite human—continues to live in the United States.

Intellectual Racism

Homo sapiens (Latin: "man who knows") is the scientific name for the human species; more specifically, humans are the subspecies *Homo sapiens sapiens*, to differentiate them from what is believed to be their direct ancestor, *Homo sapiens idaltu*. The appellation *Homo sapiens* was coined by Carl Linnaeus, a Swedish physician, botanist, and zoologist. In his treatise *Systema Naturae* (1767), Linnaeus created the system used for categorizing life forms into species, genus, family, and so forth. He was also a pioneer in defining the concept of race as applied to humans. Within *Homo sapiens* Linnaeus proposed a typology of five distinct species, which corresponded generally to racial groups. From the beginning, classifying groups into races raised the question, "Which races are superior?"

Linnaeus not only became the first scientist to conceptualize a racial typology of humans and write it within a broader classification scheme, he also became one of the first scientists to offer scientific support for the establishment of racial hierarchies. Much of his work with botany was groundbreaking. Indeed, some of it reflected a pioneering genius, but his classifying of humans into discrete categories was simply wrong. Whether intended or not, his work laid the foundation for the pseudoscience now understood as scientific racism, which became a justification for modern race-based horrors, including but not limited to the near extermination of the indigenous peoples of the Americas, the enslavement of Africans and African Americans, the Holocaust, and other genocides.

Linnaeus and those who followed him ranked white people at the top of the racial hierarchy, and ranked black people at or near the bottom, just above the nonhuman primates. Ranking black people immediately above monkeys and apes made it easy to compare black people to monkeys and apes, and eventually to drop blacks into the nonhuman primate grouping. Franz Ignaz Pruner, a medical doctor who studied blacks in Egypt, claimed in an 1861 document that the skeletons of Negroes are characterized by prognathism (jaw protrusions), which he saw as proof of a Negro-ape connection. Pruner also claimed that the brains of Negroes and apes were similar—and, he added, both Negroes and apes have a shortened big toe.[4] In that same year, the year the Civil War began, John

During the Jim Crow period it was common for black children to be shown without clothes on postcards, trade cards, and posters. This postcard was copyrighted in 1905.

H. Van Evrie, a physician, wrote: "There is a certain resemblance between the negro and the orang-outang. The latter is the most advanced species of the simidae or ape family, while the negro is the lowest in the scale of the human creation, and the approximation to each other, though of course eternally incomplete, is certainly striking."[5]

German scholars led the scientific racism movement of the 1800s, and their writings were tools for the white Americans who desired to rationalize slavery and other forms of racial oppression. Scientist Karl Vogt, in his *Lectures of Man*, claimed that Negroes and whites were so different that they constituted extreme human types, and that the difference between them was greater than the difference between two species of apes. He argued that Negroes and whites constituted two distinct species.[6] The German biologist Ernst Haeckel divided humans into ten races. Not surprisingly, he ranked Caucasians at the top. Haeckel called Negroes "four-handed apes," claiming that they had ape-like toes useful for climbing trees and holding on to branches.[7] Christoph Meiners, a philosopher and historian, divided human beings into two broad categories: the "beautiful white race" and the "ugly black race." In his book *The Outline of History of Mankind,* he argued that the ugly races were inferior, immoral, animal-like, and given to terrible vices.[8]

Samuel George Morton, an American natural scientist and physician, claimed that Negroes had much smaller brains than whites.[9] One of his many followers was Josiah C. Nott, a physician and enslaver of black people. Nott claimed that "the negro achieves his greatest perfection, physical and moral, and also his greatest longevity, in a state of slavery."[10] Nott has been accused of fabricating research: distorting facial and skull features to "prove" a close relationship between African peoples and chimpanzees.[11]

One of the more interesting developments in the history of science came from the attempts by Christian theorists to reconcile their theological beliefs with their race-based beliefs, while incorporating ideas from science. In 1867, Buckner H. Payne, under the pen name Ariel, wrote *The Negro: What Is His Ethnological Status?*, in which he argued that white Adam and Eve "could never be the father or mother of the kinky-headed, low forehead, flat nose, thick lip and black-skinned negro."[12] In 1891, William Campbell, using the pen name Caucasian, wrote *Anthropology for the People: A Refutation of the Theory of the Adamic Origin of All Races.* He agreed that Negroes did not descend from (white) Adam and were "inferior creations."[13]

The widespread acceptance of the belief that black people were simian-like is evidenced by an entry in the 1889 edition of *Encyclopaedia Britannica* that stated that the African race occupied "the lowest position

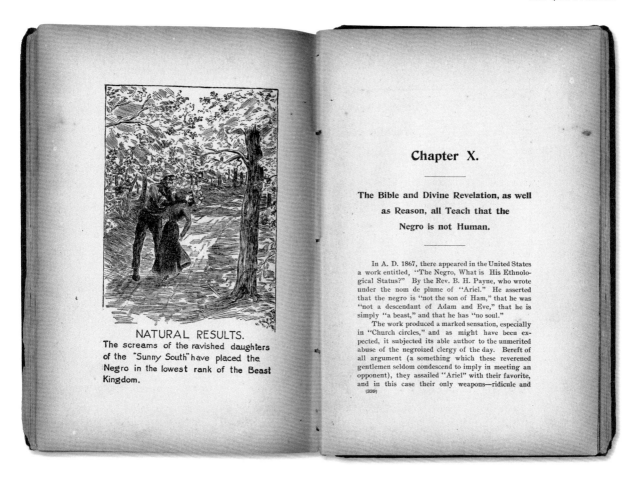

NATURAL RESULTS.

The screams of the ravished daughters of the "Sunny South" have placed the Negro in the lowest rank of the Beast Kingdom.

Chapter X.

The Bible and Divine Revelation, as well as Reason, all Teach that the Negro is not Human.

In A. D. 1867, there appeared in the United States a work entitled, "The Negro, What is His Ethnological Status?" By the Rev. B. H. Payne, who wrote under the nom de plume of "Ariel." He asserted that the negro is "not the son of Ham," that he was "not a descendant of Adam and Eve," that he is simply "a beast," and that he has "no soul."

The work produced a marked sensation, especially in "Church circles," and as might have been expected, it subjected its able author to the unmerited abuse of the negroized clergy of the day. Bereft of all argument (a something which these reverened gentlemen seldom condescend to imply in meeting an opponent), they assailed "Ariel" with their favorite, and in this case their only weapons—ridicule and

(339)

---

of the evolutionary scale, thus affording the best material for the comparative study of the highest anthropoids and the human species."[14] Placing them in an encyclopedia made these beliefs accessible to a broader population and made them legitimate in the minds of the general public, which read the words as fact, not as the fiction of white supremacists.

Newspaper stories also used simian references to describe blacks suspected or convicted of committing crimes. In 1856, for example, a newspaper described two suspects as "two black niggers, one an old ape looking darkie, and the other a young one."[15] An 1876 story began "The negro, or Ape, Henry, who is at the Poor House of this county, went into a negro church one evening last week and hollowed 'Shoot!'"[16] In 1904, Charles Smith, a black man suspected of being "the masked burglar of Providence" was described in the *New York Times* as "black as coal and of uncouth form, being built like a baboon."[17] In 1920, Andrew Jackson, a black man, was executed for raping a white woman. Jackson was described in a newspaper story as a "negro of gorilla proportions and intelligence."[18] In 1927, James Hamilton, a black man in Pennsylvania,

These are pages 338–39 in Charles Carroll's *The Negro a Beast.*

was arrested on a disorderly charge. He was described as the "gorilla man."[19] In 1935, Oscar Wilson, a black man accused of killing a woman in a New York park, was described in newspapers as "the ape man."[20]

In 1900, the American Book and Bible House published a strange but popular book by Charles Carroll. The full title of Carroll's book was *The Negro a Beast . . . or . . . In the Image of God. The Reasoner of the Age, the Revelator of the Century! The Bible as it is! The Negro and His Relation to the Human Family! . . . The Negro not the Son of Ham.* According to the book's subtitle, "The Negro [is] a beast, but created with articulate speech and hands, that he may be of service to his master—the White man." Like Payne and Campbell before him, Carroll claimed that the white race was made in the image and likeness of God, and Adam gave birth to the white race only, while Negroes are pre-Adamite creatures that are too beastlike, immoral, and ugly to have been made in God's image. The Negroes, according to Carroll, were created with other animals, before God created humans. Carroll's interpretation of human races was, as such, significantly different from the one proposed by Linnaeus. Claire Jean Kim summarizes Carroll's approach:

> Carroll ridicules both the "atheistic theory of Natural Development" (Darwinism) and "Enlightened Christianity" which together teach that although there are five varieties or races of man, they are all part of a single human species. This is heresy, Carroll contends, because it tears down the barriers that God set up between man, whom He made in His image, and the ape, and brings man down to the level of the ape by saying that he descended from the latter. The Negro, Carroll insists, was formed separately from the white man, is not part of the Adamic family, and is an ape.[21]

Some scientists attempted to prove that Negroes were inferior but human. In some instances, they accomplished their goal by comparing black people to monkeys and apes. While these scientists and philosophers used their writings to "prove" that black people belonged to a lower race, Carroll went one step further. Using a jumbled, mishmash interpretation of the Christian Bible, history, and pseudoscience, Carroll argued that Negroes were nonhuman beasts, literally apes. Carroll saw the Negro as the head of the ape family, a man-like ape, a pre-Adamic, soulless beast. He considered gibbons, orangutans, chimpanzees, and gorillas to be "negro-like apes."

Sexual relations between whites (humans) and Negroes (apes) were, therefore, unnatural and a sin. Race mixing—or rather, species mixing—was an insult to God and spoiled His creation plan. According to Carroll, the sexual mixing of whites and blacks led to the errors of atheism and

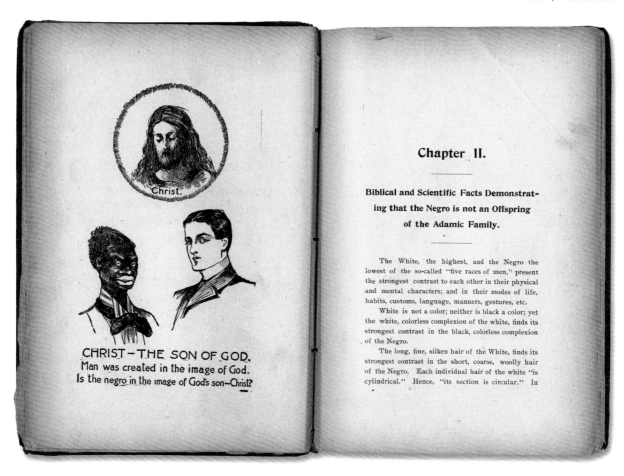

CHRIST—THE SON OF GOD.
Man was created in the image of God.
Is the negro in the image of God's son—Christ?

Chapter II.

Biblical and Scientific Facts Demonstrating that the Negro is not an Offspring of the Adamic Family.

The White, the highest, and the Negro the lowest of the so-called "five races of men," present the strongest contrast to each other in their physical and mental characters; and in their modes of life, habits, customs, language, manners, gestures, etc.

White is not a color; neither is black a color; yet the white, colorless complexion of the white, finds its strongest contrast in the black, colorless complexion of the Negro.

The long, fine, silken hair of the White, finds its strongest contrast in the short, coarse, woolly hair of the Negro. Each individual hair of the white "is cylindrical." Hence, "its section is circular." In

evolution, and to the production of human-animal hybrids (mulattoes) who did not have the right to live because they "were the rapists and criminals of the present time."[22] For Carroll, black people were not metaphoric beasts, they were literally beasts, apes with the capacity and inclination to wreak havoc in heaven and on earth.

More than a century after Carroll wrote *The Negro a Beast*, another writer, Kenneth Smith, used his understanding of the Christian creation story to hypothesize about the origins of black people. In *The True Origin of Man*, Smith argues that the first white people were Adam and Eve—with pure white skin, snow-white hair, and blue eyes.[23] Whites were created first and black (and other dark-skinned) people were created through the sinful behavior of Cain, the son of Adam and Eve, who had sexual relations with a female ape. Carroll was a white man. Smith is an African American.

Smith gained national attention when he sued the West Virginia Department of Education for teaching his daughter evolution, which is, in his view, a religion. In the complaint he argues that teaching evolution in the state's public schools constitutes "the propagation of religious

These are pages 44–45 in *The Negro a Beast*.

By permission of Herr Carl Hagenbeck] *[Hamburg*

NEGRO BOY AND APES

*An interesting picture of a Negro boy, with a young Chimpanzee (left side of figure)
and young Orang-utan (right side of figure)*

faith."[24] Smith's lawsuit was also motivated by his frustration with education officials who refused to approve *The True Origin of Man* as a textbook to be used in public schools. His lawsuit and his writings have resulted in him receiving a great deal of ridicule on the internet.

Ota Benga

White people liked to stare at Ota Benga, liked it so much they paid twenty-five cents for the privilege. They also dressed in their Sunday best to see him. Benga was young, probably twenty-three years old. He had been married twice. Both his wives were dead. But the white faces that came to see him did not care about his age or his wives. They only cared about what they believed he represented. They wanted to be entertained by something new. In a world before television and the internet, staring at Benga was entertainment, a mass attraction featured in the Bronx Zoo Monkey House in 1906. Today, it would be widely considered not only cruel but boring to watch this man sit or walk or shoot a bow and arrow or play with animals.

Some of the white people threw things at Benga. He was not in a position to effectively defend himself. He was, after all, a small man, weighing a little more than 100 pounds and standing about four feet eleven inches tall. And he was separated from them by language. He was from a tribe in the Congo and did not speak English well. Sometimes native speakers believe that someone in their culture who does not speak the native language well, or at all, must be less intelligent. The people who paid to stare at Benga thought he was dumb. They debated whether he could learn. They marveled at his perceived stupidity. They were fascinated by his every intelligible action, as if to say, "My, there are some things he can do. There are things that he does in the same ways that we do."

For the twenty-five-cent entrance fee, visitors felt entitled to yell at Benga. They called him stupid and ugly. They laughed at him, laughed at his teeth, filed to sharpened points, a decorative custom of his tribe in the Congo. When they could get close to him, the people who paid to see him chased him, and when they caught him they poked him in the ribs, tripped him.[25] They burned him with cigars. They were having fun. They called him names—savage, primitive, pygmy, little nigger—including names that questioned his humanness, most notably, "monkey boy." On September 16, 1906, forty thousand visitors, almost all whites, went to see the "savage little man" or "savage little animal."

A white American, in 1906, looking at this so-called pygmy, would have been tempted to think of him as a savage—or worse, as a missing link between humans and monkeys or apes. Was he not proof of an earlier stage of human evolution? The white American would certainly have

This is a reproduction of a photograph taken by or for Carl Hagenbeck (1844–1913), a German merchant who supplied European zoos with wild animals and "primitive" people for display.

45

reason to think in this way. After all, Benga was displayed in the New York Zoological Park, more familiarly known as the Bronx Zoo. Above the cage hung a sign that proclaimed "The Missing Link." This was propaganda in action. Benga was "sold" or "rented" as a public service announcement for the theory of evolution in general, and for white supremacy in particular.

The little black man that the white people paid to see and jeer was locked in a cage-like space, with an orangutan for a companion. He was delivered to the zoo by Samuel Phillips Verner, a failed Christian missionary and pseudoscientist who pretended to be Benga's friend.[26] Benga was received by William Temple Hornaday, the zoo's director, who saw an opportunity to make money and gain fame. He claimed that the exhibit was a valuable spectacle for visitors. Madison Grant, secretary of the New York Zoological Society, supported the exhibit. A decade later, he would gain national prominence as the author of *The Passing of the Great Race*, which expounds a theory of Nordic (white) superiority and argues in favor of eugenics programs.[27]

Benga was alone.

The *New York Times*—which would later be known as a liberal newspaper—sounded very much like a tabloid produced by Charles Carroll, Samuel George Morton, and Josiah C. Nott. When a group of local black clergymen complained about Benga's confinement in the cage, the *Times* wondered what the fuss was about. Was he not being fed? Was this not his appointed station in life? An editorial in the newspaper stated:

> We do not quite understand all the emotion which others are expressing in the matter. . . . It is absurd to make moan over the imagined humiliation and degradation Benga is suffering. The pygmies . . . are very low in the human scale, and the suggestion that Benga should be in a school instead of a cage ignores the high probability that school would be a place . . . from which he could draw no advantage whatever. The idea that men are all much alike except as they have had or lacked opportunities for getting an education out of books is now far out of date.[28]

Black clergy visited Benga. They were dismayed to see him being displayed in a cage as proof of evolution. The *Times* criticized their activism, criticizing them for not embracing evolution. In a revealing quote, one that harkened back to claims raised in *The Negro a Beast*, one of the ministers, J.H. Gordon, said, "Our race, we think, is depressed enough, without exhibiting one of us with the apes. . . . We think we are worthy of being considered human beings, with souls."[29]

White people paid to stare at Benga for several weeks. The staring stopped when the black ministers gained his release and placed Benga

This is a postcard from 1943.

in the Howard Colored Orphan Asylum, a church-sponsored orphanage. Later, he moved to Lynchburg, Virginia, where he lived with a local family. To fit in, he wore the clothes that other Americans wore, he went to a school to learn to read and write English, his teeth were capped, and he got a job.

On March 20, 1916, at the age of thirty-two, almost a decade after the white people tricked him into sharing a cage with an orangutan, Benga built a ceremonial fire, chipped off the caps on his teeth, and shot himself in the heart with a gun. After that, no one, white or black, could stare at Benga.

In-Group Insults

It is an unfortunate truth that groups that are debased—in words, images, and actions—often show evidence of internalizing the debasement, including using the slurs that the dominant group uses. This self- and group-loathing is illustrated by black people referring to one another, especially perceived rivals or enemies, as simians. An early example involved two of the most prominent black figures in this country's history: W.E.B. Du Bois and Marcus Garvey.

William Edward Burghardt Du Bois was a scholar and activist renowned as a prolific author—including his book *The Souls of Black Folk*—and as a founder of the National Association for the Advancement of Colored People (NAACP) in 1909. He grew up in Great Barrington, Massachusetts, a community that did not have the harsh violent expressions of racism found in the Deep South. He completed graduate work at the University of Berlin and Harvard, where he was the first African American to earn a doctorate. Du Bois was the leading spokesperson for African American rights during the first half of the twentieth century.

Marcus Garvey was one of Du Bois's rivals as a leader of black people. Garvey, born in Jamaica, was a black nationalist and founder of the United Negro Improvement Association (UNIA). At a time when black people were seen matter-of-factly as ignorant and ugly, Garvey encouraged black people to see themselves as beautiful, intelligent empire builders. Unlike Du Bois, who for most of his life was a radical integrationist, Garvey was an avowed separatist, who hoped to build a unified nation of people of pure African ancestry.

Garvey and Du Bois did not respect each other as leaders or as "race men." The dark-skinned Garvey wanted to include only racially pure blacks in his movement; he insisted that authentic black leadership could only come from pure blacks.[30] His approach meant that mixed-race African Americans like Du Bois were excluded as leaders of black people. The animosity between the two men was personal and nasty. Du

Bois, in an article that criticized Garvey and the UNIA, referred to Garvey as a "little, fat, black man; ugly, but with intelligent eyes and a big head." Garvey responded by saying, "if there is any ugliness in the Negro race it would be reflected more through Du Bois than Marcus Garvey, in that he himself tells us that he is a little Dutch, a little French, and a little Negro. Why, in fact, the man is a monstrosity."[31] On another occasion Garvey referred to Du Bois as a "pale shame."[32] Garvey's present-day followers claim that Du Bois referred to Garvey as a gorilla.

Du Bois may or may not have called Garvey a gorilla, but there is no doubt that a well-known black American did refer to a black man as a gorilla. Muhammad Ali is considered one of the top boxers in history. Nicknamed "The Greatest," Ali won the heavyweight championship on three occasions: in 1964, 1974, and 1978. His nickname could be attributed to his performance in several historic boxing matches. On February 25, 1964, Ali, then known as Cassius Clay, defeated Sonny Liston in what was perceived to be a major upset. Liston learned to box while in prison serving time for armed robbery. He was the most feared boxer of his time, maybe of all time. White writers described him as a thug, a bully, a union goon, and a gorilla.[33] Clay was a brash-talking pretty boy and few writers or observers gave him a chance against the "black brute." Clay defeated Liston and, in his words, "shook up the world."

On February 27, 1964, Clay announced that he was a member of the Nation of Islam, which many Americans considered a militant religious/political sect. A week later, Elijah Muhammad, the leader of the Nation of Islam, proclaimed that Clay would be renamed Muhammad Ali.

The United States was at war in Vietnam in 1966, and Ali refused to be inducted into the armed forces. He was denied a boxing license and stripped of his passport. He was barred from fighting from March 1967 to October 1970. During those years Ali traveled the country speaking about his moral and religious right to oppose fighting in the war. His stand made him a villain to some, but for others, including many present-day observers, he was a rebel hero, a courageous man willing to sacrifice professional gain.

In 1971, the U.S. Supreme Court overturned his conviction in a unanimous 8–0 ruling. After several warm-up fights, Ali fought Joe Frazier, the champion, in what was billed as the "Fight of the Century." Before the fight, Ali proclaimed loudly that Frazier was "too ugly to be champ" and "too dumb to be champ." He accused Frazier of being an Uncle Tom, a sellout, a white man's Negro. Frazier, hurt and offended, seethed. It was a close fight. In the final round, Frazier knocked Ali down with a vicious left hook. Ali got off the mat but lost by a unanimous decision, his first professional defeat. They would fight twice more, and both times Ali won

49

THE NATIONAL TATTLER

★★★★★
WEEKLY
SPECIAL
15¢

PROVOCATIVE FEATURES OF UNUSUAL INTEREST

VOL. 6, NO. 24—JUNE 11, 1967

Most Shocking Story You Have Ever Read

NEGRO WOMAN HAS APE BABY

And Nearly Died From The Pain!

Official Tape-Recorded Confessions of
THE BOSTON STRANGLER

I MOLESTED HER WITH AN ICE TRAY

in grueling battles. Before each fight Ali cruelly taunted Frazier. Their last fight occurred on October 1, 1975. It was held in the Philippines and billed as the "Thrilla in Manila." Before the fight Ali rhymed, "It will be a killa and a chilla and a thrilla, when I get the gorilla in Manila." Ali won the fight, one of the most brutal bouts in modern boxing history, when Frazier did not answer the bell in the final round. Both men left the ring physically and emotionally spent—and, one of them left the ring consumed with hatred for the man, the black man, who had called him an Uncle Tom and a gorilla. In Frazier's words, "I hated Ali. God might not like me talking that way, but it's in my heart. I hated that man. First two fights, he tried to make me a white man. Then he tried to make me a nigger. How would you like it if your kids came home from school crying, because everyone was calling their daddy a gorilla?"[34]

Black Athletes as Monkeys and Apes

The ascendancy of the African American athlete was one of the most significant cultural changes in the United States in the twentieth century. Despite being banned from Major League Baseball (MLB), the National Basketball Association (NBA), and the National Football League (NFL) during the first half of the century, by the end of the twentieth century, African Americans were among the most accomplished professional base-ball players, and their dominance was so great in the NBA and NFL, both in numbers and performances, that those leagues were increasingly seen as predominantly black leagues. The prevalence of black athletes in the country's three major sports, as well as boxing and track and field, made African Americans the sports heroes for much of the nation. Despite their celebrity status and great wealth, some black athletes, especially those with dark skin, experience traditional racism—including being called a monkey or ape.

Rodney Cline "Rod" Carew is a member of the MLB Hall of Fame. He played from 1967 to 1985 for the Minnesota Twins and the California Angels and was selected to play in the All-Star Game every year except his last season. The sweet-swinging Carew was a seven-time batting champion, finishing his career with 3,053 hits and a lifetime batting average of .328, one of the highest all-time marks. A dark-skinned Panamanian American, Carew caused a stir in 1970 when it was announced that he was engaged to marry Marilynn Levy, a white woman. He received hate mail addressed to "Dear nigger ape." The letters contained obscenities, racial taunts, and threats to "get rid of you and your Jew bitch." Carew said, "The really scary thing is that the letters are not just from one nut."[35]

Patrick Ewing, who played professionally for the New York Knicks, has been called an ape and a gorilla since his days as a college player

This tabloid newspaper was published in 1967.

at Georgetown University in the early 1980s.[36] He was an easy target: seven feet tall, with a slightly awkward gait, dark skin, and painfully shy because of his Jamaican accent. When the Georgetown basketball team took the court as visitors against Providence, one of the home team fans raised a sign that read "EWING CAN'T READ." This might be interpreted as an allusion to the "dumb jock" stereotype, or it might have been a suggestion that Ewing was dumb like a lower primate. John Thompson, Ewing's coach, pulled the Georgetown basketball team off the court until the sign was removed. At a game against Villanova, fans held up similar signs. One raised bedsheet read, "EWING IS AN APE." During pregame introductions, someone threw a banana peel on the court when Ewing's name was announced. Ewing was called ape and gorilla throughout his college tenure and his professional career. Decades after he left Georgetown he remains the African American athlete most often portrayed as a monkey or ape in photoshopped memes on the internet.

African American women, especially ones with bodies that are perceived to be less feminine, have been described as simian-like by fans and by other athletes. One of the most highly publicized incidents occurred in 1988 and involved two gifted athletes: Florence Griffith "Flo-Jo" Joyner and Jackie Joyner-Kersee, both Olympic gold medalist track stars. Flo-Jo is considered the fastest woman of all time, and Joyner-Kersee is considered one of the best overall female athletes in the history of the United States. Their careers were dogged by rumors that they used human growth hormones and other performance-enhancing drugs. In one particularly ugly moment, Joaquim Cruz, a middle-distance runner for Brazil, claimed that the women must be using the drugs because, "Florence . . . today she looks more like a man than a woman." He added that Jackie Joyner-Kersee "looks like a gorilla, so these people, they must be doing something that isn't normal to gain all these muscles."[37] Cruz later apologized for the remarks, but Joyner-Kersee, hurt to the point of tears, considered retiring.

Serena Williams and her sister Venus are African American women who have dominated professional tennis worldwide. The physical appearances of both women are often described in unflattering ways. Sports announcer Sid Rosenberg, in an attempt at humor, called Venus Williams "an animal" and said that "she and Serena had a better shot of posing nude in *National Geographic* than in *Playboy*."[38] Serena, the physically larger and more accomplished of the sisters is often slurred with words that link her to simians. In 2005, white radio sports host Tony Veitch said of Serena, "Do you know where the apes come from? She is a reminder."[39] Following every major tennis victory, the Williams sisters, especially Serena, are subjected to comparisons with monkeys and apes. After

This 1930s object may have
been used to mock Negro
League baseball players.

reviewing Twitter comments made after Serena won the U.S. Open in 2014—including "If Obama had a son he would look like her" and "Drug test them chimpanzees"—Tiffanie Drayton wrote:

> This paints a more clear picture of a modern White America that is not only racially intolerant but openly hateful. Through that lens, Serena's strength cannot be appreciated as the strength of a woman because she is a Black woman—an animal at best and Obama's son at worst. A vile, disgusting monkey with an attitude problem. The racial stereotypes invoked within those comment threads are attached to names and faces of individuals who are real. People whose profile pictures are sweet images of little, inno-cent children and babies, soldiers, both young and middle-aged White men and women smiling at the world in simple head shots. White people who obviously do not view Black people as people.[40]

In some instances it is not clear if the linking of black people with simians reflects racial malice. During a Monday Night Football telecast on September 5, 1983, Howard Cosell, one of America's most famous and controversial sportscasters, said of Alvin Garrett, an African American player with the Washington Redskins, "That little monkey gets loose, doesn't he?"[41] Cosell's comments led to charges of racism and demands that he issue an apology. Garrett asked Cosell to apologize, in part, because he wanted the locker room "pranks" to stop. "I come back [to the locker room] to put my pants on and there's a banana in my pocket. One day, somebody taped five or six bananas up in my locker. They're putting them everywhere."[42] Cosell refused to apologize. He trumpeted his support of black American athletes, including Muhammad Ali, to prove he was not a racist. Moreover, he claimed that "monkey" was a term of endearment that he sometimes used to reference diminutive athletes, including whites. Cosell may not have used the word as a racial slur—there are claims that he also used the term to refer to his relatives—but he left the Monday Night Football booth following the 1983 season.

Cosell was not the only sportscaster to refer to an African American athlete as a monkey. Billy Packer, a basketball analyst for CBS, also used a simian name to refer to Allen Iverson, a star African American athlete. Packer, describing a replay that showed Iverson making a difficult shot despite being fouled, said, "You're talking about a tough monkey."[43]

A more recent incident involving what might be "accidental racism" involved Lebron James, one of the best basketball players of his genera-tion. In March 2008, James became the first African American male to be on the cover of *Vogue* magazine, a cover he shared with the Brazilian model Gisele Bundchen. On the cover, shot by photographer Annie

Leibovitz, James's six-foot-nine-inch frame is slightly hunched over, simian-like. His mouth is open, teeth bared, and he appears to be growling. With one hand he dribbles a basketball, his other arm wrapped around the waist of the white model. The cover shot bears a strong resemblance to a World War I propaganda poster and also to a poster for the 1933 film *King Kong*.[44] James's large body and menacing body language evoke fears of the black brute, the savage who seeks to sexually assault white women, and it revives the imagery of black men as simian, in this case a gorilla. The people responsible for the *Vogue* cover may not have intended to make a racial statement—Leibovitz is known for borrowing iconic imagery from old movies—but the cover did send a message. There are others whose intentions are clearer and more direct.

John Rocker, a relief pitcher for the Atlanta Braves, made national news in an interview published in the December 27, 1999, issue of *Sports Illustrated*. The reporter, Jeff Pearlman, wrote that during the interview Rocker referred to Randall Simon, a black teammate from Curaçao, as a fat monkey. In response to a question about whether he would play for one of the two New York baseball teams, Rocker spewed a rant that managed to offend most New Yorkers.

> I'd retire first. It's the most hectic, nerve-racking city. Imagine having to take the 7 Train to the ballpark looking like you're riding through Beirut next to some kid with purple hair, next to some queer with AIDS, right next to some dude who just got out of jail for the fourth time, right next to some 20-year-old mom with four kids. It's depressing. . . . The biggest thing I don't like about New York are the foreigners. You can walk an entire block in Times Square and not hear anybody speaking English. Asians and Koreans and Vietnamese and Indians and Russians and Spanish people and everything up there. How the hell did they get in this country?[45]

Hockey is the major professional team sport in the United States with the fewest African Americans (or African Canadians). The first black man to sign a National Hockey League (NHL) contract was Art Dorrington, with the New York Rangers in 1950, but he never played beyond the minor league level. The first black man to play in the NHL was Willie Eldon O'Ree, a black Canadian, who made his NHL debut with the Boston Bruins against the Montreal Canadiens, on January 18, 1958. He played in two games that year and came back in 1961 to play forty-three games. He scored four goals and ten assists in his NHL career, all in 1961. O'Ree, the "Jackie Robinson of ice hockey," faced racial taunts from fans, especially fans in the United States.

After O'Ree's brief two-year NHL career ended, there were no black players in the league until Mike Robert Marson, another Canadian, was drafted by the Washington Capitals in 1974. Fans taunted him with slurs: "nigger," "coon," "spear-chucker," and "monkey."[46] Today, the relatively few black and multiracial players in the NHL are still sometimes targeted with racial slurs by opponents and opposing fans, and these racial taunts commonly involve simian slurs. In 1997, Craig Berube, a white player, received a one-game suspension for calling Peter Worrell, who is black, a monkey. The next year Darcy Tucker, a Tampa Bay Lightning player, called Worrell an ape. Worrell, who experienced racism from his earliest days as a hockey player, said:

> Anything I get up here [in the NHL] is laughable. To say some-
> thing about a player's race or religion, that's cowardly. But it's
> something I've dealt with my whole life. At first, I used to cry. But
> I learned at an extremely early age that, what can they do from
> the stands? I use that as a motivation. If they say, "Hey, nigger,
> you can't play hockey. Go play ball. Go to the jungle," then I think,
> "How 'bout I throw a clean body check on your son."[47]

Kevin Weekes, an African Canadian hockey announcer and former goaltender, had a banana thrown at him during a playoff game in 2002.[48] In 2011, an Ontario fan threw a banana at Wayne Simmonds, a black player. The fan was fined $200. Gary Bettman, commissioner of the NHL, said, "The obviously stupid and ignorant action by one individual is in no way representative of our fans or the people of London, Ontario."[49]

Racism expressed in language that compares black people to simians, especially monkeys and apes, is not limited to the United States. Soccer, arguably the most popular sport worldwide, has witnessed a steady stream of simian slurs and taunts against players with dark skin. In 2005, Barcelona player Samuel Eto was mocked by fans who made "monkey noises" and threw peanuts on the pitch (field). In 2008, black players for Olympique Marseille faced abuse by Russian fans, who threw bananas on the pitch and made monkey chants. In 2011, Roberto Carlos, a black player, had bananas thrown at him in games played in the Russian Premier League. In 2009, Mario Balotelli, an Italian footballer of Ghanaian descent, was subjected to racial abuse from fans. In 2012, Spanish fans directed monkey chants against him. Black players are subjected to racial abuse throughout European soccer leagues.

The Obamas as Monkeys

By the winter of 2008, Barack Hussein Obama, a multiracial black-identified Illinois senator, had emerged as a leading candidate for the

Obama Monkey Doll, 2008

This is an Obama Monkey
Doll made in 2008.

OBAMA IN
08

presidency of the United States. Mike Norman, owner of Mulligan's Food and Spirits bar in Marietta, Georgia, gained a measure of national notoriety by selling T-shirts that featured Curious George, a cartoon monkey, peeling a banana, with "Obama in '08" underneath. He argued that although blacks were sometimes compared to monkeys before and during the Jim Crow period, the T-shirts should not be viewed as racist because Obama and the cartoon monkey "look so much alike."[50] Civil rights activists and Senator Obama's supporters protested in front of Norman's business. In June, a Utah couple, the Lawsons, created a stuffed sock monkey doll dressed as and named after Obama. As with Norman, the Lawsons claimed that their creation was not meant to be racist but instead was the result of "a charming association between a candidate and a toy we had when we were little."[51] The sock monkey, advertised as "cute and cuddly," offended some Americans and amused others.

The T-shirts and sock monkeys were two of many examples of portrayals of Obama or members of his family as monkeys or apes. One YouTube video focused on a man holding the Curious George Obama monkey, the doll is wearing a hat made from an Obama campaign sticker. While he and others laugh, the man says of the monkey, "This is little Hussein who wanted to see truth and good Americans." He shakes the doll defiantly at protesters (across the street) who are chanting, "Racists, racists, racists."[52] A crasser linking of Obama to monkeys is found in a video, "Michelle Obama Without Makeup," that caricatured her as an ape.

In 2008, Barack Obama was elected president of the United States, becoming the first African American to hold the office. He was reelected in 2012. The election of a man with brown skin to the nation's highest elected office was not celebrated in all quarters of the country. Indeed, Obama's candidacy and subsequent election shone a light on a simple truth: in the United States, race is still a master status—a status that trumps others. Obama's political ascendancy provoked raw emotions, including vulgar race-fueled bitterness that expressed itself in a centuries-old racial trope: the portrayal of black people as more monkey than human.

There are dozens—maybe hundreds—of internet memes depicting Barack Obama or Michelle Obama as monkeys or apes. Between 2008 and 2011, police officials and city officials in Ferguson, Missouri, shared emails that derided and ridiculed black people. One of them included a black-and-white photograph of President Ronald Reagan feeding a baby chimpanzee, with the caption, "Rare photo of Ronald Reagan babysitting Barack Obama in early 1962."[53] The discovery of the emails further stained the reputation of Ferguson police, adding credibility to the claims of local black residents that the police routinely discriminate against

This shirt was made in 2008.   **59**

black people. In 2011, Marilyn Davenport, a Republican official in Orange County, California, sent out an email that showed three chimps, an adult male, an adult female, and an infant. Obama's face has been photoshopped onto the body of the infant. The photograph's caption reads, "Now you know why no birth certificate."[54]

  In some instances, the linking of President Obama to simians is done indirectly, often in the form of insinuations. In 2013, Ann Coulter, a political activist and provocateur, appeared on the Fox News Channel program *Hannity* to discuss the Obama administration's response to the Syrian crisis. In the course of the seven-minute segment, she said that Russian President Vladimir Putin "is making a monkey out of Obama," that the crisis may have been orchestrated "to make Obama look like a monkey" and that Putin "made Obama a monkey" on several occasions since the president's reelection.[55] A press release from the National Center for Public Policy Research criticized Coulter.

> While Coulter is free to choose her idioms, it appeared obvious her word choice was purposefully meant to provoke controversy. Even host Sean Hannity called out Coulter on her syntax three times during the relatively short segment, specifically asking at one point: "Why are you saying that? Because you know people are going to criticize you for using that term against the President. . . . Are you trying to be provocative?" Obviously taken aback, Coulter paused and denied Hannity's assertion, but then subsequently used the term "ragdoll" to characterize Putin as "playing with" Obama.[56]

In March 2014, Donald Rumsfeld, defense secretary under George W. Bush, claimed that a "trained ape" could have done a better job securing diplomatic relations with Afghanistan than did the Obama administration. In 2014, the North Korean government, angry about the release of the film *The Interview*, lashed out at President Barack Obama, whom they blamed for the movie.[57] "Obama always goes reckless in words and deeds like a monkey in a tropical forest." It was not the first time North Korean authorities directed racially charged insults at Obama. In May 2014, the official North Korean news agency referred to the president as a "crossbreed" and "wicked black monkey" after he met with South Korean President Park Geun-hye.[58]

  In 2015, Patrick Rushing, mayor of Airway Heights, Washington, posted a Facebook comment that read "Gorilla face Michelle, can't disagree with that. That woman is not attractive except to monkey man Barack. Check out them ears. LOL."[59] Despite pressure from the local city council, Mayor Rushing refused to resign, citing his right to free speech. In that same year Rodner Figueroa, an Emmy-winning host, said on the

Univision show *El Gordo y La Flaca*, "You know Michelle Obama looks like she is from the cast of *The Planet of the Apes*."[60] He was fired.

In 2009, the *New York Post* printed a cartoon that sparked national critique and criticism. The cartoon showed two white police officers, one with his gun pointed, smoke coming from the barrel. On the ground is a rabid chimpanzee, with two bullet holes to the chest, apparently dead from the policeman's gunfire. One officer, the nonshooter, says, "They'll have to find someone else to write the next stimulus bill." The cartoon was an apparent reference to two current events: a Connecticut police officer had recently shot and killed a two-hundred-pound chimpanzee after it savagely mauled a friend of its owner, and there was a national debate about the federal stimulus bill championed by President Obama. The cartoon was on page 12 of the newspaper. On page 11, there was a photograph of the president signing the stimulus bill into law.

The *Post* was assailed as being either naive or intentionally racially insensitive. Al Sharpton, an activist and television host, helped lead a protest rally outside the Manhattan offices of the newspaper. After receiving criticism, the *Post* apologized but defended the cartoon, "It was meant to mock an ineptly written federal stimulus bill."[61] Sharpton, speaking for people who believed the cartoon had a racial subtext, said:

> The cartoon in today's *New York Post* is troubling at best given the historic racist attacks of African-Americans as being synonymous with monkeys. One has to question whether the cartoonist is making a less than casual reference to this when in the cartoon they have police saying after shooting a chimpanzee that "Now they will have to find someone else to write the stimulus bill.
>
> Being that the stimulus bill has been the first legislative victory of President Barack Obama (the first African American president) and has become synonymous with him it is not a reach to wonder are they inferring that a monkey wrote the last bill?[62]

An Association That Won't Die

In 1970, Lester Maddox, an ardent and vicious supporter of racial segregation, got into an argument with Charles Diggs, one of nine African Americans in the U.S. House of Representatives. Before becoming governor of Georgia, Maddox had gained national attention by refusing to serve black customers in his Pickrick restaurant, in defiance of the 1964 Civil Rights Act. He threatened to beat with an axe handle any black person who entered his restaurant. Later, he marketed and distributed miniature axe handles (pickricks). On the day he got into the argument with Congressman Diggs, Governor Maddox was distributing the axe

CELEBRITY PRODUCTIONS, Inc. Presents A
P.A. POWERS
COMICOLOR
CARTOON
LITTLE Black SAMBO
Produced by
UB IWERKS
Processed by
NECOLOR

handles in a House of Congress dining room. During the dispute, Maddox implied that Diggs was a baboon. Maddox is dead but the racist linking of black people to simians has not died, as is made evident by the incidents listed below.

- In 2011 New York University, the largest private university in the United States, was ordered to pay $210,000 and furnish other relief to settle a race and national origin harassment and retaliation lawsuit filed by the U.S. Equal Employment Opportunity Commission (EEOC). According to the suit, the supervisor of a mailroom at the University regularly addressed an employee, a native of Ghana, with slurs such as "monkey" and "gorilla" and insults such as "Go back to your cage" and "Do you want a banana?"[63]

- Jemele Hill is a sports reporter and host for ESPN. In 2013 Hill, a black woman, was the target of an angry male listener upset because she was appearing on the ESPN radio show *The Herd* with host Colin Cowherd. In a handwritten letter, the listener called Hill a "thick-lipped gorilla," and a "bitch." The letter also states, "For 2 days now I've sat here (at work) with your 'Herd' show on—and I wanna puke. Hell I don't like women broadcasters to begin with, yet alone bitch 'jungle-bunnies'"... (what's she doing on the air anyway?—She doesn't even like golf [and said so on the air])—That's no sports person. This 'spear-chucker' needs to go away."[64]

- In 2015, Joseph Goodrow, a Tulane University Police Department administrator referred to an African American lieutenant on the force as a gorilla in the presence of visiting accreditation officials. Goodrow, who is white and serves as the professional standards manager for the university's police force, told the visitors, "I'd like to introduce you to my gorilla," referring to the black officer.[65]

- In 2015, the Jim Crow Museum received an email reading: "When will monkeys like the ones at 'jimcrowmuseum', STOP their disgusting black lies? The pure blondes with blue eyes are the Real whites and they are not equal to mongrel and niggers. I command that ugly and savage monkeys like you stop your non sense about the Magnificent white race and get the hell back to the jungle of africa and join your ape cousins there. GOD IS THE CREATOR OF THE GREAT WHITE RACE— and NOT the ugly black subhumans; the devil, satan is your creator, therefore, get back to afriac and butt-naked worship

Although the image on the mousepad is from the 1930s, the mousepad was produced in 2004.

your ancestors—those devil and dragg ugly black self out of Eurpeans countries. GOD will one day destroy savage criminals as blacks away from HIS chose WHITE-European people and obama, holder, blacklivesmatter, al sharpton, jessie jackson and all those stupid mongrel liberals out there will not be able to scream for your ugly nappy-haired self—for they too will be judge and condemn by GOD for all their atrocitties against the white that they so jealous of. Back to africa where blacks belong and end your disgusting lies today. Niggers."

Recent research conducted by social psychologists reveals that some whites demonstrate a subconscious association of black people with apes. Phillip Atibal Goff, a psychology professor at Pennsylvania State University, and his research team conducted several studies, using college-age students as subjects.[66] They found that participants—even those with no stated prejudices or knowledge of the historical images—were quicker to associate black people with apes than they were to associate white people with apes. In the first three studies, researchers subliminally flashed images of black or white male faces on a screen for a fraction of a second to "prime" the participants, who could identify blurry ape drawings much faster after they were primed with black faces than with white faces. The researchers believe this association is held in place through "implicit knowledge," the result of a lifetime of conditioning via the long history of stereotyped antiblack imagery that depicts blacks as less than human.

In another experiment, the researchers subliminally primed the subjects by showing words that are associated with apes—monkey, gorilla, chimp—or violent cats associated with Africa—lion, cheetah, and tiger. The subjects were next shown a short video of police officers violently beating a man. The man's race could not be determined by watching the two-minute video. The video clip described the man being beaten as "a loving husband and father" but also an individual with a history of committing violent crimes who may have been high on drugs when the police arrested him. Some of the video clips included a photograph of a white man and some included a picture of a black man. Participants who believed the subject was a white man were no more likely to condone the beating when they were primed with ape or "big cat words." But those who thought the suspect was a black man were more likely to justify the beating if they had been primed with ape words than with big cat words.[67] These research experiments demonstrate that the association of black people with apes lies in the subconscious of some contemporary Americans, which may offer clues to the differential treatment of black people by whites, including police officers.

A Personal Story

In 2003, I was sitting in my basement watching old cartoons. Not for pleasure. I was conducting research for a documentary explaining my work with racist artifacts and racist imagery. Cartoons are a sneaky and pernicious way of spreading racial ideas. The ones I was watching spanned the 1930s to the 1950s. They were little more than propaganda as entertainment—animated stories supporting Jim Crow segregation. The black characters were grotesquely caricatured as Toms, mammies, Sambos, savages, and pickanninies—people unfit to be treated as first-class citizens. I was watching the cartoons in my basement because I needed the peace and quiet that one sometimes finds in a basement.

I did not notice my youngest daughter Gabrielle Lynne enter the room. She started laughing. I turned to see her pointing at the television. "Daddy," she said, "those monkeys are so funny." I told her that those were not monkeys, they were supposed to be people. Again, she laughed, "No, Daddy, you're fooling me. Those are monkeys. People don't look like that." They were not monkeys; they were lies, distortions, animated justifications for mistreating black people. We talked for a while, but she was only seven or eight years old and not yet able to understand what I was telling

This is a toy for children, blocks to be stacked, circa 1930s.

her. I was so shaken by the incident that we included the account in the finished documentary, *Jim Crow's Museum*.

My experience that day reminds me of something that Martin Luther King Jr. wrote in his "Letter from Birmingham Jail." He was trying to explain to the white clergy of Birmingham—and more broadly to all people—that it is exhausting to be told to wait for rights that others take for granted. In a fit of passionate brilliance he listed a litany of injustices that make waiting intolerable: lynchings, beatings, police brutality, poverty, and daily racist slights. Among the injustices were:

> When you suddenly find your tongue twisted and your speech stammering as you seek to explain to your six-year-old daughter why she can't go to the public amusement park that has just been advertised on television, and see tears welling up in her eyes when she is told that Funtown is closed to colored children, and see ominous clouds of inferiority beginning to form in her little mental sky, and see her beginning to distort her personality by developing an unconscious bitterness toward white people; when you have to concoct an answer for a five-year-old son who is asking: "Daddy, why do white people treat colored people so mean?"[68]

It is more than a half century since King wrote those words. The cartoons that I watched in my basement are now banned from network television and the Funtowns of this nation are open to all who can afford tickets, but the "ominous clouds of inferiority" still form in the "little mental sky" of too many black children. I too had my tongue twisted as I told my children the stories of my youth—of what it was like living in the last years of Jim Crow segregation. And I confess that I continue to stammer as I try to find the words to express my hurt when black worshippers are killed in a church or young black boys are killed by police officers—or by other young black boys. These are difficult stories to tell, but they must be told—and they must be accompanied by the stories of black people who accomplished great things against staggering odds. These stories should be told to children as soon as they are old enough to understand words.

CHAPTER THREE
Watermelon Cravers

"Why do I always think of niggers and buck-and-wing dancing
whenever I see watermelon?"

—Carl Sandburg[1]

The Jim Crow Museum has hundreds of images of African Americans—
usually with very dark skin, blood-red grinning lips, and raggedy clothes—
eating watermelons, stealing watermelons, fighting over watermelons,
even being transformed into watermelons. The museum houses a 1917
book called *The Great Turkey-Stealing Case of Watermelon County.*[2] This
thin volume is a manual for amateurs performing a minstrel show. The
characters have names that mock black people: Booker T. Washington
Wiseman, John Abraham Caesar Lincoln, and Cicero Napoleon B. Smith.
The dialogue is barely discernable and often racially coarse: "Ef dat 'oman
could distingwitch one nigguh out-uh a million on a berry dark night,
she mus' a had a pe'iscope."[3] This is racial stereotyping as community-
bonding entertainment.

Most Americans would probably be surprised to learn that African
Americans are underrepresented as watermelon eaters. Black people
represent about 13 percent of the U.S. population yet account for 11
percent of the watermelon consumption.[4] The problem is not that African
Americans are shown eating watermelons on thousands, if not millions,
of material objects. Rather the problem is that blacks are portrayed as
contented coons, Toms, mammies, and pickaninnies, with all their hopes,
dreams, and fears sated by eating watermelons. Why worry about individual racism or persistent patterns of institutional racism and economic

and health disparities when you can eat a watermelon? The association of blacks with watermelons is, at its root, a mean-spirited but functional attempt to insult black people and justify their mistreatment.

Origins

Watermelons (*Citrullus lanatus*) originated in Africa. Thousands of years before the transatlantic slave trade brought Africans to colonial America to be enslaved, watermelons grew wild in the Kalahari Desert in southern Africa, covering much of present-day Botswana and parts of Namibia and South Africa.[5] Traders passing through the desert began to sell the seeds along their trade routes, spreading watermelons throughout Africa. Watermelons were cultivated in Egypt nearly five thousand years ago. Watermelon seeds were found in the tomb of Tutankhamun, an Egyptian pharaoh who ruled from 1332 to 1323 BC. Merchant ships carried watermelon seeds from Egypt to other Mediterranean basin countries. By the tenth century, the Chinese were growing watermelons. The Moors introduced watermelons to Europe in the thirteenth century.

It is likely that there were multiple introductions of watermelons into what is today the United States. African explorers may have introduced

This toy was popular in the 1980s.

the watermelon to the "New World" thousands of years before Christopher Columbus ventured across the Atlantic Ocean. The Spanish were growing watermelons in the southeastern United States by the late 1500s. For example, in 1576 a farmer named Juan Serrana testified in court that the soil of Santa Elena Island was good for growing maize, pumpkins, and watermelons.[6] Santa Elena was a Spanish settlement on what is now Parris Island, South Carolina. Watermelon seeds were also brought on the ships that carried enslaved Africans to the United States.

Once watermelons were introduced into this country, their popularity spread among the groups that ate them: the newly arrived Europeans, indigenous peoples, and enslaved Africans. In 1629, a New Englander observed that in New England "we abound with . . . sundries sorts of fruits as musk-millions, water-millions." The indigenous people of America were growing watermelons by the 1660s. Volney H. Jones, a leading ethnobotanist, identified two kinds of watermelon seeds that were recovered in an area near Albuquerque, dating from 1626 and 1675.[7]

Africans and their descendants ate the same fruit and vegetables that their enslavers ate, including watermelons. The enslaved Africans were sometimes allowed to cultivate garden plots to grow food, such as sweet potatoes, yams, plantains, and small patches of watermelons for personal use, and in rare instances they were allowed to sell the food.[8] Some enslavers believed that they were being "kind masters" by allowing the enslaved people to eat watermelon. According to William Black, a contemporary writer:

> When an Alabama overseer cut open watermelons for the slaves under his watch, he expected the children to run to get their slice. One boy, Henry Barnes, refused to run, and once he did get his piece he would run off to the slave quarters to eat out of the white people's sight. His mother would then whip him, he remembered, "fo' being so stubborn." The whites wanted Barnes to play the part of the watermelon-craving, juice-dribbling pickaninny. His refusal undermined the tenuous relationship between master and slave.[9]

It is common to argue that the negative association of Africans and African Americans with watermelons began during slavery. For example, Keith M. Woods from the Poynter Institute wrote:

> Since the earliest days of plantation slavery, the caricature of the dark-skinned black child, his too red lips stretched to grotesque extremes as they opened to chomp down on watermelon, was a staple of racism's diet. Over time, the watermelon became a

symbol of the broader denigration of black people. It became part of the image perpetuated by a white culture bent upon bolstering the myth of superiority by depicting the inferior race as lazy, simple-minded pickaninnies interested only in such mindless pleasures as a slice of sweet watermelon.[10]

Woods's contention that the "watermelon became a symbol of the broader denigration of black people" is correct. There is, however, scant evidence that it played this role in the early days of slavery. His analysis may be influenced by the presence of thousands of material objects—most notably postcards, trade cards, and paintings—that show slaves leisurely eating or lustily devouring watermelons. But many of these images were created after slavery ended. The narrative that black people are lazy, ignorant, and childish existed throughout slavery. It is not, however, clear when eating watermelon became a symbol of that supposed laziness, ignorance, and childishness. What is true is that the link between black people and watermelons was established during the last years of slavery. In 1853, for example, a writer contended that "'Happy as a nigger with a watermelon,' is the term now used by Young America to express the highest state of enjoyment."[11]

Another writer has offered the possibility that although enslaved black people may have been associated with watermelons, that association was not negative—or as negative as it would become—until after Emancipation:

> Black people grew, ate, and sold watermelons during slavery, but now when they did so it was a threat to the racial order. To whites, it seemed now as if blacks were flaunting their newfound freedom, living off their own land, selling watermelons in the market, and—worst of all—enjoying watermelon together in the public square. One white family in Houston was devastated when their nanny Clara left their household shortly after her emancipation in 1865. Henry Evans, a young white boy to whom Clara had likely been a second mother, cried for days after she left. But when he bumped into her on the street one day, he rejected her attempt to make peace. When Clara offered him some watermelon, Henry told her that "he would not eat what free negroes ate."[12]

It would be difficult to overstate the bitterness that many Southerners felt after the Civil War. Many of their cities were devastated and the "Southern way" had been, at least temporarily, dismantled. The sight of free black people doing whatever free people do outraged white Southerners. It is plausible that whites who saw black people eating

CHRISTMAS SERIES PUBL. A.H.

"If the man in the moon were a Coon"

watermelon subconsciously viewed the act as symbolic of lazy "niggers" who no longer "knew their place." In what might be the first printed illustration of the negative association of newly freed black people and watermelon, an 1869 issue of Frank Leslie's *Illustrated Newspaper* published a cartoon showing five black boys reveling in watermelon eating. An accompanying article explained: "The Southern negro in no particular more palpably exhibits his epicurean tastes than in his excessive fondness for watermelons. The juvenile freedman is especially intense in his partiality for that refreshing fruit."[13] In 1895, a white newspaper writer joked that white people in Mississippi are "working themselves to death to keep the idle free niggers in watermelons and chickens."[14]

Entertainment as Racism: Minstrelsy

The depiction of black people as dimwitted, happy grubbers of watermelons was popularized by blackface minstrelsy, which came into existence and enjoyed great national prominence during the last three decades of slavery. Minstrel shows were this country's first distinctive theatrical form, combining comedic skits, dancing, music, and variety acts, performed early on by white people in blackface (burnt cork or greasepaint) and later by black people, also in blackface makeup. Often performed

This postcard was published by A.H. and marked "Christmas Series," undated. **71**

6821. ENVY.

This is an early twentieth-century postcard by the Detroit Publishing Co.

before all-white audiences, minstrel shows painted black people as ignorant, lazy, (and sometimes) dangerous cultural parasites. These "nigger shows" lasted from the 1840s to the early 1900s.[15] Even as the professional shows gradually disappeared, their influence could still be seen in amateur shows, vaudeville, radio, television, and motion pictures.

In 1799, Johann Christian Gottlieb Graupner, a musician and educator, sang "The Negro Boy" while wearing blackface makeup. His performance occurred at the end of the second act of a play called *Oroonoko; or, the Royal Slave*.[16] One might argue that Graupner's performance as "the Gay Negro Boy"[17] should have earned him the title Father of American Minstrelsy. It did not. That distinction belongs to Thomas Dartmouth "Daddy" Rice, who "gave the first entertainment in which a blackface performer was not only the main actor, but the entire act,"[18] and it was Rice who was the first face of blackface minstrelsy in the United States.

Rice was born to poor parents in the Lower East Side of Manhattan. As a teenager he was trained as an apprentice woodcarver, but he rejected that occupation to become an actor. By the time he was nineteen years old, he was an itinerant actor, appearing as a stock player in several New York theaters and on frontier stages in the Ohio Valley.

The story of how Rice created the character that would make him famous is part legend and part truth. In 1828, Rice worked at the Louisville Theatre, playing run-of-the-mill parts. According to some stories, it was while in Louisville that he happened upon an elderly enslaved black man "crooning an odd melody and doing a curious shuffling step each time he reached the chorus of his little song."[19] The words to the song include the refrain:

> First on de heel tap, den on de toe,
> Ebery time I wheel about I jump Jim Crow.
> Wheel about and turn about and do jis so,
> And every time I weel about I jump Jim Crow.

Rice saw an opportunity. He created a skit where he pretended to be the enslaved man. He rewrote parts of the man's song. Then, dressed in blackface and wearing ragged clothes, Rice performed on stage as Jim Crow, an ignorant plantation slave. Almost immediately, his "Negro impersonation" became an astounding success, performed before sellout crowds in the United States, London, and Dublin. The song that Rice sang was an instant success and was widely distributed. Jim Crow, the carefree plantation darky, became a stock character in 1840s minstrel shows. Later, he was joined by other characters, most notably Zip Coon, a free black man, flamboyantly dressed, unwittingly spouting malapropisms.

Success breeds imitation. In the 1830s, many struggling white actors and singers began performing in blackface makeup as "Negro

This postcard is postmarked Brighton, a small, mostly white suburb near Detroit. This postcard has no other identifying information.

specialists."[20] Like Rice, they portrayed black people in racially offensive ways. Rice and his early imitators gave one-person performances, but in 1843, four white men from New York appeared as a group. Calling themselves the Virginia Minstrels, they too performed with blackened faces and mockingly exaggerated the speech and behavior of black people. The Virginia Minstrels used violins, castanets, banjos, bones, and tambourines. Their routine was successful and helped to invent the entertainment form known as the minstrel show. Shortly thereafter, "Jim Crow became a popular name for any Negro."[21]

In 1845, the Christy Minstrels originated many features of the minstrel show, including the seating of the blackface performers in a semicircle on stage, with the tambourine player (Mr. Tambo) at one end and the bones player (Mr. Bones) at the other, singing songs and engaging in humorous—sometimes risqué—banter with the performer in the middle seat (Mr. Interlocutor). In a little more than a decade, the minstrel show had gone from brief burlesques and comic entr'actes to a full-fledged entertainment form. Carl Wittke, an unabashed supporter of blackface minstrel shows, wrote:

> The stage Negro loved watermelons and ate them in a particular way. He turned out to be an expert wielder of the razor, a weapon which he always had ready for use on special social occasions as crap games, of which the stage Negro was passionately fond. In minstrelsy, the Negro type had all these characteristics and more . . . the Negro's alleged love for the grand manner led him to use words so long that he not only did not understand their meaning . . . it was this type of darky that the white minstrels strove to imitate or, better stated perhaps, created and perpetuated.[22]

Minstrel shows were make-believe displays spreading make-believe stories, though their audiences often erroneously believed that they were seeing realistic depictions of black people—their attitudes, tastes, values, and behavior. In the North, most of the white blackface performers had never been on a Southern slave plantation, and neither had the members of their audiences. But they imagined a land where enslavers were kind and slaves were happy. After the Civil War, minstrel shows fed the national nostalgia for the "good old days." According to John Strausbaugh, a contemporary writer, "The minstrel South was another fantasy onto which White folks could project their desires—a lost pre-industrial paradise where 'the sun shines bright' and the 'the darkies are gay' and 'de time is neber dreary.' A mythic Eden filled with ripe watermelon and stacks of steaming hoecakes, smiling mammies, kindly massas, wily catfish and ringing banjos."[23]

Sheet music for the coon song, "Enjoy Yourselves," words by Dave Reed Jr., music by Chas. B. Ward, 1897.

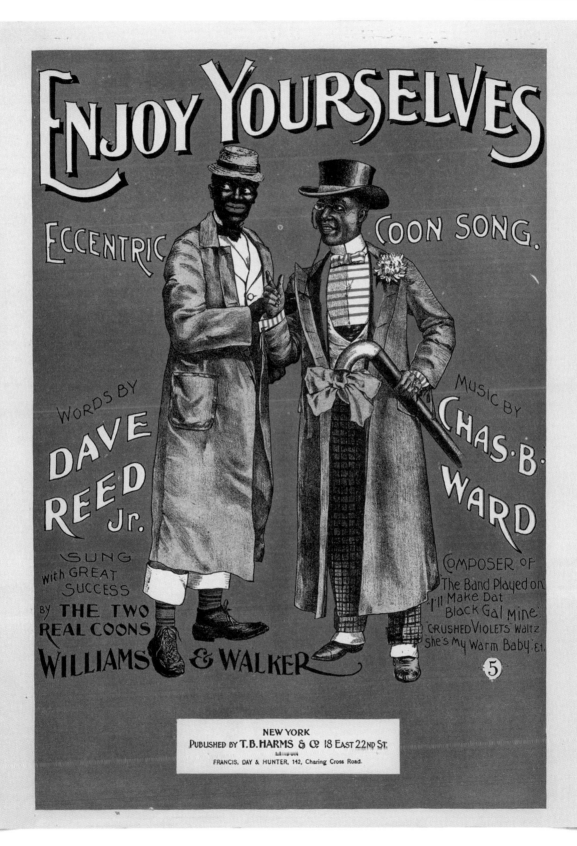

Although the portrayals of black people in minstrel shows were counterfeit, their impact was real. Minstrelsy helped shape white America's attitudes toward black people. The dimwitted, too often happy "black person" on the minstrel stage was an argument against the need for treating real black people as first-class citizens. Minstrel shows assuaged the consciences of white Americans by portraying black people as either contented slaves or childish buffoons. Both portrayals functioned as justifications and support for slavery, and later for Jim Crow segregation.

During the early years of minstrelsy, black actors were not allowed to perform on stage in minstrel shows. That privilege was reserved for white actors with their faces blackened. In those instances when black people were allowed to sit in the audience—in segregated seating—they were witnesses to a racist spectacle set to music. Frederick Douglass, the abolitionist and statesmen, angrily denounced minstrel shows. In the *North Star*, his antislavery newspaper, Douglass wrote: "We believe he [the editor of a rival paper] does not object to the 'Virginia Minstrels,' 'Christy's Minstrels,' the 'Ethiopian Serenaders,' or any of the filthy scum of white society, who have stolen from us a complexion denied them by nature, in which to make money, and pander to corrupt taste of their white fellow citizens."[24]

Douglass's critique of white blackface minstrels could have been extended to the black minstrels, many of whom blackened their already dark faces and played the fool on stage. Worse yet, they were the primary promoters of coon songs, a genre of music popular in the United States from 1880s to 1920s. These songs, in keeping with the older minstrel portrayals of black people, often featured "watermelon- and chicken-loving rural buffoons."[25] Minstrel shows "depended on caricatures of blacks in songs and dances, but the coon song transcended the minstrel shows by occupying a place in saloons and homes."[26] An American family could sit in their parlor and listen and dance to "My Watermelon Boy" (1899),

This 1907 postcard shows the sender and the recipient interacting with the racist imagery on the card.

which had these words: "He's a common nigger of a very common kind/ And he loves a melon from the heart right to the rind . . . I loves to see him roll up his eyes/When watermelon that boy does spy/No coon can win me, no use to try/Cause I love my watermelon boy."[27]

Cinematic Portrayals

The negative association of blacks with watermelons was an established part of American culture by the late 1800s, and it had flourished as a stereotype by the early 1900s. The "blacks love watermelon" story was cemented in the culture, in part, with the development of film, which from its beginning portrayed blacks as being obsessed with watermelons. *The Watermelon Contest* (1896) was the first of many short-short films—seventeen seconds long—showing black people greedily consuming watermelons. The film was remade as *Watermelon Contest* (1900), because so many copies of the original were struck that it damaged the negative. It was extended to over a minute. *A Watermelon Feast* (1896), produced by American Mutoscope, showed a black family "reveling in a feast of the favorite food of their race."[28] *Eating Watermelon for a Prize*

Al Jolson (born Asa Yoelson; May 26, 1886–October 23, 1950) was a singer, film actor, and comedian. At the peak of his career, he was dubbed "The World's Greatest Entertainer." Jolson owed much of his fame and fortune to his blackface performances.

(1903) was a free-for-all showing black men eating, fighting, and washing with watermelons. In *Who Said Watermelon?* (1903), an old black man is happy because he has a big watermelon, but his happiness turns to sadness when a group of boys try to steal the watermelon. These very short films focus on single scenes—single racist scenes.[29]

The Watermelon Patch (1905) is a ten-and-a-half-minute kinetoscope film.[30] It begins with several black men crawling on their hands and knees as they steal watermelons from a patch, and behind them are two scarecrows. Unbeknownst to the thieves, the scarecrows are really white men in disguise. The black men are so obsessed with the watermelons that they do not realize they have entered a trap. The white men shed their scarecrow clothing, revealing skeleton suits. The black men, fearing that skeletons have come to life, run through woodlands, cornfields, and dirt roads, several of them carrying watermelons. The scene shifts to the families of the thieves, who are enthusiastically dancing to banjo music in a cabin. One of the watermelon thieves shows up, a watermelon triumphantly raised above his head. The dancing stops. The watermelon is dropped on the floor and the black people scramble to get pieces. The next scene shows two black men, seated side by side, making faces while hungrily eating watermelon. White vigilantes with tracking dogs eventually find the cabin. They nail the door shut, seal up the windows, and plug the chimney. The black people inside, still eating watermelon, are oblivious to the danger. Soon they are battling smoke inhalation—one woman is both gasping for air and chomping on a slice of watermelon. The movie ends with the black people escaping through the roof and through a window that somehow was opened.

Gone with the Wind (1939) glorifies slavery and Southern slaveholders while simultaneously depicting black characters as one-dimensional caricatures: mammies, Toms, and pickaninnies. During the film's production, Butterfly McQueen, who played the role of Scarlett O'Hara's slave, refused to eat a watermelon. Years later she recounted, "I did everything they asked me to, except I wouldn't let Scarlett slap me, and I wouldn't eat the watermelon, which is silly. I could have ate it and spat out the seeds and sang but I was going through a phase."[31]

The narrative that black people are obsessed with watermelons also showed up in early (and not so early) cartoons. One example is Betty Boop's *Making Stars* (1935).[32] In this cartoon, Betty Boop emcees a stage show presenting "future stars"—singing and dancing infants. One of the performing acts is The Colorful 3, three black babies, portrayed as pickaninnies, with very dark skin, bulging eyes, and oversized white, minstrel-like lips. They dance onto the stage wearing separate diapers but sharing a large diaper pin. Being conjoined frustrates them and they begin to

This sheet music for a Malcolm Williams composition was produced in 1899. The song was often advertised as a "Coontoon Carnival."

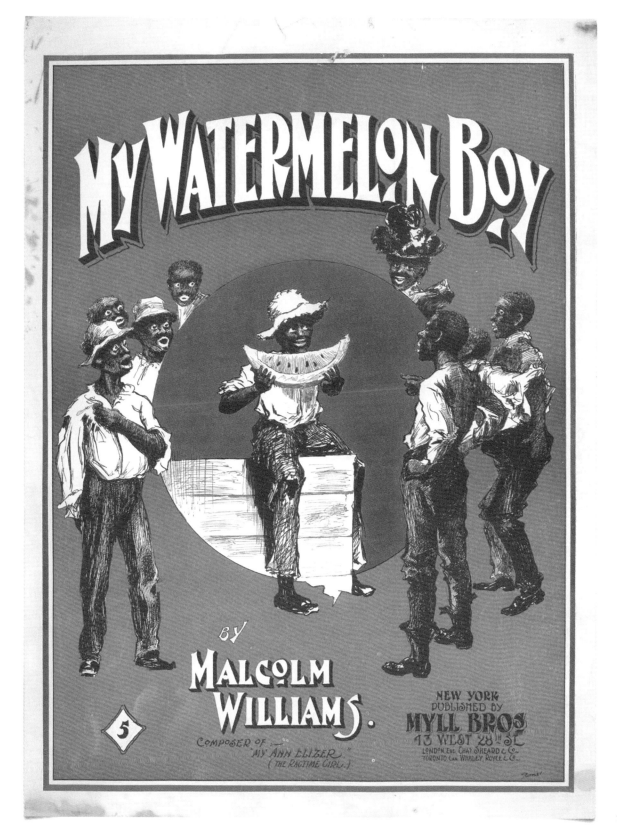

tearfully sing "Hi De Ho," a refrain made famous by Cab Calloway's 1931 song "Minnie the Moocher." The crying stops when a white hand brings a large watermelon slice near them. They exit the stage, excitedly chasing the watermelon. In the audience, a different black child points to the stage. He is held by a black woman caricatured as a mammy. The child wants watermelon, so he begins to cry and sing the "Hi De Ho" refrain. She reaches into a bag on the floor and pulls out a slice of watermelon. Now happy, the black child spits watermelon seeds, rapid-fire, at the back of the head of a white man sitting in front of them.

Scrub Me Mama with a Boogie Beat (1941) is arguably the most anti-black cartoon ever made.[33] Produced by Universal Pictures, it begins with an orchestral rendition of Stephen Foster's "Old Folks at Home," reminiscent of the rural South as depicted in many blackface minstrel performances. The setting is Lazy Town, populated by mammies, Toms, Sambos, coons, and pickaninnies, all too indolent to engage in normal activities. Even the animals in Lazy Town are lethargic. Everything changes when a light-skinned woman arrives and starts singing "Scrub Me Mama with a Boogie Beat"—a bawdy, jazzy tune made famous in the noncartoon world by the Andrews Sisters in 1941. The residents of Lazy Town, inspired by the woman and the song's rhythm, begin playing musical instruments and dancing provocatively. By the time she leaves, the community sounds like Harlem. In one scene a black male devours a huge slice of watermelon to the rhythm of the theme song. His large grotesquely shaped mouth, the color of the watermelon, melds into the watermelon.

In the 1948 cartoon *Half-Pint Pygmy*, the two main characters are talking bears, George and Junior.[34] In response to a newspaper article offering a "$10,000 reward for capture of world's smallest pigmy [*sic*]," the two bears "head to Pygmy country." When they arrive they find a Pygmy village and locate the smallest Pygmy. He is the size of a mouse, thick-lipped, with a bone through his hair. They chase him into a hole in a tree. They try to lure him out with a large slice of watermelon. When the Pygmy sees the watermelon he becomes a crazed beast: his hair stands up and saliva shoots from his mouth, which grows in size and becomes machine-like as he devours both the watermelon and the arm of the bear holding it.

The depictions of black people in movies and cartoons reveal more about the people who made the films than they do about black people. Presenting black people in humiliating and demeaning ways in the early days of film was evidence of the acceptance of coarse and vulgar racial stereotypes. These antiblack portrayals mirrored and reinforced the attitudes of white theatergoers while simultaneously instilling and

"Jinks! I could 'a sworn I saw a leetle darkey in the Melon-patch."
Copyright 1897 by Strohmeyer & Wyman.

shaping antiblack attitudes in other members of the white in-group. Black people were fodder for cheap laughs—matter-of-fact laughs of superiority.

This tendency to use black people for laughs has not died. One recent example is the movie *The Heat* (2013), a comedy about the working relationship between Sarah Ashburn, an uptight FBI agent played by Sandra Bullock, and Shannon Mullins, a foul-mouthed Boston police officer played by Melissa McCarthy.[35] There is a scene that evokes old associations of blacks with watermelons. Mullins chases Rojas, a young black male, and eventually stops him by hitting him in the back with a watermelon. This exchange ensues:

ROJAS: Lady, what the hell did you throw at me?
MULLINS: A watermelon.
ROJAS: A watermelon! Oh, hell! Ah, see, I told you you was a racist!
MULLINS: Yeah, I tried to hit you with my car. What's that make me? Yeah, let's see what you got . . .
[Mullins checks his trouser pockets]
MULLINS: Oh, look at this! Look at this! Not even my birthday!
[she takes out little bags of drugs]
ROJAS: Hey, man! You planted that shit on me, man!
MULLINS: Yeah, I planted that shit.
ROJAS: You planted that on me! I'm innocent!
MULLINS: Shut up before I beat you with a watermelon. Get up!

This stereograph card is from 1897. It is one of many popular culture images that portray black people as watermelon thieves.

81

African Americans have used the watermelon as a means to deconstruct patterns of racism. In the 1960s, Dick Gregory, a black activist and comedian, nettled his mostly white audiences with stories that linked watermelon eating with civil rights protests and poked fun at racism. During one performance he joked about flying back and forth between comedy engagements and protest demonstrations: "I don't know if my commuting is affecting the airlines, but now the stewardess comes up the aisle saying 'coffee, tea, or watermelon.'"[36]

> I booked two first-class seats on a plane back home to Chicago. The tickets were in the names of D. Gregory and W. Melon. No doubt the ticket agent thought I was traveling with a wealthy friend from Pittsburgh. I boarded the plane with my watermelon under my arm. I carefully fastened the seat belt around the melon in the seat next to me and acted like there was nothing unusual. Every time someone would look as though he was getting up the nerve to ask about it, my expression discouraged the question. I guess folks were thinking, "We knew Dick Gregory had a lot of kids, but this is ridiculous!"[37]

Watermelon Man (1970) is a blunt, satirical comedy-drama directed by Melvin Van Peebles.[38] It tells the story of Jeff Gerber, a loutish, racially prejudiced white insurance salesman in the 1960s, who wakes up one morning to discover that he has inexplicably metamorphosed into a black man, a very dark man. At first, Jeff believes he is dreaming. Then he worries that he spent too much time under a tanning machine. Confused and in a state of panic, he tries to wash the black off. That does not work. He goes to a doctor, who cannot help him, and suggests that he visit a black physician. Jeff goes to the "colored part of town" in order to find "the stuff they use in order to make themselves look white." All of his attempts to change his skin fail.

Jeff's position on America's racial hierarchy has changed and he now has a vantage point from the bottom up. He chases a bus, and a police officer stops him and accuses him of stealing. Why? Because why else would a black man be running? He gets threatening calls at home from a man telling him to "move out, nigger." His wife Althea is understandably confused by Jeff's new appearance, and though she considers herself a liberal, she asks if she should hide the family's money and serves him fried chicken and watermelon for dinner. His boss likes the idea of having a "Negro" salesman. His white secretary now finds him sexually appealing. He arrives home one evening to find the racists who made the threatening phone calls. They desperately want him out of the neighborhood and offer him $50,000 for his home. Jeff plays on their racism

This newspaper supplement appeared in the *New York American and Journal*, in 1902. It shows Bert Williams, the well-known African American performer, in blackface makeup and a coon costume. **83**

and their fear that his black-skinned presence will decrease the value of their homes and gets the price raised to $100,000, a great sum at that time. Althea sends their children to live with relatives and later decides that she cannot live with a black husband. Finally accepting his fate, Jeff quits his job, rents an apartment, and starts an insurance company to cater to a black clientele.

In 1996, Cheryl Dunye raised the ire of many political conservatives with her mockumentary, *Watermelon Woman*.[39] The movie follows the life of Cheryl, played by herself, a young black woman working as a video store employee who wants to be a director. She decides to make a documentary about Fae Richards, an obscure 1930s black film actress popularly known as "the Watermelon Woman." Cheryl discovers that Fae, who often played stereotypical mammy roles in Hollywood films, was the secret lover of a white director, Martha Paige. While researching and probing the meaning and mysteries of Fae Richards's life, Cheryl experiences drama in her own life. Her love affair with Diana, a white woman, creates conflict with her black friend Tamara, who wonders aloud about Cheryl's commitment to the black community. Much of this mockumentary consists of interviews, including one with well-known social critic Camille Paglia, who engages in a self-parodying rant praising blacks for eating watermelon and adds, "If the watermelon symbolizes African American culture, and rightly so, look what white middle-class feminism stands for: anorexia and bulimia." *Watermelon Woman* is a low-budget masterpiece. Although Fae Richards is fictional, the issues of racism and homophobia are real. Senator Jesse Helms, preoccupied with the film's single and brief sex scene, referred to the film as "flotsam floating around in a sewer."[40]

Blacks and Watermelons in Print

During the late nineteenth and early twentieth centuries, the watermelon emerged as a major symbol in the iconography of racism in the United States. The negative association of black people and watermelons was reinforced through household goods, particularly kitchen accessories. The Jim Crow Museum has many three-dimensional objects showing African Americans eating watermelons, including banks, plates, wall hangings, aprons, towels, ashtrays, toys, firecrackers, cookie jars, match holders, dolls, souvenirs, doorstops, lawn jockeys, and novelty objects.

The connection of blacks and watermelons was also popularized in printed materials, especially books, sheet music, comic books and strips, posters, stereoscopic cards, trade cards, and postcards. As with household goods, the sheer volume of these objects makes them almost ubiquitous in the United States. For example, *Pore Lil Mose* (1901), a serial comic strip by Richard F. Outcault about a pickaninny, shows Lil Mose's family seal—which has a chicken, straight razor, dice, and watermelon. In a 1902 strip, Lil Mose sits at a soda fountain and says, "I want watermelon syrup."

A 1907 postcard shows a cartoon caricature of a black man leaning against a fence wearing a yellow hat, his eyes closed. His enormous red lips are open, ready to eat a huge slice of watermelon. There is a knife in the watermelon the slice was cut from. The caption reads, "You can plainly see how miserable I am." This is a not-so-subtle reference to the question of whether turn-of-the-century black people were content with their lowly societal status. Another early 1900s postcard shows a black child sitting on the ground with a slice of watermelon in his lap. The text on the postcard dehumanizes the child:

> "WHO SAID WATERMELON?"
> George Washington Watermelon Columbus Brown
> I'se black as any little coon in town.
> At eating melon I can put a pig to shame
> For Watermelon am my middle name.

One particularly disturbing postcard, from Curt Teich & Company, shows a cartoon black girl with medium brown skin, her cheeks blushing. She is a cute pickaninny, standing in a watermelon patch between two large watermelons. Although she looks to be very young, certainly prepubescent, her enlarged stomach and sly grin suggests that she may be pregnant. The text reads, "Oh—I is not! It must be sumthin' I et!!" This combines antiblack stereotypes—in this case, the supposed hypersexuality of black females (even children) and the fictional obsession of black people with watermelons.

In the 1940s, Marvel Comics produced *The Young Allies*. One of the characters, Whitewash Jones, was caricatured with huge red lips and bugged eyes, and in the first issue introduced himself, "Whitewash Jones, who can make a harmonica talk! Yeah, Man! I is also good on de watermelon."[41]

Watermelon as a Symbol of White Resistance

The watermelon (with its association with blacks) has been used as a symbol of white resistance to black progress and black protest. One highly documented example involved Jackie Robinson. From the late 1800s to the mid-1940s, Major League Baseball was a white man's game.[42] Robinson signed a contract to play with the Brooklyn Dodgers, making him the first black American to play in the major leagues in the modern era, breaking the "gentlemen's agreement" of the 1880s, which banned black players and relegated them to the Negro Leagues. In 1946, he played

with the Montreal Royals, a Dodger farm team. The next year Robinson was called up to the majors. On the field, he faced racist taunts from opponents. Baseball fans expressed their displeasure by throwing trash, tomatoes, rocks—and, of course, watermelon slices—at him. They feared, and rightly so, that Robinson's integration of Major League Baseball would increase the likelihood that other forms of racial segregation would be challenged and eventually ended.

Two decades after Robinson broke baseball's color line, James Larnell Harris, a quarterback from Grambling State University, a historically black college in Louisiana, became the first African American to start as a quarterback on opening day for a professional football team, the Buffalo Bills. His achievement was not universally hailed. In the late 1960s and early 1970s, the quarterback position was considered a white man's position. As well as death threats, Harris received letters with drawings of nooses and watermelons.

The harassment of Robinson, Harris, and other black athletes was appalling but not fatal. On August 23, 1989, Yusuf K. Hawkins, a black teenager, and three friends went to the Brooklyn neighborhood of

This trade card is from 1882.

Bensonhurst to buy a car. The black boys were confronted by between ten and thirty angry white youths, some wielding baseball bats. The white boys erroneously believed that Hawkins and his friends were there to date white girls. One of the white youths shot Hawkins twice in the chest, killing him. Shortly thereafter, several hundred black protesters marched through the largely Italian working-class neighborhood to denounce the killing. The demonstrators were met by Bensonhurst residents, watermelons raised above their heads, shouting, "Niggers, go home." This was certainly not the first or last time that whites had used watermelons to simultaneously degrade and express their disapproval of black people.

In 1974, Judge W. Arthur Garrity ordered the Boston School Committee to desegregate the city's schools. The committee refused. Garrity put the schools under federal receivership and enacted a plan to use busing to desegregate the schools. Rioting began as black students arrived at South Boston High School. White protesters carried signs with racist slogans and hurled bottles and watermelons at the buses carrying the black children.[43]

The negative association of blacks with watermelons sometimes surfaces in the political arena. In 2001, a debate in the Mississippi statehouse on whether the state flag, which included a Confederate battle emblem in one corner, should be retired collapsed into shouting diatribes. An African American senator was mocked with references to a watermelon as he spoke, and another was told he was lucky his ancestors were slaves. This racial mocking was mild compared to the belittling of President Obama.

In 2014, the *Boston Herald* apologized for publishing a cartoon depicting a White House intruder, sitting in the president's bathtub and asking, "Have you tried the new watermelon flavored toothpaste?" The cartoonist, Jerry Holbert, said the watermelon reference was inadvertent. He claimed that he was naive about any racial undertones and "wasn't thinking along those lines at all."[44]

Holbert's naiveté is surprising given the newspaper accounts of Americans who received national attention after they drew connections between President Obama and watermelons. In 2008, a California Republican group's newsletter showed him pictured on a $10 food stamp, surrounded by a bucket of Kentucky Fried Chicken, barbeque ribs, Kool-Aid, and a watermelon. Another example involved Darwin Holly, an employee of TAMKO Building Products in southern Missouri. In 2009, while at a company picnic, Holly grabbed a slice of watermelon and said to a few colleagues, "I'm going to sit down and eat my 'Obama fruit.'" A little over a week later Holly was fired for violating TAMKO's racial harassment policy.[45] In 2009, Dean Grose, mayor of Los Alamitos, was

87

roundly criticized for sending an email that depicted the White House lawn planted with watermelons, under the title "No Easter egg hunt this year."[46] In 2012, Danny Hafley, a Kentucky man, put up a life-sized effigy of the president holding a watermelon. The Obama figure initially had a sign asking people to pray that Obama did not destroy the United States.[47]

Maybe Holbert was unaware of the many material objects that link President Obama with watermelons, such as the T-shirt that shows a white woman holding a large watermelon, with the words "I Voted for Barack Obama & all I got was this Lousy Watermelon." The internet is littered with crude photoshopped images of Obama with watermelons: exiting Air Force One cradling a watermelon, sitting in the Oval Office with a watermelon on his lap, addressing Congress while holding a watermelon, and innumerable other memes, similarly insulting and dismissive.

Still Getting Laughs

"Well, Uncle Tony, the end of the world hasn't come yet?" "No Mas' John, an' I was just thinking how good de Lord is to us poor niggers to put it off till arter watermelon season." That joke appeared in an 1870 newspaper.[48] There were many nigger-watermelon jokes in American newspapers in the late 1800s, and these jokes have not completely disappeared from the

This statue (circa 1940s) was a part of a large collection donated to the Jim Crow Museum by the family of Otis Vaughn, a longtime collector of so-called black memorabilia.

society. The antiblack jokes told in contemporary society often include watermelons and a level of disdain toward African Americans that is reminiscent of the racial hatred common in the 1800s, and these jokes are hardened by including racial slurs.[49]

> A redneck is driving down the road one day and sees a sign that says coon season is in. He goes a bit further down the road and sees a field of niggers picking watermelons. He stops, takes out his gun and starts shooting. A cop comes up and asks him what he's doing so he says, "I saw a sign back there that said coon season was in!" The cop says, "Yea, but you're hunting in a baited field!"[50]

> What's the difference between a truckload of watermelons and a truckload of nigger babies? You can't unload watermelons with a pitchfork![51]

The laughing at and mocking of black people is frequently found on college campuses, including behaviors that are suggestive of the Jim Crow period, with fraternities often the culprits. In 2001, two Auburn University fraternities, Delta Sigma Phi and Beta Theta Pi, were suspended for hosting a Halloween party. Costumes included a student dressed in full Ku Klux Klan regalia, other students wearing blackface makeup, and students wearing the shirts of Omega Psi Phi, a national black fraternity. Pictures of the party surfaced on the internet. In one of the pictures, a white student in blackface makeup is being lynched by the "Klansman" and

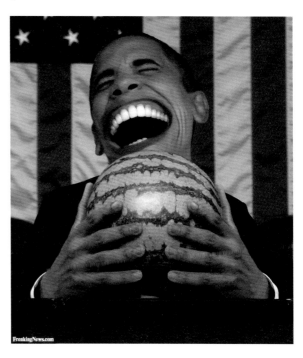

One of the many anti-Obama memes on the internet in 2017.

another student. That same year the Alpha Tau Omega fraternity hosted a party that included a student in blackface wearing a straw hat on his knees picking cotton. Another student dressed as a policeman held a toy gun to the head of a white student wearing blackface makeup.

On March 7, 2015, members of the University of Oklahoma chapter of Sigma Alpha Epsilon (SAE), dressed in formal wear and riding on a bus, were videotaped singing, "There will never be a nigger in SAE; there will never be a nigger in SAE. You can hang them from a tree, but he can never sign with me. There will never be a nigger in SAE." The video was released on the internet and caused a national furor. SAE, the only national fraternity created in the antebellum South, has a long history of mocking black people. In 1987, the SAE chapter at the

University of Wisconsin–Madison held a "Martin Luther Coon" party on the national holiday celebrating King's birthday. The price of admission was fried chicken and watermelons.[52]

Not all of the mocking of black people by white fraternities involved watermelons, but some did. In 1986, the University of Wisconsin chapter of Kappa Sigma had a Harlem Room party, where white students dressed in blackface served watermelon punch, painted graffiti on the surrounding walls, and placed garbage on the floor.[53] In 2010, members of several fraternities at the University of California at San Diego hosted a "Compton Cookout" to belittle Black History Month. The party's invitation encouraged all participants to wear chains, don cheap clothes, and speak loudly. The invitation for the off campus event urged attendees to come dressed as "ghetto chicks" and promised that fried chicken and watermelon were on the menu. In 2014, an Arizona State University fraternity, Tau Kappa Epsilon, hosted a Martin Luther King Jr. party. Participants wore loose basketball jerseys, flashed gang signs, and drank from hollowed-out watermelon "cups."

Watermelons and Symbols

A racist society produces racist objects and racializes other objects. The watermelon is illustrative. A watermelon has no intrinsic meaning. It can be seen as a useless thing that lies in a field. It can be appreciated as a desirable fruit or vegetable. It can be imbued with racial significance. For more than a century and a half, the watermelon has been a staple in America's racist diet. The depiction of black people eating watermelon has been a shorthand way of saying that black people are unclean (the fruit is messy to eat), lazy (it is easy to grow), childish (watermelons are sweet and colorful),[54] overly indulgent (especially with their sexual appetites), and lacking ambition (the watermelon presented as satiating all needs). The popular culture connection between blacks and watermelons is so strong and so negative that many black people will not eat watermelon in public, especially in the presence of white people.

Joe Louis (real name Joseph Louis Barrow) is widely regarded as one of the greatest boxers in history. He was the World Heavyweight Champion from 1937 to 1949, participating in twenty-six championship fights and winning twenty-five of them. Louis was a powerful puncher and a skilled tactician in the ring. In 2005, the International Boxing Research Organization ranked him as the #1 heavyweight boxer of all time. Louis, nicknamed the "Brown Bomber," was ranked #1 on *The Ring* magazine's list of "The 100 Greatest Punchers of All-Time."

Louis is best known for his title fights against Max Schmeling, a German citizen. The Louis-Schmeling fights occurred in the 1930s, during

This postcard was
90 postmarked in 1909.

a time of brewing conflicts between the United States and Germany. The fights came to symbolize the struggle between democracy (the United States) and fascism (Germany). Schmeling won the first match, on June 19, 1936, by knocking out Louis in the twelfth round at a bout held at Yankee Stadium. After the victory, Schmeling became a darling of Hitler's Third Reich, "proof" of Aryan supremacy. Two years later, on June 22, 1939, Louis gained revenge and became an American hero by knocking out Schmeling in their second bout.

A year before the first Schmeling fight, Louis traveled to New York to fight Primo Carnera, an Italian boxer and former World Heavyweight Boxing Champion. During a photo shoot to promote the fight, one of the white reporters brought a watermelon (or a slice) and asked Louis to pose eating it. Louis refused. The reporter persisted. Louis again refused. The reporter pressed the issue. Louis explained that he did not like watermelon, though he did.

Louis was an undefeated boxing star, a superior athlete. Although mild-mannered, he was a man of great charisma. In a few years he would become one of the most recognized men in the world, but at that photo shoot in 1935, a white reporter sought to demean him, reduce him with a stereotype, to make him simply another racialized cliché. The tools of oppression were a watermelon and a camera. Louis, already revered in African American communities, would have disappointed many of his black countrymen had he allowed himself to be photographed with the watermelon.

The racial watermelon racial trope has long haunted black people, including prominent African Americans. In 1948, Martin Luther King Jr. left Morehouse College, a historically black institution in Atlanta, to attend Crozer Theological Seminary in Chester, Pennsylvania. In many ways King was leaving the safety of a "black world." Soon after arriving at Crozer, King was invited to an outing where watermelon was being served. He remembered, "I didn't want to be seen eating it because of the association in many people's minds between Negroes and watermelons. It was silly, I know, but it shows how white prejudices can affect a Negro."[55] Malcolm X, also known as el-Hajj Malik el-Shabazz, was a powerful and courageous advocate for the rights of black people. His indictment of U.S. culture, especially white people's racial attitudes, was harsh and unrelenting. Articulating concepts of race pride, black nationalism, and (sometimes) racial hatred, he spoke to and for black people who were angry and disillusioned. King and Malcolm X differed in many ways, including in their approaches to handling white-on-black violence and institutional racism. Like King, Malcolm X would not eat watermelon in public. One biographer wrote, "For some reason, I remember him saying

he loved watermelon, but rarely ate it anyplace other than home to avoid stereotyping."[56]

Whereas King and Malcolm X were reluctant to eat watermelon in public (especially in the presence of white people), James Baldwin, one of their contemporaries, had an even more tortured relationship with the fruit. Baldwin, a deeply reflective novelist and social critic, spoke often about how pre–civil rights movement America taught blacks to hate themselves. In the following quote he links this self-hatred with all things black, including watermelons: "I was ashamed of where I came from and where I had been. I was ashamed of the life in the Negro church, ashamed of my father, ashamed of the Blues, ashamed of Jazz, and, of course, ashamed of watermelons: all of the stereotypes that the country inflicts of Negroes, that all we eat is watermelon or we all do nothing but sing the Blues."[57]

A Personal Story

In April 2012, a reconceptualized Jim Crow Museum was relocated to a larger space. Previously, it had been located in a five-hundred-square-foot room that functioned more as visual storage than as an actual museum. The new facility afforded us the opportunity to place the objects in their

This is a shirt sold on the internet in 2016.

proper (and accurate) historical contexts. Equally important, it gave us the physical space to have meaningful dialogues. There is a section that we call the "Room of Dialogue." In that area we have, I believe, meaningful discussions about race, race relations, and racism.

In 2012, we had visitors from Queensland, Australia. They were scholars interested in using the Jim Crow Museum as a template for creating a museum in Australia that dealt with the many ways that Aborigines were mistreated in that country. It was an absolute pleasure to discuss the possibilities and challenges of building a museum, especially one designed to undermine racial oppression.

At some point in their visit, I noticed that one of our guests—a man of Aboriginal descent—had left the main group and was standing alone near a showcase. I did not want to disturb him but wanted to make sure he knew I was present if he wanted to talk. As I approached him, I could see that he was crying. He was looking at the figure of a black child, heavily and grotesquely caricatured, holding a piece of watermelon. It was not, in my opinion, the most offensive object in the museum—the museum has a lynching tree—but it moved him greatly. We talked . . . well, mostly he talked and I listened. And I was reminded that people bring their own worldviews, sensitivities, and experiences to the museum. What struck me as a relatively mundane object for him evoked something much deeper. I know what it is like to look at a piece and be reminded of a hurt, an unkind word, a nasty encounter, and be moved to tears, to want to be left alone, to almost hear, literally hear, the objects, to need time to make sense of the horrible stories reflected in the objects.

CHAPTER FOUR
Razor-Toting Criminals

"What white man, while the memory of this tragic event should
last, would trust his throat again beneath a Negro's razor?"
—Charles Waddell Chesnutt[1]

In the 1940s two social scientists, Gordon Allport and Leo Postman, conducted an experiment to understand how rumors spread. In the experiment, subjects were shown a slide of a black man, dressed in suit and tie.
He is standing and talking to a casually dressed white man, also standing.
The white man has a straight razor in his hand. There are other people
in the image: all white, all seated. The subjects who were shown the
illustration were instructed to describe it to others who had not seen it.
Those who heard the description were asked to pass on their descriptions.
Those who heard the story third-hand were asked to recount it; in more
than half the accounts it was the black man who held the razor; in some
instances he was described as brandishing it violently.[2]

In that same decade the fledgling civil rights movement earned
important early victories against the racial hierarchy that dominated
much of the southern and border states. A. Philip Randolph won conces-
sions from President Roosevelt by organizing a mass protest. The NAACP
won significant victories, laying the foundation for the *Brown v. Board
of Education* decision. In 1947, Jackie Robinson became the first black
man to play Major League Baseball in the modern era. In 1948, President
Truman ordered the armed services to begin to desegregate. The United
States was changing slowly, begrudgingly, but old racial ideas lingered,
including the belief that blacks were innately prone to violence. A symbol

COPYRIGHT, 1882.

of that violence was the straight razor, presumably the weapon of choice of black people. To better understand the link between black people, criminal portrayals, and straight razors one may begin by examining the role that minstrel shows and coon songs played in establishing and popularizing the link.

Razor-toting Coons

Zip Coon was one of the early stock characters in professional minstrel shows. First performed by George Dixon in 1834, Zip Coon came into existence during the last three decades of slavery and the beginning of the minstrel period. During slavery, the character was used to demonstrate that black men, especially those living in northern cities, should be enslaved, not gallivanting around towns pretending to be white men—genteel, urban white men. On stage, the Zip Coon character (performed most often by a white man in blackface makeup) wore a gaudy combination of formal wear—a long-tailed jacket, a frilly lace shirt, a top hat, and jewelry. He was the "uppity nigger" who did not know his place. This ludicrous black dandy not only dressed like a fool but talked like one. Audiences, made up mostly of white people, laughed at Zip Coon as he spoke with a combination of (supposed) black dialect and malapropisms. Here is a sample of Zip Coon's speech: "Transcendentalism is dat spiritual cognoscence ob psychological irrefragibility, connected wid conscientient ademtion ob incolumbient spirituality and etherialized connection—which is deribed ob . . . inwisible atoms dat become anatom-ically tattable . . ."[3]

After slavery ended, white people continued to sit in the audiences of minstrel shows, satisfying their desire for entertainment by laughing at Zip Coon and other antiblack stage personas. Beneath the laughter lay an intertwined loathing and fear of the newly freed black people. Had not slavery contained the innate savagery of blacks? What now? Would black people take revenge for their enslavement? One of the manifestations of this fear was the redefining of the Zip Coon caricature—on the entertainment stage and beyond.

In his early days Zip Coon was portrayed as a stupid inferior, silly and easily dismissed but not dangerous. By the 1880s, shortly after Radical Reconstruction, Zip Coon and other coon-like characters were redefined as razor-wielding thugs. Through this representation, all black people, especially black men, were depicted as hard-partying, habitually violent social deviants. Zip Coon came to symbolize scary black people, and the straight razor symbolized coons.

Zip Coon metaphorically left the minstrel stage and found new life in coon songs around 1880.[4] These racist songs became a national craze

This trade card was produced in 1882.

for a generation of Americans. In the 1890s, there were more than six hundred coon songs published, some of them selling millions of copies.[5] Not coincidently, this decade has been described as the nadir of the black experience in the United States, a period that witnessed the "cumulative weakening of resistance to racism."[6] While black people were being denied the vote with literacy tests and poll taxes and were lynched in public spectacles, coon songs, whether performed by whites or blacks, portrayed black people as cultural parasites, unfit to vote, attend racially integrated schools, enjoy public accommodations and, in some instances, unfit to live.

In coon songs "blacks began to appear as not only ignorant and indolent, but also devoid of honesty or personal honor, given to drunkenness and gambling, utterly without ambition, sensuous, libidinous, even lascivious."[7] The "minstrel Negro" would wrestle you for a watermelon; the post-Reconstruction "coon Negro" would cut your throat to take your watermelon. Most coon songs were written by white people, but some of the most racist versions were written by black people. In "The Coon's Trade Mark," written by black performers Bert Williams and George Walker, the coon's character is assessed harshly:

Now listen and a fact I'll show,
A pointer that all do not know,
As certain and sure as Holy Writ,
And not a coon's exempt from it.
Now you've heard about birds of a feather:
Four things you'll always find together,
Regardless of condition of sun or moon,
A watermelon, razor, a chicken and a coon!

Three gemmen of color, one day did steal
A melon for their noon-day meal;
A lesson in fractions, with razors gave,
For an equal share each coon did crave;
Till a runaway team dashed past the door,
'Twas a load of chickens, they waited no more,
But rushed pell-mell the fowls to assail,
Not a pullet was left to tell the tale.

The Blue-Vein Club chose Dark-town Hall,
The proper place for their full-dress ball;
Had watermelons and chickens galore,
So the hall was crowded to the door.

A peddler stood near the entrance, quite
Three tubs of razors he sold that night:
Each coon bought one, with a grateful smile;
They'd rather be dead than out of style.

Chorus
All coons need their razors when they go to fight,
A chicken and a coon are fast friends on a cloudy night!
Ev'rybody shout this trademark, ev'rybody sing this tune:
A watermelon, razor, a chicken and a coon![8]

The lyrics in "The Coon's Trade Mark" were intended to be funny, and while it is true that the people who listened and danced to the offbeat rhythms of the song were entertained, they were also digesting racial propaganda, sadly, in this case, performed by two black men. Even a cursory examination of the song reveals racial stereotypes: black men as dangerous, chicken-obsessed, watermelon thieves. The use of the words "Blue-Vein Club," referencing light-skinned people, and "Dark-town Hall," referencing dark-skinned people, are the songwriters' way of reinforcing the idea that "not a coon's exempt" from being a chicken-thieving, watermelon-craving criminal. And even when black people attend a "full-dress ball" they buy "three tubs of razors." To be a black person, especially a black man, is to pursue style, and style means, among other things, having a straight razor. The razors featured in the songs symbolized the belief that black people had a tendency to engage in vicious, mindless violence.

As racial propaganda, "The Coon's Trade Mark" represented a more vile caricature of black people than did many coon songs, but it was hardly the only antiblack song. A song that paints an equally dark image of black people was "Coon Dat Carried De Razor" (also known as "De Coon Dat Had De Razor"), which depicts black men as so violent and blood-thirsty that a white police officer is afraid to arrest them.

Went to a ball de oder night,
At Susie Simkin's hut;
Whar de coons all carry razors,
And how dem niggers cut,
Horace Jinks got in a row
With slow foot Jim Frazier;
"Take care," squealed out old Sallie Gum,
"Dat coon has got a razor"
Dey cut poor Johnny's coat-tail off,

Dey carved him to de fat;
Dey chopped his ear clean off his head,
Den cut his beaver hat.
Aunt Hannah said: "For gracious sake,
You'll kill poor Johnny Frazier,"
But he never noticed here at all,
But slashed 'round wid dat razor.

Coons come flying down the stairs
Gals all hollered murder;
Johnny Frazier he fell down,
He couldn't fall no further.
Horace he rushed for de mokes,
And old policeman Hazier
Said: I aint gwine to take dat coon,
For he has got a razor.[9]

One of the major differences between the razor-toting coon and the razor-toting brute is that the former reserves his violence for other black people; coon songs would not have been as popular if the lyrics included descriptions of black men carving whites "to de fat" or chopping the ears of a white man "clean off his head." Coon songs used black-on-black crime as entertainment and as proof of both black people's inferiority and white people's superiority.

In 1905, William H. Councill, the president of the Agricultural and Mechanical College for Negroes at Normal, Alabama, denounced coon songs. It is revealing that his censure embraces the antiblack rhetoric often spewed by white people: "The coon songs are against us; they make sentiment against us. Make the young negroes burn coon songs and go to the songs of our mothers and fathers. Teach them about God. The cake-walking negro is a disgrace to the race; he is a monkey; he is the 'jim crow' negro; he is the insulter of women. He furnishes the class who are lynched."[10]

Some stereotypes die, others morph. Almost a hundred years after the coon songs dominated the American consciousness, Jim Croce, a white singer, wrote and performed "Bad, Bad Leroy Brown." The song, which became a hit in 1973, was inspired by Croce's relationship with a man whom he befriended while both served in the army. Croce did not identify the race of Leroy Brown in the song or in interviews; however, the song's lyrics portray a character that bears a striking resemblance to the black men portrayed in coon songs. Leroy is a name stereotypically associated with black men.[11] He is flashy—"he like his fancy clothes"—and

This is sheet music for one of the most popular coon songs of the 1880s. Notice the bully's dandified dress, the chicken, and the oversized straight razor.

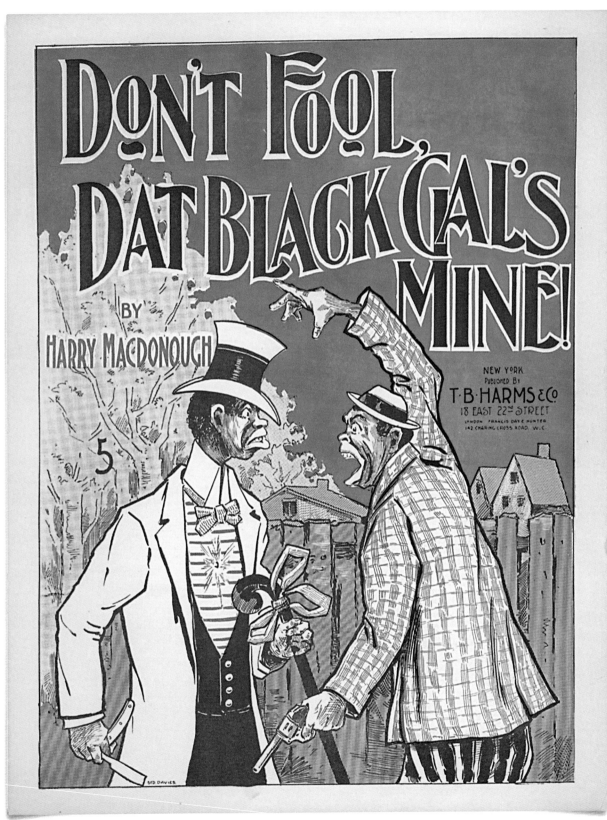

a braggart, like the 1890s Zip Coon dandy. He has a penchant for "shootin' dice" and fighting over a "girl that looked nice." In the 1970s, these were all well-assimilated antiblack racial tropes.

Croce went further. In order to make Leroy Brown a real badass, he wrote and sang: "He got a .32 gun in his pocket for fun. He got a razor in his shoe." The black man portrayed in the coon songs may not have had a gun "for fun," but he definitely would have had a razor, and he might have hidden it in his shoe. There is no evidence that Croce wrote his song to offend black people; indeed, he may have written and performed the song as homage to a friend, as he sometimes claimed. Nevertheless, the imagery in the song reinforces decades-old racial stereotypes about scary black men with flashing straight razors.

Razor-Toting Brutes

During the centuries of slavery, it benefited the larger white society to think of (and portray) black people as docile Toms, mammies, Sambos, and pickaninnies, but there was always a competing narrative: some black people, perhaps most black people, were innately savage, animalistic, destructive, and potentially criminal. Enslavers slept with their guns, rarely left white women alone on plantations, paid patrollers to act as police and vigilantes, and severely and savagely punished rebellious slaves. Even with these and other measures, the fear that the "brutish" nature of black people, especially men, would be directed against whites did not go away.

Slavery was a cruel and barbaric system: slave families were denied stability; their unions were not legally or officially seen as marriages; family members were separated, often for their entire lifetimes; most were denied opportunities for education; as property, they were bought, sold, traded, and degraded. Moreover, the slaves were witnesses to and victims of modeled violence of almost incomprehensible brutality— brandings, rapes, castrations, limb amputations, and, in many instances, daily beatings. Frederick Douglass, who had once been a slave, referred to the beatings he received as discipline:

> I was somewhat unmanageable when I first went there, but a few months of this discipline tamed me. Mr. Covey succeeded in breaking me. I was broken in body, soul, and spirit. My natural elasticity was crushed, my intellect languished, the disposition to read departed, the cheerful spark that lingered about my eye died; the dark night of slavery closed in upon me, and behold a man transformed into a brute!

When Douglass used the term "brute" he meant a being who was not allowed to be fully human—a man who was not allowed to learn,

This is sheet music to an 1897 coon song. It has the chorus:
"'Low no foolin' wid a gal of mine!
Coons, remember, she ain't in yo' line;
Fo' I'se de only one wid her can shine,
Yo' nigger! Yo' nigger! Don't fool! dat black gal's mine!"

This postcard was produced by Tichnor Bros. Inc., Boston, serial no. 556, circa 1940s.

to dream, to hope and work for a better tomorrow. To the people who enslaved him, Douglass was born a brute. Beating him did not make him a brute; that was what you did to brutes to keep them under control, to decrease the likelihood that they would one day hurt you.

When slavery ended, most of the former slaves emerged illiterate and poor, still living in a society where white people believed them to be inherently and immutably inferior in all ways that matter. Not only were black people confused and uncertain about their futures, so were Southern whites, especially the people angry about slavery's end. It seems almost inevitable that antiblack terrorist groups—most notably the Ku Klux Klan—would come forth to try to restore a slavery-like social order. And it is hardly surprising that white people's assessment of black people as brutish by nature fed white fear that without the "civilizing discipline" of slavery, black people would engage in wanton antiwhite violence.

Less than a generation after slavery ended, the nation was listening to coon songs that posited the criminality of black people, music that propagated the belief that all black people were potentially dangerous. These songs universally spoke of black people hurting other black people and reinforced beliefs about their innate criminality and propensity for criminal savagery, a savagery no longer suppressed by enslavement. The characterization of Africans and their American descendants as black beasts and black brutes capable of unspeakable violence was reinforced by newspaper accounts of black criminals, some of whom hurt people with straight razors.

Los Angeles Herald
August 17, 1905
NEGRO ATTACKS CHINESE COOK WITH A RAZOR
The kitchen of Hotel Hollywood was the scene of a small riot last evening, the contending factions being the Chinese chef, Sam, and some of the negro waiters. The trouble started over a special order given by a waiter, which the chef refused to fill, claiming the waiter wanted it himself. The negro, becoming enraged, picked up a heavy chair and badly cut and bruised the cook, who fled to the office for safety. While in refuge there, word came from the kitchen that the negro would kill him If he came back. Despite all efforts to prevent him, the chef reached the kitchen, where he was set upon and badly cut in the sides and back by a razor in the hands of the waiter. The participants were soon separated, but not until the Chinese was severely injured. He is resting easily today. The negro escaped with a few scratches.[12]

High Point Enterprise
February 9, 1914
NEGRO SLASHED WITH RAZOR—WOUNDS SERIOUS
It seems that a negro, Harvey Hunter, has been visiting the home of another negro, Bud Lindsay, without the latter's consent. Bud warned him to keep away, but Harvey persisted in his intentions. They met early Saturday night on the railroad near the tool house when some words ensued. Harvey drew his razor but Bud Lindsay was too quick, and drawing another razor slashed Hunter's throat cutting it almost ear to ear.[13]

Accounts like ones above reinforced the portrayal of black men as razor-toting coons who attacked other black people or people of color. But the real fear among whites was that some black people were not coons but brutes, meaning they would extend the violence to white victims.

Brooklyn Eagle
July 20, 1901
BLOOD WAS SPILLED FREELY
During a race riot that took place last night on the Bowery, Coney Island, several colored men and one white man were severely

slashed with razors and knives and another negro was rendered unconscious with a brick. The police were called out to quell the riot and several of them found it a difficult undertaking, as they had to pick their way between the negroes who were running about armed with razors. The white man who was cut is Paul Matley, a special policeman who is employed at Lawrence's concert hall, at the corner of Bowery and Jones' walk, and in front of which place most of the cutting was done. Lots of blood was spilled and the boardwalks are well sprinkled with it.[14]

Daily Arkansas Gazette
October 1, 1905
MRS. LEHMAN LOEB CUT BY NEGRO THIEF
Mrs. Lehman Loeb was attacked and seriously injured by John Mays, a negro, yesterday afternoon in her home, 809 West Third street. Mrs. Loeb's throat was cut, her arm severely slashed, and it was by only a small margin that she escaped with her life.[15]

Eugene Guard
October 24, 1922
NEGRO BURGLAR ATTACKS WHITE MAN WITH RAZOR
Seattle—Attacked by a negro burglar armed with a razor in the hallway of an apartment here early today. W.J. Clark, 39, a merchant, was severely gashed about the arms and body before the negro fled. Clarke surprised the man in the act of tearing a pay phone from the wall. He grappled with him and after a desperate fight threw him down the front stairs.[16]

Newspaper accounts of "colored men" or "negroes" with razors and knives added the veneer of validity to the racial ideas of men like Charles Henry Smith, who wrote in the 1890s, "A bad negro is the most horrible creature upon the earth, the most brutal and merciless."[17] Smith's real concern was that black men had too much liberty and that this was reflected in "the alarming frequency of the most brutal outrages upon white women and children." Smith was neither the first nor the last white writer to assume that the "black brute" was not content to brandish and use a straight razor to settle disputes. The brute was not just a violent criminal, he committed a specific violent crime: rape, including the rape of white women.[18]

The brute caricature thus became a justification for the lynchings of black men. Smith argued that the "brutality of the white retaliation against black rapists and murderers was more than justified by the

May Irwin was a leading coon shouter (one who sings in the manner of a blackface minstrel). Her performance of the Charles Trevathan hit "The Bully Song" (1896) was influential in establishing the stereotype of the razor-toting, belligerent black male.

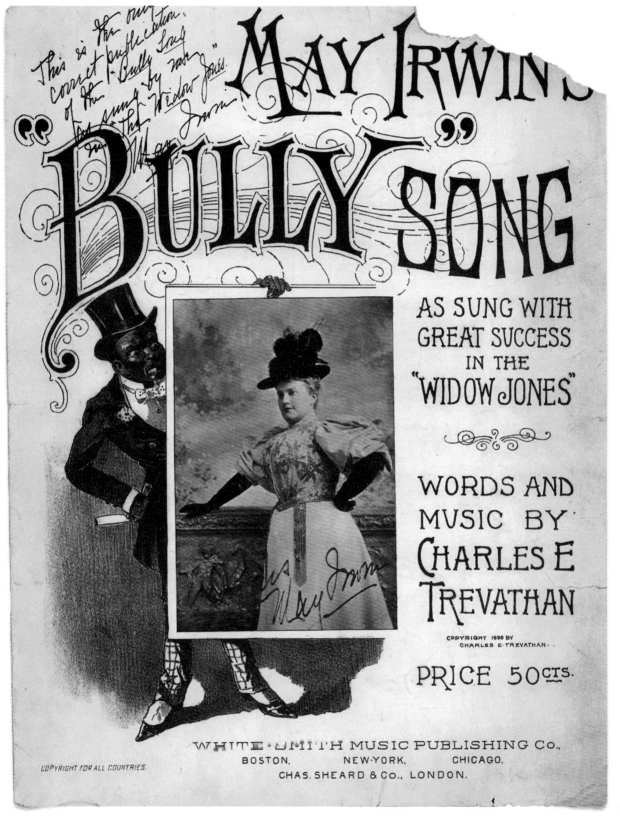

increasing 'horror and brutality' of the crimes allegedly committed by blacks."[19] This was racial propaganda. Most of the black people lynched were not accused of these crimes, and the ones who were accused were often lynched without the benefit of criminal trials. The cry to "protect the virtue of white women" was the public rationalization for the brutal lynchings of hundreds, maybe thousands, of black men. Ben Tillman, a senator from South Carolina, was one of many white politicians who used the protection of white women as a campaign platform. He claimed that "civilized men" were justified in wanting to "kill, kill, kill the creature in human form who has deflowered a white woman." His words were echoed in 1926 by an anonymous East Texas man who said, "God will burn . . . the Big African Brute in Hot Hell for molesting our God-like pure snowwhite angelic American Women."[20] One white writer, defending the lynching of what he called "a black brute" in Monroe, Louisiana, stated:

> The people of Monroe want to discourage brutal crimes commit-
> ted by the negro, and at present it seems the previous means of
> disposing of such cases is about the best and quickest way, and just
> as long as the negro commits rape and murder, here or elsewhere
> in the South, just that long will he be lynched and mobbed. Now if
> you want to stop lynching in Louisiana, first do something to stop
> the negro from committing crimes that justifies his neck being
> broke and then there will be no more lynchings.[21]

Lynching black men for the supposed crime of raping white women represented both hypocrisy and projection. White men raped black women, almost at will, during the centuries of slavery, and they continued to rape black women when slavery ended. During the Memphis race riot in 1866, white men robbed, beat, and killed black people, torched their homes, gang-raped black women at gunpoint, and attempted to rape a female child. In 1871, during Reconstruction, Harriet Smirl, the wife of a black Republican politician, was gang-raped. The rapists told her to make sure her husband voted for Democratic candidates.[22] When black men tried to protect their wives, daughters, and sisters from being raped, they were sadistically beaten. The raping of black women by white men— rape as a weapon of racial terror—continued throughout the lynching period. White crowds numbering in the hundreds, sometimes thousands, lynched black men for unsubstantiated and often false claims of rape crimes against white women while ignoring the thousands of black women raped by white men.

On February 20, 1892, Edward Coy, a thirty-two-year-old black man (sometimes identified as a mulatto) was killed by a white mob who claimed that he had raped Mrs. Henry [Julia] Jewell, a white woman

23

living in Texarkana, Arkansas. The mob pronounced him guilty, tied him to a tree, whittled the flesh from his body, poured coal oil over him, and made Jewell set the torch to his body. Although she was "generally known to have been criminally intimate with Coy for more than a year" she was treated as a white woman victimized by a black brute.[23] Even as the mob cut off hunks of his flesh, Coy maintained that the sexual relationship was consensual. As Jewell applied the torch to him, he turned to her and asked how could she burn him after they had been "sweet hearting" so long.[24] Newspapers referred to Coy as a "negro brute" and described Jewell as "a respectable farmer's wife, with a five-months-old babe at her breast."[25]

It would be difficult to accurately measure the extent to which black men raped white women in the early 1900s, especially in the Deep South. Accusation of raping a white woman was treated as proof of a black man's guilt. Also, all sexual contact between a black man and a white woman was treated as rape. Black men and white women did engage in consensual sexual relations, but if discovered the black man was treated as a rapist, deserving of death for engaging in an act of "horror and brutality." Moreover, the official records kept by white law enforcement officers, especially those in southern and border states, cannot be trusted because the lawmen were often complicit with or active participants in lynchings.

This postcard was sold in the 1940s.

There were instances when black men did commit violent crimes against white people, including rape or attempted rape. And sometimes a single violent crime became an excuse for whites to attack entire black communities. For example, on July 4, 1908, Clergy Ballard, a white man, awoke to find a man in his home standing near his daughter's bed. The intruder ran. Ballard caught him outside the home and they fought. During the struggle the man slashed Ballard's throat with a straight razor. Before dying, Ballard identified his assailant as Joe James, a young black man. The white residents of the town found and beat James before police arrested him.

The residents were inflamed when they read in the local newspaper that Ballard had died preventing his daughter from being raped.[26] Soon afterward, there was another report of a black man, George Richardson, sexually assaulting a white woman. In this instance, the police tried to protect Joe James and George Richardson from a lynch mob. The officer informed the mob that the men had been moved to an undisclosed location and that they would receive a trial. The angry mob lynched two uninvolved black men, William Donegan and Scott Burton.

Lynching two innocent black men did not quell the white mob's bloodthirst. The whites robbed gun stores to acquire ammunition. They destroyed businesses and homes owned by black people, who fought back, returning gunfire. The mob shot and killed six black people, lynched two other blacks, and caused thousands of dollars' worth of property damage. The sad events occurred in Springfield, Illinois, and sent a message to the nation's black people: you are not safe in a northern city.

Origin of a Stereotype

In most racial stereotypes there is a kernel of truth. At no time from the period of slavery through the 1970s did a majority of black people carry straight razors. But some did. Even during slavery, when the enslaved population was not allowed to own or even possess weapons, some slaves had straight razors. There is a scene in the movie *Django Unchained* where Calvin Candie, the cruel and ruthless enslaver who runs the Candie plantation, wonders aloud why the black man who served as his father's barber never took revenge on his enslaver:

> This is Ben. He's an old joe that lived around here for a long time, and I do mean a long damn time. Old Ben here took care of my daddy and my daddy's daddy. Till he up and keeled over one day, old Ben took care of me. Growin' up the son of a huge plantation owner in Mississippi puts a white man in contact with a whole lotta black faces. I spent my whole life here, right here in Candieland,

This postcard mocks black men as dandified coons, postmarked 1900.

surrounded by black faces. Now seein' 'em every day, day in and day out, I only had one question: Why don't they kill us? Now right out there on that porch, three times a week for fifty years, old Ben here would shave my daddy with a straight razor. Now, if I was old Ben, I woulda cut my daddy's goddamn throat, an' it wouldn't-a taken me no fifty years of doin' neither. But he never did.[27]

Candie used the story about Ben to suggest that black people are inherently incapable of rebellion because there is a flaw in their brains, something that produces excessive submissiveness. The fictional character's argument is undermined by many real-life events, for example, there were more than 250 slave revolts. One of the slaves who participated in Nat Turner's rebellion, a revolt that led to the deaths of sixty whites, killed a white enslaver with a straight razor.

Candie's comments draw attention to an early group of black men who were identified with straight razors. Like Old Ben in *Django Unchained*, some slaves served as barbers for their enslavers. There are multiple testimonies of white men allowing slaves to shave them—to hold a straight razor against their faces. In the North, wealthy white businessmen also used free blacks as barbers. After the Civil War, the barber profession was one of the few occupations where a black man could earn a decent

This is a "LAFF-GRAM" postcard published by Baxtone, in Amarillo, Texas, date unknown.

living. The association of black people with straight razors may have been popularized with coon songs, but it probably began with the black barbers, both slaves and freemen, who shaved the faces of white men.

After slavery ended, many black barbers continued to only serve white customers, some gaining both wealth and political influence. George Myers, a black barber in Cleveland, Ohio, counted among his clients William McKinley, who became president of the United States. Quincy Mills, a contemporary historian, claims that some black barbers used the profits from their barbershops to found life insurance companies such as Atlanta Life and North Carolina Mutual, and that wealthy black barbers were "central figures of the black political class, bar none."[28] Eventually, black barbers began to cater to a black clientele and the black barbershop became an iconic symbol of the African American community.

While it is likely that the presence of black barbers helped link straight razors and black people in the white imagination, the minstrel shows and coon songs popularized this association, made it negative, and broadened it to include all black people, even children. This is illustrated in the sheet music for "Hie away, ole satan," from 1885. The cover shows a drawing of a horned Satan. A black mother tries to protect her infant from Satan. The infant, lying in a crib, is armed with an open straight razor that is nearly double his size. Images like this one continued to be produced in this country into the next century and sometimes appeared in mainstream publications. A cartoon that appeared in the January 1941 issue of *Esquire* magazine is illustrative. It shows a wedding scene, presumably a military nuptial. The newly married couple, two black people, march through a line of saluters, but instead of being saluted by raised rifles they are saluted by raised hands holding straight razors. The bride is so heavily caricatured that she looks more simian than human. The straight razor was the typical weapon of choice in portrayals of black people, if not in actual cases of black violence.

Weapon of Choice

The first gun control laws in the United States were slave codes that banned African Americans from owning or bearing arms. The Virginia slave code of 1680 made disarmament of black people mandatory, ruling, "It shall not be lawfull for any negroe or other slave to carry or arme himselfe with any club, staffe, gunn, sword or any other weapon of defence or offence." This prohibition was repeated in the 1705 Virginia slave code, requiring that "no slave go armed with gun, sword, club, staff, or other weapon."[29] After the Civil War ended, whites in southern and border states added "Black Codes" to their state constitutions to strip away the rights gained by black people. One of the rights taken from the newly freed black people was the right to own guns. For example, a Black Code in Alabama in January 1866 made it a crime for black people to own or carry firearms or other deadly weapons and prohibited "any person to sell, give, or lend fire-arms or ammunition of any description whatever" to any black person. According to Thomas Eddlem, a contemporary writer:

> Mississippi's Black Codes provided a $10 fine . . . for black ownership or possession of guns, but in Florida the penalty for an African-American owning a gun was positively medieval. Florida stipulated that black gun owners would be required to "stand in the pillory . . . for one hour, and then whipped with thirty-nine lashes on the bare back." Thirty-nine lashes was also the standard penalty under slave codes in many of the Southern states for gun ownership. South Carolina also prescribed "corporal punishment" for blacks owning guns.[30]

A related attempt (though not technically a Black Code) occurred in Tennessee in 1870. White legislators signed into law "An Act to Preserve the Peace and Prevent Homicide," sometimes called the Saturday Night Special ban. The new law banned the sale of all handguns except the "Army and Navy model handgun," a gun which many whites owned or could afford to buy, but was too expensive for most black people to purchase. B. Bruce-Briggs, a gun historian, wrote in the *Public Interest*, "It is difficult to escape the conclusion that the Saturday Night Special is emphasized because it is cheap and being sold to a particular class of people. The name is sufficient evidence—the reference is to 'niggertown Saturday night.'"[31]

Throughout slavery and into the beginning of the twentieth century, black people were either legally denied the right to own guns or punished for owning guns. It was not surprising that a black person denied a gun might use a straight razor for protection: "However, the razor, an indispensable tool of personal hygiene, could not realistically be banned as a weapon. A black man could buy one without arousing suspicion and it was so flat as to be undetectable when kept in a pocket. Later, this oversight would be addressed by making it illegal to carry a razor unless one was also carrying a shaving brush—an item much more difficult to conceal."[32]

From slavery through the 1940s African Americans, especially members of the lower classes, were routinely depicted as prone to criminal behavior. Hundreds of newspaper articles told stories about "razor-wielding negro brutes." These newspaper accounts were rarely supplemented by sociological research. One exception was a 1962 article by

Leroy G. Schultz entitled "Why the Negro Carries Weapons." That article begins: "The Negro in the lower socio-economic group is traditionally viewed as a weapons carrier by law-enforcement personnel, on the basis of their day-to-day experience, and by laymen through humor and jokes which stereotype the Negro as a 'Rastus' wielding a razor. Are such attitudes justified?"[33]

Schultz focused his examination on black people convicted of carrying weapons in Saint Louis in 1958. He identified fifty blacks who were convicted of these offenses—and who were referred for presentence investigation. Schultz then conducted intensive interviews of these persons. He concluded that the weapon carriers came from all ages—not predominantly one of youth or delinquency—tended to come from the poorly educated lower classes, were primarily migrants from the rural South, for the most part had prior criminal records, and were "not to any appreciable degree a razor carrier."[34] The overwhelming majority of the black people arrested for carrying a weapon were arrested as a result of a police search—and the search was precipitated by the police officer's contention that the person was guilty of disturbing the peace.

Straight Razors and Black People in Film

Although the flashing straight razor was by the early 1900s a symbol of black criminality, the stereotype did not commonly appear in early film. In *Pokes and Jabbs*, a 1916 comedy, a white man decides to play a prank on a woman he desires as a romantic interest.[35] He colors his face with black greasepaint and pretends to be a black man. Later, he acts as if he is going to assault her. She, believing him to be a black rapist, runs. He gives chase and threatens her with a straight razor. She begs for mercy. He grabs a towel and wipes the greasepaint from his face, revealing his real identity. This frivolous film was one of the few examples of a "black" person seen brandishing a razor in movies through the 1920s. Anthony Balducci, a film historian, wrote:

> Black men were almost never portrayed as brutes in silent film comedy. The absence of the black brute is not surprising because the silly fellows who made these films were not trying to make a critical commentary on the modern black community. Not that everyone would agree with my perspective. Others have made the point that the black brute was too disturbing for popular enter tainment. They claim that the image of the docile black servant was more acceptable to white audiences, who liked to see a black man kept in his place. . . . In the 1920s, the idea of a black man menacingly brandishing a straight razor was a source of anxiety

RICHARDS & PRINGLE'S
FAMOUS
GEORGIA MINSTRELS

"I'M GOIN' TO GIT DAT MAN"

This is an advertisement poster for a minstrel show, circa 1900.

for white people, who imagined walking down a street at night and a black man jumping out of the shadows to stab or cut them. Stories of criminal acts by blacks were given prominence in newspapers and magazines of the day. But this was never reflected in films except in rare instances.[36]

In the 1940s, one could find references to razor-toting coons on the small screen. In the Tom and Jerry cartoon series there is a character called Mammy Two Shoes, a stereotypical mammy. In the episode "Lonesome Mouse," from 1943, a terrified Mammy Two Shoes climbs a stool to avoid a mouse. The mouse shakes the stool and her clothes begin to fall off. The shaking also dislodges a diamond ring, false teeth, a pair of dice, and a straight razor. Puppetoons were a series of animated puppet films made in England in the 1930s and in the United States in the 1940s. One of the Puppetoon characters was a black boy, Jasper.[37] In 1946, a *Hollywood Quarterly* article protested that the Jasper shorts presented a "razor-totin', ghost-haunted, chicken-stealin' concept of the American Negro."[38]

Stepin Fetchit was the archetypal movie coon: a slow-walking, slow-talking, lazy ne'er do well. In *Charlie Chan in Egypt* (1935), he added to his coon resume. In the film Fetchit, won by his boss in a dice game, sits idle all day, reminisces about southern living, and brandishes a straight razor in a scuffle. In the film *Pinky* (1949), a white-looking multiracial female is threatened by a dark-skinned black woman with a straight razor.[39] In 1949, the boxer-turned-actor Canada Lee said of the media, "With rare exceptions, it is the lazy gambler, the shiftless, thieving, razor-wielding Negro that has come to represent the totality of Negro life."[40]

Many of the portrayals of blacks with straight razors were created in the 1970s or later, but the films are set in prior decades. For example, in *Lady Sings the Blues* (1972), a biographical film about jazz singer Billie Holiday, when Billie's lover tries to stop her from shooting heroin she attacks him with a straight razor. *J.D.'s Revenge* (1976) is a blaxploitation horror film set in the 1970s. Early in the movie, the audience is shown a scene from the 1940s where a street hustler brutally slashes a woman to death with a straight razor. The scene reoccurs as a perpetual flashback throughout the movie. *The Bingo Long Traveling All-Stars & Motor Kings* (1976) is a film about a semiprofessional baseball team. The team is made up of black ballplayers, some of whom have major-league talent, but all are barred because of the ban against black players. In one scene, a black player is kidnapped and slashed with a razor. In *The Color Purple* (1985), a movie set during the Jim Crow era, Celie, a black woman abused by Mister, her black husband, is justifiably tempted to cut his throat with

a straight razor as she shaves him. *Harlem Nights* (1989) is a comedy/drama set in the waning years of Prohibition. The film centers on the activities of black gangsters who run a nightclub, Club Sugar Ray, which includes a brothel. The madam of the brothel and one of the gangsters get into a fight. Initially, she gets the best of him. He reverses his fortunes by hitting her with a garbage can. Angrily, she pulls a straight razor from her bra. *Hoodlum* (1997) is a crime drama set in the 1920s amid a war between an emerging black mafia in Harlem and an Italian and Jewish mafia. In one scene, the leader of the Harlem gangsters orders his men to slice open a man's throat.[41]

Blaxploitation movies, popular in the 1970s, were a reaction to old cinematic stereotypes: ignorant coons, loyal mammies, docile Toms, and animalistic children, all nonthreatening to whites. The blaxploitation movies rejected those antiblack stereotypes and substituted a new set: political insurgents, pimps, whores, and drug dealers—in the main, a group dangerous to both black people and white people. The straight razor made a comeback in these films. For example, *Black Caesar*, a 1973 crime drama, tells the story of Tommy Gibbs, a black gangster. As a child growing up in Harlem, he was brutally beaten by a white police officer. The incident scarred Gibbs and led him to a life in crime. As an adult, he exacts revenge

This shirt was sold on the internet in 2016.

for the beating. He kills a white man who is in a black barbershop getting shaved with a straight razor. The white man grabs the straight razor from the black barber and tries to attack Gibbs. He fails. Gibbs shoots him. The white man falls back into the barber's chair, his body covered with blood. Gibbs finishes shaving the now dead man. In other blaxploitation movies, a razor blade is used instead of a straight razor. In *Coffy* (1973) the black heroine hides razor blades in her afro. She later removes them to defend herself against a white man who tries to kill her.[42]

In *Angel Heart* (1987), set in the 1950s, a black character, Toots Sweet, slashes Harry Angel, a white character, with a razor. Angel takes the razor and uses it to threaten Sweet, unless he gives him information. Angel's action points to a little-recognized theme in film: the use of razors and straight razors by whites against black people. In *Mississippi Burning* (1988), there is the real-world account of Judge Edward Aaron (named Homer Wilkes in the film) who was "taken for a ride" by three white boys. They took him to a shack and took out a razor blade, spread his legs, sliced off his scrotum, and put it in a coffee cup. In *Soul Vengeance* (sometimes called *Welcome Home Brother Charles*), a 1975 blaxploitation movie, a black man is arrested by two Los Angeles Police Department officers. They take him to an alley. One of the policemen racially taunts and beats the man, then attempts to castrate him with a straight razor. Later, it is revealed that the offending officer's wife is in a sexual relationship with a different black man, and the officer knows it. *Soul Vengeance* is a low-budget, critically panned film, but it told a truth: black men were castrated with knives and straight razors for having consensual sexual relations with white women.[43]

Not Dead, Yet

The caricaturing of black men, and sometimes black women, as coons (who attack black people) or brutes (who attack white people) with razors outlived coon songs. In the 1920s, an Ohio woman was found murdered. The only clue at the crime scene was a broken razor. Seven black men were arrested because the razor was identified as a "Negro" weapon. The murderer was later found to not be a "Negro."[44]

It is common for individuals to participate in their own degradation, either because they have internalized the negative images or because they have found ways to financially benefit from acting out the degradation. For example, in the 1930s, Charley Henry, a black promoter, organized the Zulu Cannibal Giants, a semiprofessional black baseball team. Emphasizing comedy over athletic skill, players on the team wore war paint, grass skirts, and headdresses. Pandering to white America's stereotypical beliefs about black people, the players entertained fans with

This sheet music shows that black women were also depicted as razor-toting coons, circa 1900.

comedic acts that included cannibal fights (with spears) and a crap game with players threatening cheaters with straight razors.[45]

Stereotypes may be removed from one category (group) and placed on another category (group). Black people in the 1920s were considered inferior athletes relative to whites; today those stereotypical associations are reversed. Sometimes stereotypes appear to die but are actually reborn as new variations of old themes. Think of the "brute" caricature that emerged in the United States during Reconstruction. This idea of the scary, badass societal threat never really died. Indeed, one can argue that it is today the dominant popular cultural image of young urban black men.

What about the straight razor? Today, one rarely sees the straight razor used as a symbol of black violence unless it involves a film set in an earlier decade. Black men, like Michael Brown or the looters televised after his death at the hands of police officers in Ferguson, Missouri, are still portrayed as brutes or beasts. There is still a fear of black men. But the stereotypical association of straight razors with black people, especially young men, is so rare—relative to its popularity in the 1920s—one is tempted to say that the stereotype is dead. It is not. Singer-songwriter Michelle Shocked criticized gangster rap in the pages of *Billboard* in 1992, writing: "What white folks have always believed about black men is just what the work of Ice Cube, N.W.A. and other gangster rappers confirms today. The chicken-thieving, razor-toting 'coon' of the 1890s is the drug-dealing, Uzi-toting 'nigga' of today. And then as now, the central audience for this imagery has been primarily white."[46]

Michelle Shocked might be surprised to discover that the straight razor has appeared in rap lyrics. On *The Bitch Is Back* (1992), Roxanne Shanté's second and final album, there is a song entitled "Straight Razor." The song is an abrasive, hardcore rebuke of philandering black men, who are best handled by giving them (cutting them with) a straight razor. The following lyrics are illustrative:

> You got a nigga that plays, ya walk around with a razor
> Cause you got that you can fight like Frazier
> So you duck him. Tell him good luck, and motherfuck him
> And if your butt's still stuck, you better buck him
> Tell the buck you don't need him
> And beat him up and down, don't frown
> To beat him, that's how you defeat him
> Scream and shout until you pass out
> And if he doesn't then throw his motherfuckin' ass out
> Fuck the bills he pays, leave him in pain for days
> When you give him a straight razor.[47]

The straight razor link to black criminality is not as strong as it was during the heyday of the coon song, but the association still exists. Snoop Dogg, 50 Cent, Raekwon, and Young Money are among the African American rap artists whose songs sometimes include references to razors, though it is not always clear if they are referring to straight razors or razor blades. Whether as cultural diffusion or appropriation, several prominent white musical groups, including but not limited to Motörhead, Exodus, and Chris Mills, have employed the straight razor as a symbol of cruel violence. Among the most graphic examples is the song "Straight Razor Rape" by Cancerslug, an underground horror punk/metal band. The song, which graphically and coarsely tells the story of a man who mutilates a woman's genitalia with a straight razor, concludes with lyrics that function as an ode to murder and suicide:

> Blood on my hands
> the tears in her eyes
> Please understand
> there will be peace when you die
> I know what it takes
> to make a heart ache
> a straight razor rape
> You weren't the first
> You won't be the last
> Give me a break and take your own life.[48]

Black Faces, White Crime

This chapter began with a brief examination of the role played by black-face minstrelsy in perpetuating the portrayal of blacks as criminals. That is an important story, but it is not the whole story. Minstrel performers were not the only whites who darkened their skin and pretended to be black people. From the late 1800s through the first half of the 1900s, newspapers reported stories of white criminals disguising themselves as "Negroes." Their crimes ranged from loitering to murder. In 1884, Bogan Cash, a fugitive, roamed the woods near Columbia, South Carolina. His face was "blacked with charcoal." He shot at one person.[49] There was a double killing in 1894 in Robeline, Louisiana. A man described only as a peddler heard "cries of murder" coming from a home and broke down the door "pistol in hand." He saw two black-faced men attacking a white woman. He killed them. He did not know that both would-be murderers were white women dressed in men's clothing—with their faces blackened. The women and their husbands had concocted the plan.[50] In 1902, a New Hampshire man, Thomas Marshall, was wanted for escaping a house of

correction and for the theft of a horse and wagon. He was found hiding in a woman's closet, "disguised as a negro."[51]

There are many instances of white robbers blackening their faces. In 1894, Carroll Martin, of Van Buren County in Tennessee, was murdered by two men. It was a botched robbery. Martin's daughter and granddaughter were also wounded. The assailants were "disguised as blacks."[52] In 1906, the police department of Los Angeles reported that some recent robberies, burglaries, and holdups "supposed to have been committed by negroes have been committed by white men disguised as blacks."[53] In 1913, Roy Gardner, a white criminal, blackened his face and robbed a mail truck.[54] In 1916, D.O. Downing entered a Pennsylvania bank and shot a bank teller. Downing, described as a "prominent farmer and business man," walked into the Curwensville National Bank "disguised as a negro with his hands and face blackened and carrying a revolver in each hand."[55] It is not clear whether he was there to commit a robbery or was angry with the bank's staff. In 1919, Eufala, Oklahoma, was the scene of "the first minstrel train robbery in history." The criminals, fifteen whites, "with their faces blackened with burnt cork and otherwise disguised in a way that made them look like a colored minstrel troupe" robbed the M.K. & T passenger train. The robbers were not pretending to be black people. The burnt cork was to hide their faces.[56] "Many robberies charged to colored men in Casper, Colorado, according to the chief of the police of that city, were committed by two white men and a white woman who had blackened their faces."[57] In 1935, an unidentified white man, brandishing a straight razor, robbed a mother and her daughter of $25. According to a West Virginia newspaper, he was "disguised as a negro."[58]

The white criminals who disguised themselves as blacks sometimes committed sexual crimes. In 1909, William B. Mitchell, one of the wealthiest and most prominent residents of Thomasville, Georgia, was found guilty of attempting to abduct Lucille Linton. Mitchell was "disguised as a negro woman."[59] Nancy Dawson, from Canton, Georgia, was the victim of a rape attempt in 1906. She was beaten and her clothes torn away. In the struggle she "scratched the man's face, and the stains on her fingers indicated that his face was blackened by art not by nature." Dawson managed to escape. Soon afterward, the town's white people formed a mob. They planned to lynch Lewis Bates, a black man who had been in the vicinity of the attack. He barely escaped. A white man "with his face and hands blackened" was arrested. Dawson could not identify him, so he was released.[60] In 1927, a Mississippi man was caught as he attempted to rape a white woman. The offender, identified as Mississippi Sexton, had blackened his face to commit the crime. After his arrest, Sexton said that

This early postcard was published by H.M. Rosenblatt & Company. **123**

"there was a regularly organized gang, the members of which blackened their faces to commit crimes against women."[61]

In 1909, Elmer Carr, a Dayton, Ohio, man was arrested on a charge of arson. His live-in lover Carrie Middlestetter, told the investigating police officers that Carr had committed more serious crimes. He had raped many girls and women and murdered at least three teenage girls. When he left home to commit the last murder (and maybe others), Carr was "made up as a negro."[62] Carr's crimes were revealed because of the testimony of his girlfriend. There is no way to know how many black people, primarily but not exclusively men, were punished—including being tortured and lynched—because white criminals committed acts of rape and murder with their faces blackened. An editorial in the *Pittsburgh Courier*, a black newspaper, lamented: "Every Negro knows that there is no commoner device of white criminals than to blacken their faces or for persons guilty of a crime to declare that 'two black brutes' committed it."[63]

In 1923, a white high school student in Kansas City blackened his face and attempted a robbery. He was killed in the process of committing the crime. The *New York Age* reprinted a *Dallas Express* editorial that claimed that it was common for white people to hide their crimes behind blackened faces:

> It has happened before hundreds of times yet in few cases has Fate so arranged that it has been found out. Hundreds of Negroes in all parts of America have been put behind the bars, lynched, burned at the stake and sent to their Maker in other ways because some white criminal had "sense" enough and "superior" intelligence enough to blacken his face. Statistics in proof of this assertion would stagger the most incredulous. And yet we go on our way—not serenely; not happily; far from satisfied, for we know that often we are the "goat." How long, Ah Lord, how long? This masquerading of white criminals under blackened faces accounts for much of the crime charged against the Negro in the South. It is only when the criminal is killed or captured in the commission of the act, that the ruse is exposed.[64]

An epilogue to the story of white criminals posing as black people occurred in 2010. Conrad Zdzierak, an Ohio man, pleaded guilty to one count of aggravated robbery and five counts of robbery in a plea deal with prosecutors. Zdzierak robbed a credit union, a pharmacy, and four banks. Witnesses reported that the robber was a black man, and the surveillance cameras appeared to show an African American. The witnesses were unaware that Zdzierak wore a silicone mask that gave him the appearance of a black man.[65]

A Personal Story

In the mid-1980s I was an avid collector of baseball cards. I lived in Michigan City, Indiana. About two miles from my home was a shop that sold sports cards and jewelry. In those days I often looked for sports memorabilia that I could buy and resell. So, I went to that shop. I remember two things about the clerk in the store: he was rude and dismissive, and he had a gun on his hip. I was in the store only a few minutes, then I got in my car, intending to go home.

I drove maybe two blocks before I heard police sirens. My first thought was "I know darn well I wasn't speeding." I hoped the flashing lights were meant for someone else. They were not. The police car almost hit the rear end of my car. I pulled over, my heart racing.

An officer approached my car with his gun raised. He demanded that I get out and put my hands on the hood of my car. I did. He asked if I had a gun. I told him I did not. I asked him why I was stopped. He told me to shut up and asked if there were any weapons on my person. I said no. Again, he told me to shut up, though I was no longer talking. Another police car pulled up, then a third.

I noticed people watching. They were driving by, slowly, nosily, staring at the officers and me. I hoped that no one I knew recognized me.

I can say that I don't remember how much time went by, but the truth is I don't believe I was ever aware of how long I stood there, my face to the car, my back to the officers. I could hear them whispering. I expected the worst. A year earlier I had facilitated a diversity training session with police officers in Elkhart, a nearby town. During the session one of the officers boasted that "in the old days" he and other officers stopped people, "beat them, and didn't even arrest them." I now hoped that someone, anyone, would recognize me.

And then it was over.

A police officer—not the one who aimed his gun at me—said, "You can go." My fear was replaced by anger. I told them that I wanted to know why I had been stopped. One of the officers said sternly, "Get in your car now." When I got home I called the police department to complain. The person on the other end said that I hadn't been physically injured, and I looked like the suspect who had recently robbed that sports card store—adding that he was sure that I would want to see the offender caught. I told him that the only thing he should be sure of was that something bad happened and something much worse could have happened.

In 2012, just a month before the museum was scheduled to open, I was in a car accident. It was winter, Michigan winter, but I thought the roads were fine. They were not. I drove through a patch of black ice and lost control of the car. I hit a tree head-on, driving in excess of seventy miles per hour. The airbag deployed, then exploded, the engine dropped out of the car, and the vehicle's front was pushed almost to my lap. My head hit something. I briefly lost consciousness.

Some of my friends told me that I was blessed, while other friends told me that I was lucky. I suppose they meant the same thing: I had cheated death. I had headaches and my stomach was queasy from smelling and inhaling whatever it is that comes out of an exploding airbag. But I did not die, and I was not seriously or permanently injured.

There is something about the accident that I have not shared with others. It is about the split second before the car hit the tree. My life did not flash before my eyes, nothing like that. My head was clear the entire time. I saw the tree, tried to avoid it, and when I understood that the car was going to hit it, I relaxed my body. I was not afraid. I tell this story not to make myself sound brave but to illustrate a point.

In the days that followed the accident a fear, a creeping "what if" fear, consumed me. What if the airbag had not deployed? What if I had hit the tree at a less-advantageous angle? What if the accident had occurred at night when I might have been on the road alone? I thought about my wife, my children, my friends, and all the things I wanted to do . . . and the more I thought about the people in my life and the work I wanted to complete the more afraid of became . . . afraid of what might have been.

I had a similar reaction those many years earlier in the days that followed my confrontation with the Michigan City police officers. What if I had resisted? I was, after all, innocent. What if the officer's gun had discharged? It was pointed at me. What if the officer, perceiving me as a threat, went into fight-or-flight mode—tunnel vision, auditory exclusion, the loss of fine and complex motor control, and the inability to think rationally and clearly? What if I had slipped and he perceived my slipping as a sudden, aggressive move? There are reflexes that are triggered by the perception of a threat. What if he (or they) had tried to subdue me, choke me? I likely would have defended myself. . . . It took me a while to get over the fear of all the things that might have happened.

Not long afterward, there was an article in the local newspaper detailing the arrest of the robbery suspect. He was half a foot shorter than me. I had a full head of hair, and he was almost bald. His skin was dark, while my skin was red. I thought: maybe I should have stayed in Prichard, Alabama.

CHAPTER FIVE

Menaces Who Deserve to Be Hanged

> "I ain't givin' no lifetime of misery and sweat to these pecker-woods. I'd rather die than be a slave. You, peckerwoods, that's right! You peckerwoods was oppressed in your own land. We was free and you brought us here, in chains. But now we here. And you just better know, this is just as much our land as it is your'n . . . and after you hang me, kiss my ass."
>
> —Cicero in the film *Mandingo* (1975)[1]

One of the saddest and most shameful periods in the history of the United States is the seventy or so years when hundreds—in some cases, thousands—of Americans beat, tortured, and lynched fellow Americans. Although whites were sometimes lynched, most lynching victims were African Americans.[2] A recent report documents 3,959 lynchings of black people that occurred in Alabama, Arkansas, Florida, Georgia, Kentucky, Louisiana, Mississippi, North Carolina, South Carolina, Tennessee, Texas, and Virginia between 1877 and 1950.[3] And unlike white lynching victims, the blacks who were lynched were often tortured in ways that are incomprehensible to a contemporary American. The lynchings of black people were used to support the Jim Crow racial hierarchy. With white supremacy undergirding every major societal institution, black people were lynched for petty offenses such as stealing a cow, "sassing" a white person, asking for a raise, and trying to vote, or for being accused of more serious offenses, such as raping a white woman or murdering a white person.[4] Black people accused of crimes were often lynched without the benefit of criminal trials. Lynchings were an extralegal social

control mechanism used to keep black people at the bottom of the racial hierarchy.

Not all of the lynchings involved hangings, but many did, and the hangman's noose: a rope looped and secured with multiple wrapping turns or coils, became a powerful symbol of antiblack violence in general and lynchings in particular. The hangman's noose, whether used to murder someone, to symbolically kill (as with an effigy), or simply hanging alone, remains a mark of racial intimidation. There is a narrative, thankfully not as pervasive as in the past, that black people are menaces who deserve to be publicly hanged.

A Tool of Oppression

Although black people enslaved in the United States were sometimes lynched, usually for running away or planning a rebellion, lynching as a widespread, distinctly antiblack tool of oppression emerged after the Civil War. In the years immediately following the war, the newly emancipated

Elias Clayton, Isaac McGhie, and Elmer Jackson were lynched in Duluth, Minnesota, in 1920. They were falsely accused of raping a white woman. In 2003, the city of Duluth erected a memorial to the murdered men.

black people were victimized by sustained and brutal violence. Historian Leon F. Litwack writes that "how many black men and women were beaten, flogged, mutilated, and murdered in the first years of emancipation will never be known."[5] This violence, including lynchings, was used to reestablish white supremacy and deny the newly emancipated black people first-class citizenship.

During the next several decades, lynchings increasingly became a tool of racial control. Lynchings were often seen as frontier justice for offenses ranging from cattle theft to murder, and during the late 1800s white people were lynched in the United States. But by 1900, the racial character of lynching was well established. The ratio of black lynching victims to white lynching victims was four to one from 1882 to 1889, increased to more than six to one between 1890 and 1900 and soared to more than seventeen to one after 1900.[6]

The most common justification offered for the lynching of black people was that it was a necessary evil to keep black brutes or black beasts—savages no longer restrained by enslavement—from raping white women. While most lynchings of black people did not involve allegations of rape, "the specter of violated white women lay at the center of prolynching rhetoric and instigated the most horrific lynching tortures and spectacles."[7] Rebecca Latimer Felton, the first woman in the U.S. Senate and a champion of women's suffrage, said in an 1897 speech that the biggest problem facing women on the farm was the danger of black rapists. "If it takes lynching to protect women's dearest possession from drunken, ravening beasts," she said, "then I say lynch a thousand a week."[8] Felton's views were normative among whites during the lynching period.

On August 21, 1901, the *El Paso Herald* ran a story entitled "Human Torch," which recounted the torture and killing of a man identified only as "the negro brute." With a "rope around his neck and several guns at his temples he confessed" to raping J.M. Caldwell, a white woman. A mob of three hundred men and boys dragged the black man for miles, hanged him from a tree, the lower half of his body lowered into a burning pyre. According to the newspaper:

> But this death was too merciful in the opinion of some of the mob, and the fire was allowed to die down, the negro's blackened body was lowered, and the rope removed from his neck. The writhing of the half burned animal was jeered by the mob, who seemed to enjoy the brief respite, it was so much more horrible than mere cremation. Some of the mob ran for coal oil, having to go several miles to a town to get it. A new pile of wood and brush was made, and when the coal oil came it was poured over the mass, and on

the tree. Then the distorted body of the negro was saturated with the oil, and the fire lighted. Again, the rope was put around the negro's neck and thrown over the tree limb. The oil blazed up, and almost enveloped the scene in the lurid flame. The odor of roasting flesh was sickening, and the writhing body in dying convulsions made the sparks fly. Round after round of shots were fired into the mass where the body lay, the rope having burned through.[9]

About 25 percent of the lynchings of black people involved allegations of rape, but it's important to keep in mind that all sexual relations involving black men and white women were considered illicit and therefore constituted rape. Indeed, protecting white women's "dearest possession" also included lynching black men who flirted with white women or found themselves in other inappropriate settings with white women. Keith Bowen was lynched in Aberdeen, Mississippi, in 1889. He was a black man who made the mistake of trying to enter a room where three white women were sitting and talking.[10] The entire local white community participated in his lynching, even though he was not accused of anything other than trying to enter the room. Another black man, General Lee, was lynched for knocking on the door of a white woman's home in Reevesville, South Carolina, in 1904.[11] There are other instances of black men being lynched, often after being sadistically tortured, for offenses as innocent as accidently brushing a white woman or not stepping off a sidewalk to avoid possibly touching a white woman. Ida B. Wells, an African American journalist in Memphis, published an editorial critical of lynchers and challenging the myth of an epidemic of black-on-white rapes, pointing out that black men and white women sometimes had consensual sexual relations. A white mob burned her newspaper office and threatened to lynch her.[12]

Wells would not have been the first or last black woman lynched. From the 1890s through the 1950s, at least 159 black women were lynched.[13] Laura Nelson and her son L.D. were hanged from a bridge over the North Canadian River in Okemah, Oklahoma, on May 25, 1911. Neither Laura nor her son were accused of raping a white woman, but it is evidence of the hypocrisy that undergirded the Jim Crow racist hierarchy that members of the white mob raped Laura before they lynched her.

Picnics and Spectacles

Some of the more than four thousand blacks who were lynched were lynched in settings that are appropriately described as picnic-like; more accurately, the lynchings were a cross between picnics and spectacles. In 1903, a black man was lynched in Greenville, Mississippi. A white writer

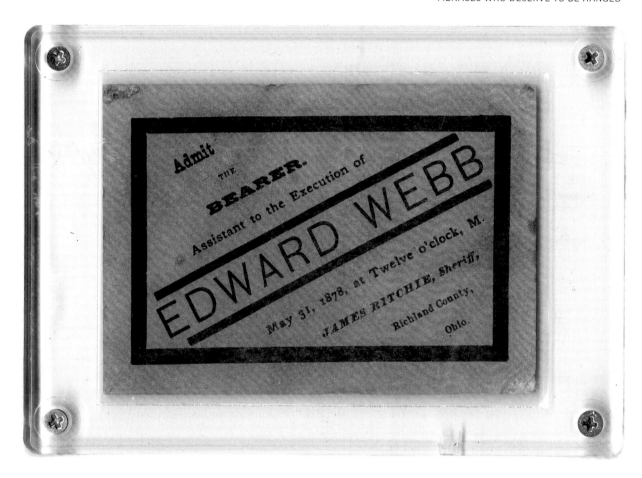

said, "Everything was very orderly, there was not a shot, but much laughing and hilarious excitement. . . . It was quite a gala occasion, and as soon as the corpse was cut down all the crowd betook themselves to the park to see a game of baseball."[14] Historian Phillip Dray wrote: "Lynching was an undeniable part of daily life, as distinctly American as baseball games and church suppers. Men brought their wives and children to the events, posed for commemorative photographs, and purchased souvenirs of the occasion as if they had been at a company picnic."[15]

Dray's use of the word "picnic" is an accurate description of some lynchings, but there is a current story about the etymology of picnic that is inaccurate. Some colleges and universities no longer refer to any campus outings as picnics. The decision was made, they argue, because the word "picnic" was derived from the Jim Crow–era practice of randomly "picking a nigger" to lynch for the entertainment of white spectators.[16] But the etymology of the word "picnic" does not suggest racist or racial overtones. It was originally a seventeenth-century French word, *pique-nique*, whose meaning was similar to the English: a social gathering where each attendee brings a share of the food. The literal meaning

In 1878, Edward Webb, described in newspapers as "a negro murderer," was hanged at Mansfield, Ohio. As this ticket suggests, his public execution was scheduled. There were thousands who wanted to view the execution but did not have tickets. The ticketless mob stormed the jail and forced Webb's hanging in their presence. **131**

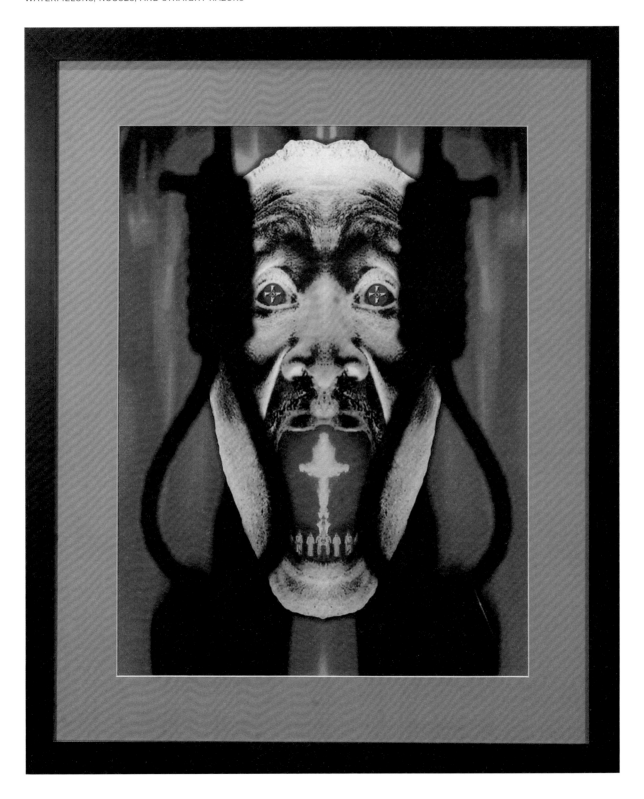

of *pique-nique*, which became our "picnic," is "each pick a bit."[17] A 1692 edition of Gilles Ménage's *Origines de la Langue Françoise* mentions *pique-nique*, but the term "picnic" did not appear in the English language until the eighteenth century.[18]

The word was not derived from "pick-a-nigger," "pick-a-nig," or similar racist phrases, but that does not weaken Dray's "company picnic" metaphor. Often the lynch mob acted with haste, but on other occasions the lynching was a long, drawn-out affair with speeches, food, and ritualistic and sadistic torture: victims were dragged behind cars, pierced with knives, burned with hot irons or blowtorches, had their fingers and toes cut off, had their eyes cut out, and were castrated—all before being hanged or burned to death. One Mississippi newspaper referred to these gruesome acts as "Negro barbeques."[19] The use of a food metaphor is unfortunately appropriate. According to Dray:

> While attendees at lynchings did not take away a plate of food, the experience of having witnessed the event was thought incomplete if one did not go home with some piece of cooked human being; and there is much anecdotal evidence of lynch crowds either consuming food and drink while taking part in the execution, or retiring en masse immediately afterward for a meal or, in the case of a notorious immolation in Pennsylvania in 1911, ice cream sundaes.[20]

At the end of the nineteenth century, Henry Smith, a mentally challenged seventeen-year-old black male, was accused of killing a white girl. Before a cheering crowd of hundreds, Smith was made to sit on a parade float drawn by four white horses. The float circled numerous times before the excited crowd tortured Smith, then burned him alive.[21] After the lynching the crowd celebrated and collected body parts as souvenirs.

All lynchings were murders and indictments against American democracy, but several lynchings were especially notable for the level of brutality inflicted on the victims. One such lynching occurred in Jackson County, Florida, on October 26, 1934. The lynching victim was Claude Neal, a black farmhand accused of raping and killing Lola Cannady, a white female. Neal's guilt was never established because he was denied a trial. Instead, he was forcibly removed from a jail and tortured before hundreds, maybe thousands, of white citizens in ways that are almost incomprehensible. A white Southerner named Howard Kooter reported on the lynching, quoting a member of the lynching party:

> "After taking the nigger to the woods about four miles from Greenwood, they cut off his penis. He was made to eat it. Then

The painting, "The Lynched," painted in 2003 by Laertis Limnidis, is part of the Jim Crow Museum's Hateful Things traveling exhibit.

they cut off his testicles and made him eat them and say he liked it. Then they sliced his sides and stomach with knives and every now and then somebody would cut off a finger or toe. Red hot irons were used on the nigger to burn him from top to bottom." From time to time during the torture a rope would be tied around Neal's neck and he was pulled up over a limb and held there until he almost choked to death when he would be let down and the torture begin all over again. After several hours of this unspeakable torture, "they decided just to kill him."[22]

In an action that foreshadowed the 1998 death of James Byrd, Neal's body was tied to the rear of a car and dragged. Hundreds of people continued the mutilation. His body was hung from an oak tree on a courthouse lawn. Souvenir collectors cut off his toes and fingers and skinned his body with knives.[23] People late to the lynching purchased pictures of Neal's mutilated corpse for fifty cents. In many cases, arguably in most cases, lynch mobs had a particular target and confined their heinous aggression to a specific person, but after Neal's lynching white mobs attacked local black people.

Neal's torturous murder served multiple purposes. It bonded local communities of whites against a common enemy: the supposed black brute. The murder reinforced the belief that "bad" black people needed to be killed, and it offered "good" white people an opportunity to perform their "civil duty." There was insanity present at the Neal lynching, but the torturous acts were not confined to crazed thugs. Respectable community leaders, including politicians, police, ministers, and teachers, participated, as did women and children. It sent the message of white supremacy to whites, demonstrating their rank at the top of the racial hierarchy, and it sent this message to black people: "violence will be used to keep you in your place." This latter message is echoed in the words of a white man in Oxford, Mississippi, in 1938, who declared that it was "about time to have another lynching. When the niggers get so they are not afraid of being lynched, it is time to put the fear in them."[24]

Innocent black men were sometimes lynched. As historian Dominic J. Capeci noted, when it came to lynching, "one black man served as well as another."[25] In 1891, Will Lewis, a black man, was taken from a caboose in Tennessee by eight masked men. They hanged him for no apparent reason.[26] Rev. J.E. Horne of Madison County, Texas, told the story of a black man who was accused of riding a horse over a little white girl, inflicting serious injuries. He was lynched. Later developments show that the mob got the wrong man and the guilty one escaped.[27] In 1900, Henry Lewis, the alleged killer of Marshall Richardson, a white man, was on the

lam with bloodhounds and a posse pursuing him. Another black man, identified as "the negro Lewis," had earlier been lynched for the crime.[28]

In 1903, a Georgia mob killed an unidentified black man, believing him to be Ed Clauss—suspected of raping a white woman. The victim was "tied to a tree and his body riddled with bullets, despite his frantic protests of innocence."[29] He was, in fact, not Ed Clauss. In 1912, Walter Johnson, a black man, was lynched in West Virginia. He was accused of the rape of Nita White, a fourteen-year-old white girl. Shortly thereafter, a local judge, prosecuting attorney, and sheriff concluded that Johnson had not committed the crime. According to newspaper reports, "The negro fell far short in dress and physical appearance of the man described by the girl."[30] In 1915, in Jackson, Mississippi, Ed Johnson, a black man, was taken by a mob—he had been in the custody of a constable on charges of stealing a cow. The mob lynched Johnson. Two days later the cow returned, having merely strayed.[31]

In 1933, an eleven-year-old white girl in Maury County, Tennessee, claimed that Cordie Cheek, a black teenager, had raped her. He had not. Cheek had refused to call a white teenager "Mister." That resulted in a fight. The white boy later paid the girl one dollar to say that Cheek had raped her. A white mob kidnapped him from his home and lynched him.[32]

On October 8, 1933, Anna Mae LaRose, a white woman, was found dead in a sugarcane field in Labadieville, Louisiana. At her funeral,

William Brown was accused of assaulting Agnes Lobeck, a white woman, in Nebraska. On September 28, 1919, he was brutally and savagely lynched in Omaha. **135**

MENACES WHO DESERVE TO BE HANGED

LaRose's stepfather accused Fred Moore, a sixteen-year-old black youth, of raping and killing LaRose. Moore was arrested and placed in the Assumption Parish Jail in Napoleonville. This did not satisfy the local white citizens. On October 11, a lynch mob kidnapped Moore from his jail cell using keys from one of the deputies. They beat the boy until he confessed to the murder. Moore also named a "Norman Jackson" as an accomplice. The mob castrated Moore. His lifeless body was hung from the Labadieville Bridge. A note was affixed to his body that said, "Niggers, let this be an example. Do not touch for 24 hours." His body was displayed until the following day. The *Chicago Defender* reported that photographs of the lynching were sold for twenty cents to "lift a mortgage" on a Labadieville church.[33] Norman Thibodaux, another black youth, was tortured and nearly lynched. Later, LaRose's stepfather confessed that he had murdered his niece.[34]

Strange Fruit

"Strange Fruit" is a euphemism for the lynched bodies of African Americans hanging and swaying from trees, poles, and bridges—people like Fred Moore. It is also the name of one of most powerful protest songs ever written, a haunting tune made famous by Billie Holiday. In the 1930s and 1940s, when political protest was rarely expressed in musical form, the song portrayed lynching in all of its brutality. Here are the words to "Strange Fruit":

> Southern trees bear strange fruit.
> Blood on the leaves and blood at the root,
> Black bodies swinging in the southern breeze,
> Strange fruit hanging from the poplar trees.
>
> Pastoral scene of the gallant south,
> The bulging eyes and the twisted mouth,
>
> Scent of magnolias, sweet and fresh,
> Then the sudden smell of burning flesh.
>
> Here is fruit for the crows to pluck,
> For the rain to gather, for the wind to suck,
> For the sun to rot, for the trees to drop,
> Here is a strange and bitter crop.

Although Holiday made the song famous, she was not the author of the heartrending lyrics. That distinction belongs to Abel Meeropol, a Jewish schoolteacher from the Bronx. Meeropol saw a gruesome photograph of

These mannequins are in the museum's Klan display.

the hanging bodies of two young black men, Thomas Shipp and Abram Smith, who were lynched on August 7, 1930, in Marion, Indiana.[35] The lynching of Shipp and Smith bore striking similarities to the Neal lynching: in broad daylight a mob took the men from the police, brutally beat them, and dragged them to be hanged near a courthouse. The photograph, taken by Lawrence Beitler, the town photographer, shows a crowd of white people, some of them smiling, with the two murdered African Americans, their bodies bloodied, hanging from a tree. One white spectator points as if to say, "This is what happens to niggers who don't stay in their places." The photo sold thousands of copies. Beitler stayed up for ten days and nights printing them.[36] Meeropol saw a copy of the photograph and it horrified and sickened him. He dealt with his horror by writing the poem "Bitter Fruit," which was published in 1937 in the *New York Teacher*, a union publication. Meeropol, a member of the American Communist Party, also later published it in the Marxist journal *New Masses*.

In early 1939, after seeing Holiday perform at the Café Society, an interracial nightclub in Greenwich Village, New York, Meeropol showed her the poem and a version that he had put to music, and which had been sung by his wife Anne. Holiday liked it and worked with Meeropol and Sonny White to turn it into her version of "Strange Fruit." She was

The Jim Crow racial hierarchy was supported by violence.

worried about singing it, even at Café Society, a place that catered to progressives. "There wasn't even a patter of applause when I finished," Holiday later wrote in her autobiography. "Then a lone person began to clap nervously. Then suddenly everybody was clapping."[37] Her rendition made an enormous impression on that first audience and on most audiences that heard her sing the disturbing ballad that would become her signature song.

The lyrics are hard to read and even harder to hear in song. Nightclub partiers, who had come to drink, dance, and have a good time, not to hear about lynched boys "swinging in the southern breeze," walked out. Some who stayed were angry at Holiday for daring to sing those words. It is easier to be angry at the messenger than it is to change a culture. But many listened, nodded and applauded, and knew that she cried the truth. The simple but poignant contrast between the "scent of magnolias" and the "sudden smell of burning flesh" brought some to tears. Some of those who cried did so because Holiday spoke a truth they didn't want to hear in song, and others because they needed someone, anyone, to tell the truth. Still others cried because it was sad to think of any mother's son hanging like fruit from a tree—dead fruit. Holiday performed the song nightly.

This is a 1905 newspaper cartoon with a casual reference to lynching.

139

In the 1930s, it was hard to make a record that testified about racial atrocities. Holiday asked her recording label, Columbia, to record the song. They refused. The executives at Columbia feared a hostile response by southern record retailers and affiliates of Columbia's co-owned radio network, CBS. Columbia did grant Holiday a one-session release from her contract to work with Commodore Records, an alternative jazz label. In 1939, she recorded "Strange Fruit" and it became her biggest seller. Singing the song both reflected and increased her pain. Her accompanist Bobby Tucker recalled that Holiday cried after every performance of "Strange Fruit." She cried because she knew the nooses were not empty.

Time magazine referred to the song as "a prime piece of propaganda" for the NAACP. The magazine was disapproving but right. Since its founding in 1909, the NAACP had waged a battle against the lynching of African Americans. "Strange Fruit" quickly became an anthem of the anti-lynching movement and the first significant song of the then fledgling civil rights movement. The song forced listeners to confront the brutality of lynching. Although many radio stations refused to play it, enough did for thousands to hear it. And, of course, Holiday traveled to sing it in places where both she and the song were welcome. "Strange Fruit" became a memorial to the voiceless victims of hate: men and women beaten, stripped, lashed, mutilated, burned, riddled with bullets, and left "hanging from the poplar trees."

Hanged in Effigy

Not all lynchings involve killing real people. Sometimes a crude representation of a person is hanged, burned, or riddled with bullets. For example, during the height of the civil rights protests in Birmingham, Alabama, in 1963, a life-sized dummy of Martin Luther King Jr. was hanged in the courtyard of a Catholic church. That year King was also hanged in effigy at the headquarters of the National States' Rights Party, a white supremacist group, also in Birmingham. Sometimes the hanging or burning of effigies is done to ridicule someone not liked and there is no real threat involved. While there is no evidence that the people involved in hanging King's effigy in Birmingham or elsewhere participated in his murder, it seems that the hanged effigies were not merely representations of ridicule or empty threats. King was shot while standing on a balcony at the Lorraine Motel in Memphis, Tennessee, on April 4, 1968.

It took a federal court ruling to gain a black person admission to the University of Mississippi, and when that black man, James Meredith, arrived on the Oxford, Mississippi, campus in 1962, he was met by death threats and rioting white students, riots which left two people dead and hundreds of others injured. The resistance to Meredith's presence on the

This 1960 effigy of a black college student was intended to scare civil rights activists.
Photo caption: Baton Rouge, La., March 30—Effigy a reaction to lunch counter sit downs—A life-size effigy with sign describing it as a Southern University student hangs from lamp post by field house at Louisiana State University here early today. Students of Southern University, a Negro school, have staged lunch counter sit downs and demonstrations in Baton Rouge this week. Fourteen have been arrested. (AP Wirephoto 1960).

(BT4) BATON ROUGE, La., March 30—EFFIGY A REACTION TO LUNCH COUNTER SIT DOWNS—A life-size effigy with sign describing it as a 'Southern University' student hangs from lamp post by field house at Louisiana State University here early today. Students of Southern University, a Negro school, have staged lunch counter sit downs and demonstrations in Baton Rouge this week. Fourteen have been arrested. (AP Wirephoto) (rwt41630mbr)1960

previously and proudly all-white campus was predictable. Meredith's attendance at the university was a frontal assault on Jim Crow segregation. On and off campus, whites threatened Meredith with all the tortures meted out to Neal, Shipp, and Smith. Meredith received one postcard signed "The Whites," which read, "Dear Nigger bastard, I hope they hang your black ass from the biggest tree around."[38] During his first weeks on campus, Meredith was hanged in effigy at least three times. The effigies of Meredith were meant to intimidate him. One writer concisely drew the link between lynchings of real black people and lynching their likenesses:

> Just as their parents and grandparents had used ritualized violence against black bodies to celebrate white supremacy, the University of Mississippi students who displayed and burned these effigies performed a ritual desecration of Meredith's body. The bodies left hanging around campus may have been filled with cotton, not the flesh and blood of African Americans, but these effigies proudly invoked a tradition of lynching that reaffirmed the same culture of white supremacy that lynching had celebrated for over one hundred years.[39]

Despite being harassed and threatened daily and attending class accompanied by armed guards, Meredith persevered and on August 18, 1963 became the first black person to graduate from the University of Mississippi. In 2006, the university, by then essentially racially integrated, erected a life-sized bronze likeness of Meredith. The statue shows a figure walking toward a seventeen-foot-tall limestone gateway topped with the words "courage," "perseverance," "opportunity," and "knowledge." On the day of the unveiling, survivors of the civil rights movement applauded the university. Representative John Lewis, who had participated in the Freedom Rides in 1961, captured the spirit of the day: "With the unveiling of this monument, we free ourselves from the chains of a difficult past. Today we can celebrate a new day, a new beginning, the birth of a new South and a new America that is more free, more fair and more just than ever before."[40]

Meredith was fortunate to be in attendance at the ceremony. In 1966, he began a March Against Fear walk. His goal was to walk from Memphis, Tennessee, to Jackson, Mississippi, to encourage voter registration and to highlight continuing racism in the South. On the second day of his solo protest, he was shot by a white gunman. During his hospitalization and recovery, leaders of major civil rights organizations set a plan to complete Meredith's march. After a short hospital stay, Meredith joined the group, which numbered about fifteen thousand marchers and became the largest civil rights march in Mississippi. In 2015, a former University

This anti-lynching cloth banner was produced by the Union Poster Service, New York City, circa 1940s.

of Mississippi student, Graeme Phillip Harris, pleaded guilty to a misdemeanor charge arising from placing a noose on the statue of Meredith.

As Meredith's entrance into the University of Mississippi demonstrates, black people who violated Jim Crow norms and customs were sometimes hanged in effigy. In 1939, the Ku Klux Klan hanged a black effigy from a telephone pole in Miami, Florida. The bloodstained effigy included a sign announcing, "This Nigger Voted."[41] In 1947, white students at Fremont High School in Los Angeles expressed their disapproval of six black youths being admitted to the school by hanging a "Negro in effigy."[42] In 1956, a black family moved into a previously all-white neighborhood in Fort Worth, Texas. They were met by at least 150 angry whites who racially taunted them and "hanged a Negro effigy" in front of their home.[43] That same year, two years after the Supreme Court struck down racial segregation in *Brown v. Board of Education*, twelve black students were admitted to the previously all-white Mansfield High School in Mansfield, Texas. The white residents of the town, upset by the prospect of black students attending the school, soon devolved into a mob.

> The mob hung an African American effigy at the top of the school's flag pole and set it on fire. Attached to each pant leg was a sign. One read, "This Negro tried to enter a white school. This would be a terrible way to die," and the other read, "Stay away, niggers." A second effigy was hung on the front of the school building. Soon afterward, the Mansfield School Board voted to "exhaust all legal remedies to delay segregation." In December 1956, the United States Supreme Court ordered the Mansfield school district to integrate immediately, but Mansfield public schools did not officially desegregate until 1965.[44]

Lynched Like Me

White people who worked to dismantle the Jim Crow racial hierarchy were occasionally hanged in effigy. For example, Joe Lapchick, while coaching the New York Knicks in the 1950s, was called a "nigger-lover" and hanged in effigy after he allowed a black player, Nat "Sweetwater" Clifton, to play in a game. In 1967, Father James Groppi, a noted civil rights activist, was hanged in effigy by a large band of white youths. The effigy included the sign, "A Good Groppi is a Dead Groppi."[45] John Howard Griffin, the author of *Black Like Me*, was also hanged in effigy.

Griffin, frustrated at the racial tensions that existed between blacks and whites in the late 1950s, made the decision to become what sociologists call a complete participant. He wanted to know what it was like to live as a black man in the Deep South, so he conducted a radical

experiment: he underwent medical treatment to temporarily darken the color of his skin.

On November 1, 1959, Griffin arrived in New Orleans, Louisiana. The next morning he met with a prominent dermatologist, explained his experiment, and asked for assistance. In a later meeting, the physician revealed to Griffin his beliefs that light-skinned blacks are more moral than darker blacks and that all blacks are inherently violent. Nonetheless, the doctor reluctantly agreed to help. After consulting with several colleagues, he recommended a medication taken orally followed by huge doses of ultraviolet rays; this treatment was similar to the way vitiligo (a disease that causes white spots to appear on the face and body) was managed. Griffin began treatment immediately, eventually also shaving his head. After enduring a series of additional treatments, he had the appearance of a black man—and confronted the racist in his mirror.

> Turning off all the lights, I went into the bathroom and closed the door. I stood in the darkness before the mirror, my hand on the light switch. I forced myself to flick it on. In the flood of light against the white tile, the face and shoulders of a stranger—a

This paperweight was sold at a Michigan flea market in 2006.

ROPE

fierce, bald, very dark Negro—glared at me from the glass. He in no way resembled me. The transformation was total and shocking. I had expected to see myself disguised, but this was something else. I was imprisoned in the flesh of an utter stranger, an unsympathetic one with whom I felt no kinship. All traces of the John Griffin I had been were wiped from existence. Even the senses underwent a change so profound it filled me with distress. . . . The completeness of this transformation appalled me.

Griffin calmed down and began his experiment. He confided his secret to Williams, a black confidant, who offered to help, including allowing Griffin to work with him at a shoeshine stand. There, Griffin got his first glimpse of what it meant to be black. He was treated as a nonperson by many of the whites whose shoes he shined. Indeed, they only looked at him when they asked if he could help them find black girls for sex. He learned the difficulty of finding places to eat and urinate. He met a black man who told of hating the ghetto so much that he frequently went to white neighborhoods to smell the clean air and look at the pretty houses.

Once he was followed by a white man who cursed and threatened him. Griffin tried to get away but the man continued to hound him with racial taunts and threats. Finally, Griffin was left no choice but to defend himself—he was a trained martial artist. At the last minute the man backed away. For the first time in his life, he felt the sting of being called a nigger.

He tried to get a job but no white employer considered him competent or trustworthy. He battled frustration. For example, on one occasion he was sitting on a park bench, and a white man told him that he should move. At first Griffin believed the man was trying to protect him from inadvertently violating Jim Crow customs. Later he realized that the man simply did not want to sit near him. He experienced rude treatment from bus drivers, restaurant workers, and others. Living as a black man in New Orleans was bad, but Williams convinced Griffin that things were worse in Mississippi and other Southern states.

Griffin traveled on Greyhound buses and occasionally hitchhiked across Louisiana, Mississippi, Alabama, and Georgia trying to see race relations through the eyes of a black man. He found out what every southern black person already knew: the Deep South had a racial hierarchy with whites on the top and blacks on the bottom. He had anticipated some prejudice and hardship, but he was shocked at the extent of it. The little courtesies and amenities that he, as a white man, had taken for granted were now prohibited to him. He couldn't find a restroom that blacks could use. It was impossible to find a job, suitable housing, or a clerk who would

This shirt was purchased in 2014 during President Obama's second term.

147

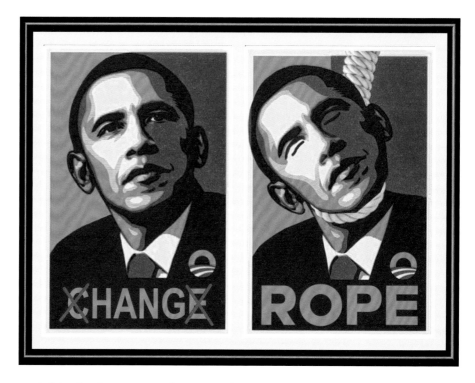

cash his checks. He was threatened. Everywhere he went whites treated him with disdain, fear, or vulgar curiosity.

He was particularly shocked when white men openly and without embarrassment asked questions about his sexual life, including one man who asked to see his genitalia. In general, Griffin met blacks who were poor, powerless, and resentful of whites, and whites who treated blacks as second-class citizens. After only a few weeks as a black man, he fell into depression and hopelessness. His experience was a powerful testament to the impact of racial prejudice and discrimination.

Griffin stopped taking his medication and using a skin dye and began alternating his racial appearance. He would visit a place as a black man and then return as a white man. Not surprisingly, when he presented as a white man, whites treated him respectfully and blacks were standoffish; when he presented as a black man, blacks treated him warmly, while whites treated him with contempt. Griffin concluded that the racial gulf between Southern blacks and whites made meaningful dialogue necessary, though highly unlikely.

Six weeks into the experiment, Griffin decided to end the project and return home. He was emotionally spent. Of course, unlike real blacks, he had always had the option to "stop being black" and reclaim his life as a white person. Even so, the experience had shaken him. He had received psychological relief by alternating his racial appearance, but he could not continue the experiment. He used the qualitative data to write "Journey

into Shame" for *Sepia* magazine, a five-part series that indicted the Jim Crow South and the system of discrimination that denigrated blacks. Later, Griffin rewrote his notes in the form of journal entries, subsequently publishing the entries as *Black Like Me*.

He became a national celebrity and villain. Griffin was interviewed on national television shows and in newsmagazines, including *Time*. His unconventional approach to understanding race relations brought him congratulatory mail from around the world, but in his hometown of Mansfield, Texas, the reaction was different. He and his family received hate mail, including threats to castrate him. An effigy of him, painted half black and half white, was burned on Main Street. A cross was burned in the schoolyard of an all-black school. The threats convinced Griffin to move his family to Mexico. For those who opposed civil rights for blacks, Griffin was a race traitor. He received death threats for the rest of his life.

In the half century since Griffin was hanged in effigy, the United States has become a more egalitarian and democratic society. De jure segregation (legal Jim Crow) has been dismantled. Black people are no longer lynched for trying to vote, attend a "white" school, move into a previously all-white neighborhood, or date a white. Race still matters, as evidenced by institutional racism and cultural norms that support

Visitors to the Jim Crow Museum learn about the relationship between violence and the Jim Crow racial hierarchy.

white privilege, but the United States that Griffin knew and studied has been radically altered. In 2008, the election of Barack Obama was hailed in many quarters as the dawning of a new society, a postracial society. But old prejudices die hard. President Obama has on many occasions been hanged in effigy. Some people contend that this is not significantly different than President George W. Bush or Governor Sarah Palin being hanged in effigy. Citizens are, the argument goes, simply expressing their disdain for a politician. Others draw a link between the hanged Obama effigies and the mistreatment of black people, especially black people who challenged the racial hierarchy.

The Noose Hanging Alone

Lynchings of black people, either literally or symbolically, reminded black people that the United States was a white man's country, and white people would use violence, including gruesome public murders, to maintain white supremacy. Although not used in all lynchings, the noose came to symbolize lynchings, and, more generally, the noose came to symbolize an unveiled threat to punish or a desire to control black people. In a 2008 event at the White House, President Bush referred to the noose as "more than a tool of murder. It was a tool of intimidation that conveyed a sense of powerlessness to millions."[46] The use of the noose to attempt to intimidate black people is not new. Jack Shuler, the author of *The Thirteenth Turn: A History of the Noose*, recounts three examples of countless such incidents: "On May 3, 1939, in Miami, a Klansman held

The museum does not focus on the Klan, but one cannot understand race relations in this country without examining the role of the Klan and other domestic terrorists.

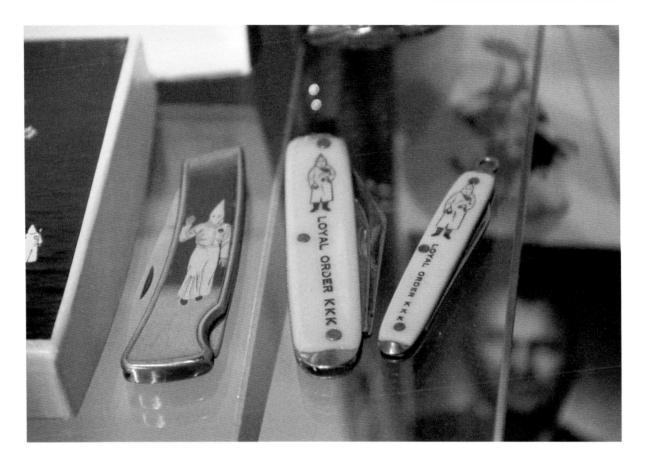

a hangman's knot outside a car window during a 'parade' through an African American neighborhood the night before a municipal election. In the late 1950s a noose was mailed to NAACP Secretary Roy Wilkins. And on Sept. 11, 1956, in Texarkana, Texas, a noose appeared, dangling in a schoolyard tree during a battle over desegregation."[47]

In March 2015, a noose was found hanging from a tree on the campus of Duke University. Campus leaders, including the president, condemned the incident. The noose sparked several public demonstrations, including roughly a thousand people who met to discuss diversity and inclusion at the University. The student responsible for hanging the noose came forward and "received a sanction through the University conduct process," which apparently included being required to write a letter to the campus. In that letter he attributed his action to a "lack of cultural awareness and joking personality."[48]

If the student is an international student, as is widely reported, then it is plausible that he was unaware of this country's use of lynchings to brutalize, control, and intimidate black people, and he might also have been unaware that the noose symbolizes those lynchings. The "joking personality" defense is often used in similar cases. For example, in 1999,

I have got to hang around here awhile. till I get my clothes.

police in Philadelphia, Pennsylvania, were called to investigate a black man's claim that white coworkers placed a noose around his neck. The victim, after a brief but anxiety provoking struggle, managed to remove the noose. The perpetrators told a union arbitration panel that their intent was "all horseplay and good fun."[49] In 2006, two African American sheriff's deputies in St. Louis, Missouri, claimed that they worked in a racially hostile environment where black employees were not promoted. Moreover, they claimed that their white supervisor refused to discipline white employees who engaged in racist acts, including displaying a noose in a prisoner holding area. The noose hanging was treated as a practical joke.[50] In 2015, a noose was found hanging in a post office in Worcester, Massachusetts. John "Mike" Powers, a district manager responsible for most of the state's postal workers, suggested that the employee who hung the noose was not making a racist statement. He called the incident a "bad joke gone bad."[51]

There are some noose hangings that may be correctly viewed as pranks, for example, every year during the Halloween season. But nooses hung or otherwise displayed in areas where black people work, attend school, or sometimes visit are not simply pranks. The initiator may not have racist intentions, but the noose—because it has become a synonym for lynchings—is often received as a racial taunt or a racist threat. The person who hangs the noose may be having fun, but the fun is not innocent. For many black people, the noose is a symbol of what was done to African Americans in the past and what may be done to a black person today.

This postcard has a 1907 postmark.

In some instances the "joking personality" rationalization is undermined by other indicators of a hostile environment. In these cases the noose may be accompanied by racist graffiti and a pattern of racial discrimination. The noose may be intended not as a threat of violence but as a visual way of expressing the sentiment: "Your life is not in danger, but we do not want you here." The following Equal Employment Opportunity Commission (EEOC) complaints involve displays of nooses or noose images in work settings.[52]

In January 2007, EEOC settled a racial harassment lawsuit against AK Steel Corporation, a Fortune 500 company, for $600,000. The evidence in that case was both severe and pervasive because the workplace featured Nazi symbols, racially graphic and threatening graffiti with messages to kill black people, displays of nooses and swastikas in work areas open to black employees, racial slurs and epithets, an open display of Ku Klux Klan videos in the employee lounge areas and circulation of political literature by David Duke, a known Klan leader.

In October 2007, EEOC obtained $290,000 from an Oklahoma-based oil drilling contractor for seven African American men who

This shirt was purchased from a Klan website in 2015. **153**

alleged that, while on an oil rig, they were subjected to a hostile work environment, which included the display of hangman nooses, derogatory racial language, and race-based name calling.

In April 2010, the EEOC settled its lawsuit against Professional Building Systems for $118,000 and significant non-monetary relief after it had identified at least twelve black employees who had been subjected to racial harassment there. According to the EEOC's complaint, at various times between mid-2005 and 2008, black employees were subjected to racial harassment that involved the creation and display of nooses; references to black employees as "boy" and by the "N-word"; and racially offensive pictures such as a picture that depicted the Ku Klux Klan looking down a well at a black man. In its complaint, the EEOC alleged that the managers of the company not only knew about the harassment and took no action to stop or prevent it, but also that a manager was one of the perpetrators of the harassment.

Ready Mix paid a total of $400,000 in compensatory damages to be apportioned among the seven class members to settle an EEOC lawsuit. The Commission had alleged Ready Mix USA LLC, doing business as Couch Ready Mix USA LLC, subjected a class of African American males at Ready Mix's Montgomery-area facilities to a racially hostile work environment. A noose was displayed in the worksite, derogatory racial language, including references to the Ku Klux Klan, was used by a direct supervisor and manager and that race-based name calling occurred. The case was settled in 2012.

In March 2012, the EEOC sued a restaurant in Menomonie, Wisconsin because its managers allegedly posted images of a noose and other racist depictions, including a dollar bill that was defaced with a noose around the neck of a black-faced George Washington, swastikas, and the image of a man in a Ku Klux Klan hood. A black employee complained and then was fired.

Ghoulish Acts

In 1918, a delegation of African American leaders met with Ruffin Golson Pleasant, governor of Louisiana. The delegation was concerned that black people were still being lynched in the state. Governor Pleasant, although conceding that lynchings "in many cases constituted murder," admonished the leaders to "go among their people and teach them not to commit crimes that would aggravate a community into breaking the law," because "sometimes the law of race becomes stronger than the law of the land."

There is no information on this postcard.

Charles M. Robertson, a black man from Shreveport, responded to the governor:

> We are here in harmony with the idea that lynching is wrong under any circumstances, whether it be applied to white or black. We have suffered by this system of lawlessness more than any other race in this country. We are being burned at the stake, hanged to the telegraph and telephone poles, hanged to trees within the shadows of our temples of justice; our fingers and ears are kept as souvenirs by that class who seem to believe in the mobs ruling the courts, rather than the courts ruling the mob. And yet, the violator of the law is rarely ever brought to the bars of justice.[53]

In 1911, Coleman Livingston Blease, governor of South Carolina, gave a speech to farmers. As an aside, he brought up the lynching of a black man. The governor said that rather than use his office to stop white men from "punishing that nigger brute" he would resign and "lead the mob."[54] That is not surprising. Blease believed that black people were inherently inferior to whites—education would "spoil" them—interracial couples should be severely punished, and lynching was necessary—not a necessary evil, simply necessary. He once buried the severed finger of a lynched man in the South Carolina gubernatorial garden. He was certainly not the only person to collect lynching relics, including the body parts of victims.

The people who participated in or witnessed the lynching of black people sometimes collected parts of the lynching tree and the clothes of the victim—and they occasionally collected body parts. In 1899, Richard Coleman, a black man accused of killing a white woman, was tortured and burned to death. Relic hunters took away teeth, bones, and flesh.[55] In 1901, George Ward, a black man, was lynched in Terre Haute, Indiana. He was accused of killing Ida Finkelstein, a white woman. A mob took him from a jail cell, dragged him to the river bridge and hung him to a beam, then burned his body "until nothing was left save a piece of the backbone and the back of the head." Teenage boys sold one of Ward's toes for a dollar, then began an impromptu auction for the other toes.[56] There was no effort on the part of authorities to intervene.

In 1899, Sam Hose, a black farmer, killed Alfred Cranford, a white man. Hose, fearing for his life, fled. Newspapers claimed that he "brutally murdered" Cranford and "assaulted his wife." While a posse was searching for him, the *Wilmington Messenger* wrote, "It is believed tonight that Hose will die fighting and thus avoid the worse in store for him."[57] Hose did not avoid the "worse in store." He was caught and a white mob of two thousand people watched his torture. His ears, fingers, and genitalia were cut off. The skin was cut from his face. His body was doused with

This image is in the "Hateful Things" exhibit. The caption reads in part "Last May [1939], in order to frighten Negroes away from the polls, the Ku Klux Klan hung this effigy in Miami."

156

kerosene and he was set afire. According to newspaper accounts, "The negro pleaded pitifully for his life while the mutilation was going on, but stood the ordeal of fire with surprising fortitude."[58] It was reported that small pieces of Hose's bone went for 25 cents "a bit of liver, crispy cooked, sold for 10 cents." His knuckles ended up on display in a store window in Atlanta.[59] Later investigations revealed that Hose had killed Cranford in self-defense and had not sexually assaulted Cranford's wife.

There is a record of what happened to Hose's knuckles, but in general there are few records of what happened to the parts cut from the bodies of other black lynching victims. What became of the severed ears, fingers, toes, and skin? Are they still displayed as conversation starters, hidden in the dusty trunks owned by elders, or long ago discarded or buried? It is hard to imagine an America where people fought over the charred severed fingers of a lynched black man, woman, or child.

The gruesome practice of collecting body parts from lynching victims is paralleled and rivaled by the practice of using the skin of black people to make shoes, wallets, belts, and other leather products. In 1831, Nat Turner, the leader of the Southampton Insurrection, was caught and hanged. He was skinned, "the hide having been tanned" and "distributed as souvenirs

This showcase houses a cartoon from *Hustler* magazine, one of the most disturbing objects displayed in the museum.

in the curiosity shops of many residents in and about Southampton."[60] There are multiple reports that a purse was made from the skin of the rebel leader.[61] Grease was made from his flesh.[62] Around the time of the Civil War, Steve Babcock, a transplanted Northerner, operated a tannery near Decatur, Alabama. He occasionally tanned the skins of black people. When asked how he could tan a human skin, Babcock responded, "Why this is not a human skin; it is only a nigger's hide. A nigger is nothin' but a beast. There hain't nothing human about him."[63] In 1878, the *New York Times* told the story of a black convict. After his death, medical students "skinned his body and tanned his hide for the purpose of making boots."[64] In 1883, a governor gave a military friend a small traveling bag "made of a negro skin tanned at Tewksbury, Massachusetts."[65] In that same year, there was a newspaper report of "tanned negro skins" being used for book bindings, pocketbooks, and satchels. A Boston tanner said that Harvard students brought him "negro skins to be tanned."[66] According to the *Semi-Weekly Citizen*, "the leading demand being for mulatto and octoroon skins."[67] An 1887 newspaper article told the story of a prominent New York physician who owned a pair of shoes made from the skin of a black man. According to the *Saint Paul Globe*, "the negro who furnished the material for the shoes bore the name of Sam Sternberg, and he was hung at Fonda, N.Y., in 1876, for the murder of a man named Parker."[68] The newspaper also recounted the story of a black man who was killed while robbing graves. His body was taken to a medical college and dissected. One of the students cut off a toe and gave it to a friend, "which it is said, possesses much of the look of a rabbit's foot."[69] According to an 1887 newspaper, there was young man who "carries a cigar case made of negro skin," a well-known surgeon with a "beautiful instrument case entirely covered with leather made from an African's skin," and a young socialite with slippers made from the skin of a black person, "whose leather invariably excites the admiration of her friends."[70]

In 1896, there was a report of a Philadelphia physician who had his shoes made from the skin of black people. He obtained the skin from a medical college. According to the *Richmond Climax*, "the result is a beautiful leather, extremely soft and pliable, very lustrous . . . the shoes are beautiful to look upon and grasp the feet kindly."[71] In 1900, skin from the amputated arm of a black man "was tanned and sent to Baltimore to be made into purses."[72] In 1912, the *St. Louis Post-Dispatch* told the story of "a physician's wife who is having a dead negro's skin tanned for a Christmas gift for her husband. A part of the negro's hide is to be made into a razor strope."[73]

There are many stories told in the Jim Crow Museum, but none are as horrible as these tales. The idea of using the skins of black people to make

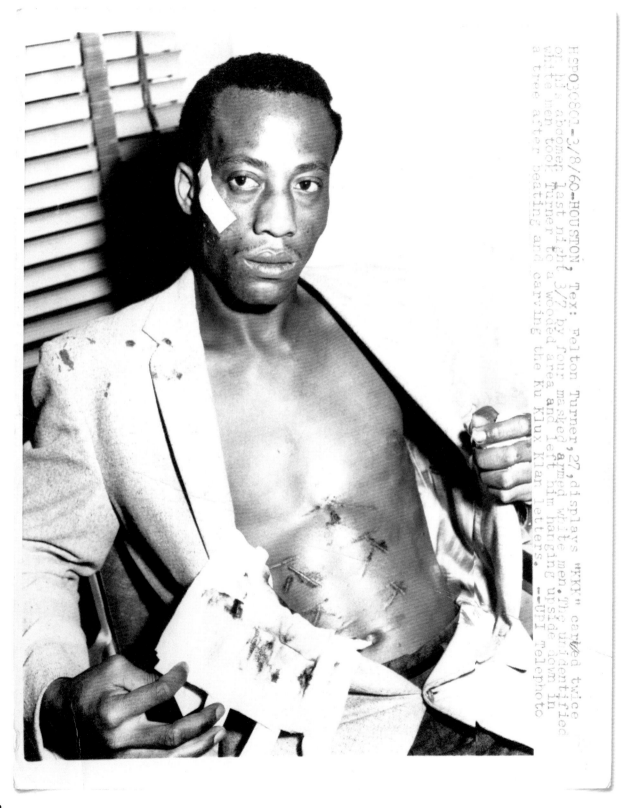

HEPO30801-3/8/60-HOUSTON, Tex: Felton Turner, 27, displays "KKK" carved twice on his abdomen last night 3/7 by four masked armed white men. The unidentified white men took Turner to a wooded area and left him hanging upside down in a tree after beating and carving the Ku Klux Klan letters. —UPI Telephoto

purses, shoes, belts, and other leather products is, of course, disgusting to contemporary Americans; however, there was a time—not so long ago—when the debasement of black Americans was so nearly complete that one could read about the skin of a black person being tanned in the same newspapers that reported the previous day's baseball box score.

A Personal Story

When the time came to select a dissertation topic, I decided to research lynchings. I was unsure what I would find—or even what I wanted to find. At most, I had some vague idea about comparing the ways that specific lynchings were reported in white newspapers and black newspapers. I hoped that immersing myself in the newspaper stories would give me some clarity and help me focus my research interest.

I knew from previous inquiries that the main library at The Ohio State University had bound copies of every issue of the *New York Times*, and equally important, the collection came with a citation index. It was a green oversized book, each page divided into two columns; the specific citations were very small. I remember the first time I looked up the word "lynching." There were dozens of lynchings cited on each page—and there were many pages covering lynchings. My plan was to start with the earliest incidents and continue until I had discerned patterns. How were the lynching victims described? What justifications were offered for the lynching? How many people attended? Participated?

Oh my goodness.

I grew up in Mobile and Prichard, two adjoining Alabama cities with long histories of racial injustice, including acts of terrorism against black people. I knew this history. I attended Jarvis Christian College, a historically black college in East Texas. The teachers there, blacks and whites, told stories about lynchings. I was not naive about this country's legacy of publicly executing black people, but I did not know as much as I thought I knew.

For more than two months I read the *Times* accounts of lynchings. These days there is much condemnation of the group referred to as the Islamic State of Iraq and Syria (ISIS). The denunciation is justified. ISIS has engaged in hate-induced, horrific, and barbaric acts of violence—but those acts are eerily similar to the lynchings that I read about in the *Times*. Lynching victims were sometimes burned at the stake. Some had spikes and nails driven into their writhing bodies. Some were stabbed with knives or slashed with straight razors. Some had their skin carved from their bodies. Some were beheaded. Spectators cheered, paid for—and sometimes fought over—the amputated fingers, toes, and genitalia of the victims. Before beginning the research, I knew that some lynchings

Felton Turner, a black man, was savagely attacked by the Klan in 1960.

had been spectacles and I knew that ghoulish atrocities had been committed, but I was not ready for what I read.

I thought about it too much, thought about it not as a researcher—thought about it as an imagined spectator . . . imagined myself as the victim. How is it that these things could have happened here? How to describe the insanity of thousands of spectators cheering as a scared, crying, begging man—the only brown face there—is doused with kerosene and set on fire. Maybe it was the sheer volume—each day reading about more lynchings, different lynchings, dying differently in the same way, but I stopped. At that time in my life I could not finish. Some knowledge is too expensive.

In the middle of the Jim Crow Museum is a full-sized replica tree. Hanging from the tree is a hangman's noose. The tree and noose are reminders that Jim Crow segregation did not work without violence. Visitors standing in the shadow of the museum's lynching display may be surprised to learn that there is a lynching-related "object" in the museum's holdings that has never been displayed.

It is about three inches long, brown, with an oblong shape. It looks like a small piece of an old leather football. It came in a thin white box, one that previously held an inexpensive piece of jewelry. It is difficult to know what to call it, this object—even calling it an "object" seems inappropriate because it is a part of a person, a souvenir collected from the mutilated body of a lynching victim.

The skin was donated to the museum by a man whose father attended a lynching. The donor received it as a child living in Illinois in the 1950s, but the father may have "collected" it earlier, probably in the 1930s. The donor was not sure if the lynching occurred in Illinois or a neighboring state; it was common for people to travel many miles to witness lynchings. When and where the desecration occurred is lost, and the donor's father died without talking about the lynching or the "souvenir."

It would be disrespectful to display the skin, not because it is visually offensive. Indeed, its appearance gives few clues to what it really is: a small piece of a person. But the museum's staff knows what it is. We know that this skin carved from the body of a lynched victim is tangible proof of the horrific torture inflicted on black people in this country. The staff also knows that the lessons about lynching in the United States can be taught without displaying the skin. If displayed, the body part, yet again, becomes fodder for entertainment, albeit horror as entertainment.

CHAPTER SIX
Hated by Dogs

"B stands for bloodhounds. On merciless fangs
The Slaveholder feel his 'property' hangs,
And the dog and the master are hot on the track,
To torture or bring the black fugitive back . . .
Say, which is the monster, the man or the beast?"

—Abel C. Thomas[1]

There is a cultural narrative that suggests that dogs are racist against black people. One can debate the extent to which dogs experience emotions, but there is little evidence that dogs possess the complex thinking and other higher cognitive functions necessary to be racist. Yet a dog can be trained or conditioned to attack black people, which is evident by the use of dogs to control the enslaved population in the United States. They were used to punish disobedient slaves on plantations, and they were used to track and attack slaves who ran away. Not only did dogs play a significant role in the tyrannical regime of slavery, but a century later dogs were used by white police officers to enforce and sustain Jim Crow segregation. And in the twenty-first century reports surfaced with evidence that police dogs in Los Angeles and other large cities are much more likely to be used to attack blacks and Latinos.[2] Dogs cannot be thinking, reasoning racists, but they can be used to attack people of color.

Slavery-Era Negro (Nigger) Dogs
In the United States dogs are idealized as faithful, pampered companions and "adopted" as family members. A staggering 83.3 million dogs

are pets in the United States. Americans spend billions of dollars on their dogs and consume romanticized representations of them as "man's best friend." First Dogs, the pets of presidents,[3] are profiled in newspapers and picture books. Rufus Thomas's "Walking the Dog," Joan Baez's "Old Blue," and Dolly Parton's "Gypsy, Joe, and Me" are among the many popular songs that mention dogs. Rin Tin Tin, Lassie, and Benji are among the dozens of dogs that have become Hollywood stars. Dogs headline an impressive list of popular family movies, such as *Turner & Hooch* (1989), *Bingo* (1991), *Beethoven* (1992), *101 Dalmatians* (1996), *Snow Dogs* (2002), *Because of Winn-Dixie* (2005), *Air Buddies* (2006), *Marley & Me* (2008), *Hachi: A Dog's Tale* (2009), *Marmaduke* (2010), and *Max* (2015).[4]

The representation of dogs as innocents who love humans unconditionally is challenged by their roles in controlling Africans and African Americans in the United States. One of the most controversial scenes in Quentin Tarantino's movie *Django Unchained* (2012) involved so-called nigger dogs, canines trained to hunt and attack black people. In the movie, Calvin Candie is the merciless owner of a ranch known as Candieland, a plantation famous for breeding Mandingos—slaves trained to fight to the death for their owner's amusement and for betting purposes. One of

Early twentieth-century postcard.

the fighters, D'Artagnan, mockingly named after the hero in *The Three Musketeers*, is a reluctant combatant who was caught running away. Candie states that his slaves cannot retire from fighting until they have won at least five matches in order for him to recoup his $500 investment in them. D'Artagnan, who is surrounded by white slave catchers and vicious hounds, refuses to fight and begs for his life. Candie shows his displeasure with D'Artagnan by "handling this nigger any way I see fit." He says to a white slave tracker, "Mr. Stonesipher, let Marsha and the bitches send D'Artagnan to nigger heaven." The dogs are loosed upon the black man, who is on his knees. Several white henchmen hoot and holler while the dogs savagely kill and apparently eat D'Artagnan. The other black fighters watch the bloody murder. Viewers of *Django Unchained*, more than a century removed from slavery, questioned the accuracy of the "dogs eating slaves" narrative.

It is difficult to generalize about slavery in the United States because the institution lasted for more than two centuries and had many variations, but there is no denying that enslavers used dogs as instruments of control and oppression. Mr. Stonesipher was a fictional slave tracker, but he had many real-world counterparts, and they used dogs to capture and torture black people escaping slavery. Ryer Emmauel, an enslaved man, stated that the white pursuers of black runaways would "let de dog bite you en taste your blood."[5] Bennett H. Barrow, an enslaver from Louisiana, kept a diary that talked about the importance of dogs in capturing runaways, as well as the violence they could inflict: "hunting Ruffins Boy Henry, came across Williams runaway caught him dogs nearly et his legs off, near killing him."[6] One enslaver expressed concern about using dogs because "they may kill a man in a very short time. Last time they had nearly torn him up."[7]

Frederick Law Olmsted, a famed architect and journalist, observed in the 1850s that "no particular breed of dogs is needed for hunting negroes: blood-hounds, fox-hounds, bull-dogs, and curs were used."[8] The dogs were trained and black people were used as training bait. According to Olmstead:

> One white man told me how they were trained for it, as if it were a common or notorious practice. They are shut up when puppies, and never allowed to see a negro except while training to catch him. A negro is made to run from them, and they are encouraged to follow him until he gets into a tree, when meat is given them. Afterwards they learn to follow any particular negro by scent, and then a shoe or a piece of clothing is taken off a negro, and they learn to find by scent who it belongs to, and to tree him, etc.[9]

Enslavers and the "nigger chasers" they hired used the dogs they could afford to buy or breed. Wealthier families could import specially bred dogs, canines known for their ferociousness and savagery. One example was the Cuban bloodhound.[10] Zachery Taylor, a military hero and the twelfth president of the United States, was one of the prosperous enslavers who imported these large, muscular mastiff/bulldog cross-bred hounds from Cuba. Most bloodhounds are known for tracking, not for savage attacks, but the Cuban bloodhounds were bred to be vicious. According to the historian John Hope Franklin, these bloodhounds "were fierce hunters, and if not constrained at the end of the chase, they would tear a man to pieces."[11] It may be coincidental but one of the earliest masks worn by the Ku Klux Klan bore a striking resemblance to the Cuban bloodhounds.

Runaway slaves were pursued by slave patrols—the slaves called them patrollers, pattyrollers, or paddy rollers: white men, armed with guns and whips, who protected the interests of enslavers by "apprehending runaways, monitoring the rigid pass requirements for blacks traversing the countryside, breaking up large gatherings and assemblies of blacks, visiting and searching slave quarters randomly, inflicting impromptu punishments, and as occasion arose, suppressing insurrections."[12] Patrollers had reputations for brutalizing black people, including beating and raping them. Each slaveholding community financed some version of these quasi-police.

One patroller, John Capeheart, a constable from Norfolk, Virginia, stated: "It was part of my business to arrest all slaves and free persons of color, who were collected in crowds at night, and lock them up. It was also part of my business to take them before the Mayor. I did this without any warrant, and at my own discretion. Next day they are examined and punished. The punishment is flogging." Capeheart received extra pay for administering the floggings, which were usually thirty-nine lashes. He was paid fifty cents for each arrest and another fifty cents for each flogging. He added, "I have flogged hundreds. I am employed by private persons to pursue fugitive slaves. I never refuse a good job of that kind."[13]

This is the infamous Cuban bloodhound. It bears a striking resemblance to one of the early Mississippi Klan costumes.

Fugitive slaves were also pursued by other slave hunters hoping to collect on a posted reward or to hire themselves out to hunt a specific runaway. These "professionals" were involved in cases where the runaway had avoided overseers and the slave patrols. It was not uncommon for the slave catchers who

"Thou art so near and yet so far"

owned dogs to advertise in local newspapers. David Turner advertised in the *Western Tennessee Democrat*: "BLOOD-HOUNDS.—I have TWO of the FINEST DOGS for CATCHING NEGROES in the Southwest. They can take the trail TWELVE HOURS after the NEGRO HAS PASSED, and catch him with ease."[14]

In 1855, the *Liberator*, an antislavery newspaper, reprinted an advertisement that had appeared in a Missouri newspaper. It is reproduced below to give readers a deeper understanding of the normalcy of using "negro dogs" or "nigger dogs" in 1855.

I would inform the citizens of Holmes County that I still have my NEGRO DOGS, and they are in good training, and ready to attend to all calls of hunting and catching RUNAWAY NEGROES, at the following rates: For hunting per day, five dollars, or if I have to travel any distance, every day will be charged for, in going and returning, as for hunting, and at the same rates. Not less than five dollars will be charged in any case where the Negroes come in before I reach the place. From fifteen to twenty-five dollars will be charged for catching, according to the trouble; if the Negro has weapons, the charge will be made according to the difficulty had in taking him,

This is a 1905 postcard that displays multiple antiblack stereotypes.

or in case he kills some of the dogs, the charge will not be governed by the above rates. I am explicit, to prevent any misunderstanding. The owner of the slave to pay all expenses in all cases. I venture to suggest to any person having a slave runaway, that the better plan is to send for the dogs forthwith when the negro goes off, if they intend sending at all, and let no other person go in the direction, if they know which way the runaway went; as many persons having other negroes to hunt over the track, and failing of success, send for the dogs, and then perhaps fail in consequence to catch their negro, and thus causelessly fault the dogs. Terms cash. If the money is not paid at the time the negro hunted for is caught, he will be held bound for the money. I can be found at home at all times, five and a half miles east of Lexington, except when hunting with the dogs.[15]

No societal institution, including the political and legal systems, afforded the enslaved population protection from being tortured by enslavers, their overseers, patrollers, or other whites. Enslavers had almost unchecked power regarding their slaves. There was nothing other than business concerns and their consciences to prevent enslavers from, in the words of the fictional Calvin Candie, "handling this nigger any way I see fit." And many enslavers saw fit to make torture integral in their relations with the enslaved population. The barbarity of enslavers and their overseers explains why many slaves ran away, risking injury or death from slave hunters and the pursuing hounds.

Most of the black people who tried to escape slavery failed and were returned to their enslavers, where they were tortured and sometimes returned to the auction block. The torture devices included: thumbscrews, which crushed bones in the fingers; tin masks with small slits that simulated suffocation in the wearer; heavy wooden and metal collars, which made all mobility difficult and painful; ropes used to hang the victim in suspension; and whips, including the cat-o'-nine-tails, to administer lashes. Of former slaves interviewed in the 1930s, half of those from the upper South and three-quarters of those from the lower South reported that they had been whipped. Slaves were also raped, branded with hot irons, dismembered, and castrated. And dogs sometimes savagely attacked the enslaved man, woman, or child.

Treated Worse than Dogs

Enslavement in the United States is correctly seen as chattel slavery, meaning, enslaved black people were legally defined as property; bought, sold, traded, and inherited—"owned" like animals and routinely treated

10813, Convicts lunch hour, Atlanta, Ga.

like animals. Public notices for the sale of slaves listed slaves and animals side by side, with comparable descriptions and prices.[16] The slaves at auction were poked and prodded. Like animals, enslaved black people were restrained and disciplined with whips and chains. Runaway slaves were frequently hunted like big game. Enslaved women were treated as breeders, their children seen as a litter. Black men, women, and children were branded like cattle. It was common for white people to refer to enslaved black people (and sometimes free black people) as brutes and beasts. Recalcitrant slaves were forced to wear collars made of metal, thick and heavy, with protruding spikes, or muzzles. The historian Carl N. Degler captured the significance of these practices:

> When a master muzzles a slave, for example, he is literally treating that slave like a dog. At the very least, the master's behavior is evidence for concluding that the master is in the process of thinking of the slave as being on the level with a dog; at the most, his behavior suggests that the source of, or impetus for the particular behavior is the belief that the slave was, from the beginning, no better than a dog and so deserves no better treatment.[17]

In some ways, enslaved black people were treated worse than dogs. When the enslaved black people said they were "treated like dogs" they meant that they were cruelly mistreated by enslavers or their overseers. Much of the abuse was physical: denial of food and rest, floggings and other physical punishment, and rape. Psychological abuse included measures, many and varied, to strip slaves of their humanity. One overseer

This stereograph card from 1896 shows a black work gang "supervised" by armed white guards.

169

forced slaves to attend the funeral of the dog he had used to hunt them when they ran away, which was his way of saying to the enslaved people, "This dog was more important, more valuable than you are."[18] Below are the words of black people who were enslaved.

> Now, if, uh, if my master wanted send me, he never say, you couldn't get a horse and ride. You walk, you know, you walk. And you be barefooted and collapse. That didn't make no difference. You wasn't no more than a dog to some of them in them days. You wasn't treated as good as they treat dogs now. But still I didn't like to talk about it. Because it makes, makes people feel bad you know. Uh, I, I could say a whole lot I don't like to say. And I won't say a whole lot more.
>
> —Fountain Hughes, enslaved in Virginia.[19]

> My marster was mean an' cruel. I hates him, hates him! The God Almighty has condemned him to eternal fiah. Of that I is certain. Ivan the cows and horses on his plantation was scared out o' their minds when he come near 'em. Oh Lordy! I can tell you plenty 'bout the things he done to us poor Niggers. We was treated no better than one o' his houn' dogs. Sometimes he didn' treat us as good as he did them. I prays to the Lord not to let me see him when I die. He had the devil in his heart.
>
> —Charlie Moses, enslaved in Mississippi.[20]

Enslaved black people were frequently legally prohibited from owning dogs. Owning pets would imply that blacks were themselves not pets—more importantly, the animals could be used as weapons against whites. One writer summarized the complex relationship between races—in this case the descendants of slaves—and pet keeping, especially dogs, this way:

> Prior to emancipation it was illegal, in many areas, for slaves to own dogs, but afterward there was a growing demand among African Americans for domestic pets. Their experience during slavery may have influenced their attraction, or lack thereof, to dogs. Because of the long-standing use of dogs to track escaped slaves or to otherwise terrorize African Americans, a phobia about dogs lingers for some people today, especially among rural southern African Americans.[21]

Nigger Dogs after Slavery

Emancipation did not end all slavery in the United States. Many black people, especially those who were rural and illiterate, found themselves enslaved in a system called peonage—also referred to as debt slavery or debt servitude. The Thirteenth Amendment prohibited involuntary servitude such as peonage for all but convicted criminals. This meant that white landholders, desiring cheap or free labor, searched for ways to make criminals of the newly freed black people. Some black people were arrested for minor charges—often vagrancy—others on trumped up charges. Once arrested, the detained person faced huge fines and court fees. They were sometimes given a choice: serve time on a chain gang or work for a local employer. In other instances, the decision was made for them. In either case, the black person was forced to work on a farm, in a

This is an early twentieth-century advertisement poster for a play.

railroad camp or a turpentine camp, or on a construction crew. The pay was nothing—the "criminal" was supposedly working off their debt to society. It is with good reason that this system has been called "slavery by another name." As was true of pre–Civil War slavery, peonage slavery often produced great cruelty.

In 1896, Alfred Griffith, a black man living in Madison County, Georgia, was unable to pay a $100 fine which had been imposed on one of his sons for the crime of disturbing public worship. Griffith was poor with barely enough money to feed and clothe his thirteen children. He did not want to see his son sent away to work on a chain gang, so he went to Lucious Pittman, a wealthy plantation owner and asked the white man to pay the $100 fine. Griffith was illiterate and unable to understand the legal contract. He signed an agreement that stated that he, his wife, and thirteen children would work on Pittman's farm until the debt was liquidated. The contract, however, gave the white man full discretion in determining when the debt was retired.

About a year after moving to the farm, Pittman and Griffith got into an argument and according to the *Washington Times*, "the negro had six bullets pumped into him, producing death." The coroner's jury rendered a verdict of justifiable homicide before Pittman was even charged. This was not surprising. The Jim Crow racial hierarchy protected whites and punished black people. As might be predicted, peonage was supported by state and county officials. The murder of Griffith did not end the nightmare for his wife and children, it intensified it. The wealthy white man (literally) kicked Mrs. Griffith off his property. But he forced the children to remain. For the next seven years the children worked from "daylight until dark and at night were chained in a room and kept under lock and key." The female children were raped and all the children were routinely and savagely beaten. Eventually, the Griffith children were rescued—and for reasons not specified placed in a jail in Atlanta. Alfred, the eldest boy, said:

> Boss, dis am de happiest time of my life. I didn't know dat I was a free nigger until I got here, an' I hain't free yit, but I'd sooner be in jail all my life dan go back to Mister Pittman's 'cause he beats and cuffs me an' all de rest of 'em er round' like wese er lot er dogs. We couldn't get er way, boss 'cause he got dem nigger dogs dat run you down an' tear yer all ter pieces.[22]

Peonage was a type of slavery and the enslavers often used the same methods as their pre–Civil War predecessors: the black people entrapped in peonage were lorded over, kept near starvation, beaten, raped, and tortured. And they were watched closely—and sometimes chained—to make

This is an early twentieth-century single-sided trade card.

sure that they did not escape. In 1880, the *Bismarck Tribune* reported that blacks in peonage "work under the supervision of a sergeant with a gun and nigger-hounds."[23]

Peonage was not the only system where "nigger hounds" were found. These dogs were also used to track black criminals, especially ones escaping from jail or prison. In 1901, the Athens, Georgia, police department had a fund set aside to pay for "nigger dogs." The dogs were owned by B.O.W. Rose, a member of the police force for twenty years. Rose was widely regarded as an expert on the training of these dogs. According to the policeman:

> The Cuban bloodhounds were introduced to hunt slaves and they were the best bloodhounds this country has ever seen. But any bloodhound is too much like the bulldog; he is brutal and ignorant; the least intelligent of dogs. Its depressed forehead, underhanging jaw and bloodshot eyes make it the personification of the savage. The bloodhound cannot be relied on as a friend, and is so without intelligence that it will attack friend or foe. This is not true of the negro dog. While it is claimed that bloodhound has a keener scent than any other dog, this is not true. The bloodhound is not particular what it pursues—just as soon chase a white man as a negro. The only way to stop the genuine bloodhound is to spill blood, and thus destroy its discriminating powers.[24]

When Rose spoke of spilled blood he meant the blood of a black person, and he preferred that the dog doing the spilling was a cross between the Cuban bloodhounds and red fox hounds of South Carolina. Rose said, "My 'nigger' dogs will not trail anything save a negro. . . . These dogs never become enthusiastic until I call nigger, then they are almost unmanageable."[25] According to the *St. Louis Post-Dispatch*, "Rose not only uses his dogs to catch negroes in Clarke County, but is frequently sent for to go to other sections of the South" and "when runs are not frequent Mr. Rose will hire a negro to give his dogs a chase."[26]

Rose was not the only law enforcement official using nigger dogs. Old Troup was the name of a dog owned by the Fulton County, Atlanta, convict camp. The dog was hailed in newspapers as "the best nigger dog in Georgia" for its prowess in treeing and capturing black prisoners who escaped the chain gangs in the early 1900s.[27] In 1908, the state of Tennessee had sixteen bloodhounds for use in capturing escaped convicts, two English-bred bloodhounds and fourteen "old-fashioned 'Georgia Red, Nigger Dogs.'"[28]

In the early 1900s, the fear and loathing of black people was normative. In at least one instance, a community wanted to proactively purchase a nigger dog, presumably to protect themselves. In 1904, the citizens of Hearne, Texas, held a fundraiser "the proceeds of which were to be used in purchasing a pair of 'nigger' dogs . . . should occasion arise now wherein the dogs are needed, they can be had on short notice."[29] It was not unheard of for white people to train and sell so-called nigger dogs, as is evident by an advertisement in the classified section of the *Houston Post* in 1910, which read: "'Nigger Dogs'—8 for sale: all young, well bred, well trained man-chasers. D.D. Hooks. Eldridge, Texas."[30]

"NIG"

Hoover Dam Mascot

A Bull and His Dogs

In 1963, Birmingham, Alabama, became the national and international face of racial segregation and white supremacy. As was true in other southern cities, a race-based hierarchy existed in Birmingham, with whites on the top and blacks at the bottom. This system of stratification was undergirded by several interrelated assumptions: whites are superior to blacks in all ways that matter, including but not limited to intelligence, morality, and civilized behavior; interracial activities must be avoided because they imply that blacks and whites are equal; "social equality" (treating black people as equals to whites) encourages interracial unions, which will undermine the culture; and, if necessary, violence should be used to maintain the status quo. Birmingham historian Pamela Sterne King summarized the "racial two-ness" of the city during Jim Crow:

> Sex between blacks and whites was illegal; every "pool room, hall, theatre, picture house, auditorium, yard, court, ballpark, or other indoor or outdoor place" was segregated; checkers, dominoes and dice could not be played by blacks and whites together; black babies could not be born on the same ward with whites; white nurses were prohibited from attending black men; store, bank and office elevators were reserved for whites; department store dressing rooms were for whites only; streetcar seating, water fountains and bathrooms were separated; eating establishments, hotels and bars could not serve both races; dead bodies were buried in different cemeteries; court room Bibles could not be sworn upon by blacks and whites; black and white athletes could not compete; tax-supported schools and libraries, parks . . . zoos and pools were segregated or denied to blacks; and railroad stations had separate waiting rooms and ticket counters.[31]

This pinback was purchased in the 1970s.

For decades the city's black residents had worked to dismantle the system of racial stratification that elevated whites above blacks economically, politically, and socially. Despite modest gains, Birmingham remained a Jim Crow city. In 1963, local activists, most notably, Frederick Lee Shuttlesworth, joined with Martin Luther King Jr., James Bevel, Wyatt Tee Walker, and other nationally known civil rights leaders to bring attention to the plight of black people in Birmingham. Their strategy, labeled the "Birmingham campaign," was a massive direct action campaign to attack the city's system of segregation by engaging in nonviolent protests: lunch counter sit-ins, marches on City Hall, and a boycott of the stores of white Birmingham merchants during the Easter season.

One of the most controversial aspects of the protests was the "Children's Crusade," which involved the participation of children in the demonstrations. In part, this was done because King's goal was to fill the city's jails. James Bevel trained college, high school, even elementary school students in the general principles of nonviolence protest. The students joined in a peaceful walk from the 16th Street Baptist Church to City Hall. On April 2, 1963, almost a thousand black students were arrested as they attempted to march into downtown Birmingham. The next day, hundreds of black students gathered to march to City Hall. Eugene "Bull" Connor, the commissioner of public safety for Birmingham, directed local police and fire departments to use extreme force to halt the demonstrations. During the next few days images of children being blasted by high-pressure fire hoses, clubbed by police officers, and attacked by police dogs appeared on television and in newspapers, triggering national and international outrage. According to one newspaper account:

> Patrolmen and police dogs broke up a Palm Sunday anti-segregation "prayer pilgrimage" Sunday and sent 600 Negroes scurrying. Screaming demonstrators fled before the snarling police dogs held on leashes by police. Several persons were bitten. Others climbed on top of automobiles to get away from the dogs. One Negro was thrown to the ground after police said he tried to kill a police dog with a knife.[32]

One of the most iconic images of the civil rights period involved a young black man and a dog. The photograph, taken by Bill Hudson, an Associated Press photographer, shows Walter Gadsden, a high school student, being attacked by a police dog. Although he was not a participant in the Children's Crusade, he was grabbed by a white police officer while a German Shepherd lunged at him. The next day the photograph appeared in newspapers across the country, including the *New York Times*. The image of Gadsden being attacked symbolized the courage of

This is a greeting card, date unknown.

young African Americans who were determined to combat racial injustice. The televised images of police brutality helped sway public opinion in favor of the civil rights protesters.

Kelly Ingram Park served as a staging ground for many of the demonstrations in Birmingham in the 1960s. Today, it is home to a sculpture exhibit called "Police and Dog Attack." The welded steel display allows visitors to walk between two walls; there is one dog on one wall and two on the other. The sculpture captures the ferociousness of the lunging dogs. James Drake, the creator of the sculpture, tried to create for visitors an experience that replicated the experiences of the protesters in the Birmingham campaign and also demonstrated the courage they had displayed.

The use of police dogs to attack blacks and other people of color continued after the civil rights movement ended. According to a story reported on the blog ThinkProgress.org, in the 1980s, the Los Angeles Sheriff's Department reportedly referred to young blacks as "dog biscuits." And in the first half of 2013, blacks and Latinos were the only ones bitten by police dogs.[33] In 2015, a video of two New Jersey police officers allowing a K9 dog to attack the face of an unarmed black man went viral. The man, thirty-two-year-old Phillip White, later died while in police custody. The Department of Justice's report on the Ferguson Police Department—a report sparked by the death of Michael Brown, a black teenager, killed by Darren Wilson, a white police officer—showed that in 100 percent of cases in which an attack dog bit a suspect and the suspect's race was reported, those bitten were black people.[34]

White Dog

The motif of ferocious dogs chasing black people has from the beginning been a theme in film. In *The Watermelon Patch* (1905), a short comedic film, dogs are used to chase black watermelon thieves. In *The Slave Hunt* (1907), a young black man who killed an enslaver is pursued by bloodhounds. He is eventually caught and killed. In the short film *Chased by Bloodhounds* (1912), an affluent white chicken breeder sets his dogs on a chase of a black man who stole a chicken. In *The Nigger* (1915), an intoxicated black man sexually assaults a white child. The child dies. There is a manhunt with bloodhounds. He is caught, lynched, and burned at the stake. In *The Birth of a Nation* (1915), Silas Lynch, a lecherous biracial villain, throttles a dog by the throat and tosses it aside. In *Uncle Tom's Cabin* (1927) Eliza, a runaway slave, is pursued by men with guns and dogs.[35]

Images of police dogs attacking black protesters are a stark reminder that dogs have been used to police populations that threaten the status quo. In the film *Sweet Sweetback's Baadasssss Song* (1971), a black militant is chased by Los Angeles police, who send several hunting dogs after him. He

This comic book was published by the Gilberton Company, New York, in 1944.

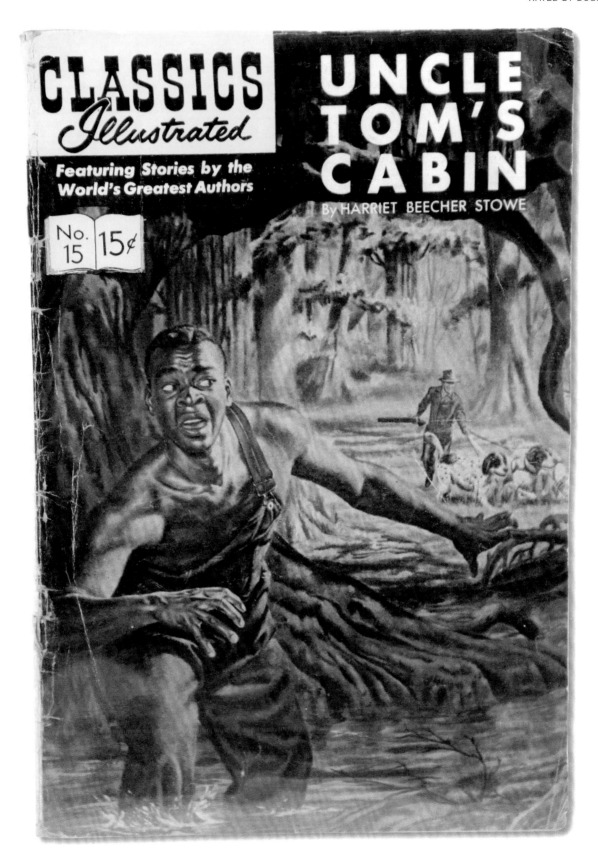

"HOT DOG"!
WHAT A "MATCH" WE'D MAKE!

escapes to Mexico, swearing to return to "collect dues." In *The Spook Who Sat by the Door* (1973), dogs are used to control angry citizens. One black character asks, "The dogs, why did they have to go and bring in the dogs?" The film *When We Were Kings* (1996) shows George Foreman arriving in Africa to fight Muhammad Ali in 1974. Foreman is accompanied by a large German Shepherd. According to the film, he lost the support of many local fans who associated him with the white Belgians, the former colonizers who used German Shepherds as attack dogs to terrorize black population.[36]

There have been many films that included the narrative that dogs are enemies of black people, but none have employed and examined the narrative more directly than *White Dog* (1982), directed by Samuel Fuller, using a screenplay that he cowrote with Curtis Hanson loosely based on Romain Gary's 1970 novel of the same title.[37] *White Dog* uses a dog trained to attack black people as a metaphor for whites who have been taught to mistreat people with dark skin.

The story begins when a young Hollywood actress, Julie Sawyer, accidentally hits a German Shepherd with her car. She takes the dog home to nurse him. Shortly thereafter, an intruder—a white male—breaks into her home and attempts to rape and beat her. She is saved by the dog, who mauls the would-be rapist. Julie believes that she has befriended an attack dog.

During daytime hours the dog is a mild-mannered canine who playfully wrestles with Julie, but at night he leaves the house and prowls for black people, returning to her covered in human blood. One night he kills a black truck driver. When Julie takes him to work, he attacks a black actress on the set. Realizing that something is wrong with the dog, she takes him to an animal trainer, a white man named Carruthers, who tells her, "Can't nobody unlearn a dog. Nobody." When leaving Carruthers's office, the dog attacks a black laborer. Carruthers shouts, "That ain't no attack dog you got. That's a white dog." Carruthers wants to see the dog destroyed. Another animal trainer, Keys, a black man who works with Carruthers, witnesses the attack and volunteers to reeducate the dog as a personal and professional challenge. He says, "If I don't break him, I will shoot him." He has tried before to break the training of white dogs, but never succeeded.

Keys, wearing protective gear, begins intensive training with the dog. He keeps the dog in a large caged dome. During their training sessions, the dog savagely attacks him. Eventually, the dog shows less aggression. The dog receives food and care from Keys. After one session there is this exchange between Julie and Keys:

> JULIE: I don't understand. One minute he's as gentle as a lamb, the next minute he's a monster.

This is an early twentieth-century Valentine's Day card.

KEYS: He's not a monster but he was made into one by a two-legged racist.

JULIE: You know, I don't understand how that can happen. I . . . I really don't. How can . . . How can someone turn a dog into a racist?

KEYS: Well, over a hundred years ago, they raised dogs to catch runaway slaves. Then they progressed . . . to track down runaway black convicts.

JULIE: What about runaway white convicts?

KEYS: (Chuckles) Well . . . almost overnight they graduated to a vicious breed of watchdogs trained to tear apart any blacks within sight.

JULIE: Does he attack any other color?

KEYS: No. Dogs live in a black-and-white world. Unlike ours, they live it visually and not racially.

JULIE: The man who owned him. How did he turn him into a racist dog?

KEYS: It's simple. Find a black wino who desperately needs a drink . . . or a black junkie who'll do anything for a fix . . . and then pay them to beat that dog of yours when he was a puppy.

One night the dog escapes. He goes to a nearby town and scavenges food. He spots a black man and begins chasing him. The man runs into a church where he is mauled to death by the dog, who is shown with a bloody mouth and fur. Keys shoots the dog with a tranquilizer. He is sickened by the sight of the black man's dead body, but opts not to turn in the dog to the authorities. He chooses to continue the training, over Julie's protests—she now wants to see the dog destroyed. Keys tells her that the training must continue so that he can learn how to cure racist dogs. He believes that curing the dog will discourage white racists from training dogs to attack black people. He continues working with the dog, but now he works without protective gear.

Eventually, Keys believes the dog is nearly cured. He prepares to give the dog a final trial and he calls Julie to be a witness. As she is leaving her house, she meets an elderly man with his two small grandchildren. He is the man who trained the dog. They have a profanity-laced argument. In the final scene, Keys, without any protective clothing (but armed with a gun) beckons the white dog to come to him. The dog rushes toward him, but does not attack. Julie hugs the dog. But the dog sees Carruthers and begins mauling him. Keys kills the dog.

Although the movie *White Dog* was an unabashed frontal assault on racism, civil rights organizations argued that the movie—in which three black people are viciously attacked by the white dog—might incite

Moore, Charles
(b. 1931)
Birmingham, 1963, Police Dog
Photography

violence against blacks. The NAACP demanded to have a representative on the set during filming. Fuller, an ardent and sincere integrationist, was insulted. He demanded that the NAACP representative be banned from the set. Afterward, rumors circulated that the movie was racist and antiblack. When the filming ended, Paramount, which owned the movie rights, did not release the picture. The studio claimed that the movie had tested poorly in Detroit. It is likely that they feared the bad publicity that would follow a boycott led by the NAACP and other civil rights organizations. In 1984, the NAACP pressured NBC to not air the

Iconic image captured by Charles Moore.

movie on television. The Criterion Collection released the original uncut film to DVD in 2008. That was the first release of the movie in the United States. Charles Taylor, writing in the *New York Times*, lamented the film's original suppression due to "the stupidity of pressure groups." Taylor defended both the movie and its direction.

> The pity of this is that "White Dog" is a profoundly antiracist film, though a despairing one. Fuller, the patriotic liberal whose muck-raking style had always demonstrated a belief in the possibility of reform, is here saying that while racism is learned, it is also a poison that can never be banished from those it infects. A tabloid artist, Fuller reveled in the juice and force of melodrama, and he has been dismissed or ridiculed by those who believe art must be subtle. . . . The dog is a killer. But a close-up of Ms. McNichol's hand lost in the inviting thickness of its fur—literally, the image of a girl and her dog—is a potent reminder of how hatred can be familiar, reassuringly close.[38]

The canine in *White Dog* is a metaphor for learned, conditioned racism. A central premise of the movie is that racists are created. Neither people nor dogs are natural racists, programmed at birth to hate others based on racial characteristics. *White Dog* focuses on how racism passes from generation to generation through deliberate teaching and receptive learning. As one reviewer wrote:

> There is no reasoning to the animal's violence against anyone with darker skin, just an artificially conditioned hair-trigger instinct. This is racial hatred in a nutshell, a programmed autonomic response to specific words, sounds or imagery that is devoid of logic or any real humanity. The white dog becomes a potent symbol of prejudicial savagery, all bared teeth and furious snarls and an uncontrolled urge to kill, not to defend its home ground or even a master to whom it has become loyal, but because of the colour of human skin.[39]

The use of a dog to address racism is handled differently in an earlier movie, *To Kill a Mockingbird* (1962), a film based on Harper Lee's Pulitzer Prize–winning novel of the same name.[40] Set in a fictional Alabama town in the 1930s, this film tells the story of a decent—even noble—white attorney who defends a black man falsely accused of raping a white woman. In one especially dramatic scene, a dog stricken with rabies is killed because of the threat that he poses to a family and to the community. The rabid dog is a metaphor for a diseased community, its members made sick by their racial hatred. Equating of racism with a disease is reminiscent of

Albert Einstein's claim that racism was "a disease of white people."[41] A more accurate connection would be that racism is like certain serious diseases, debilitating, destroying, and spreading, and the sufferers are dangerous to others.

Michael Vick

"A righteous man regardeth the life of his beast:
but the tender mercies of the wicked are cruel."

—Proverbs 12:10

There are racial differences in dog ownership; while 46 percent of all households own dogs, this number is 51 percent for whites, 53 percent for Hispanics, and 24 percent for blacks.[42] Some of these differences exist because black people are more likely to live in densely populated urban areas with less room for dogs or other pets. Beliefs exist among some African Americans that owning dogs is a white behavior and that whites care more about dogs than they care about black people. These beliefs were strengthened by the arrest and conviction of Michael Dwayne Vick, a famed football player, on a federal conspiracy charge of bankrolling a dogfighting operation from his home near Newport News, Virginia.

The Atlanta Falcons selected Vick in the 2001 National Football League (NFL) draft, marking the first time that a black quarterback had been the first overall pick. Vick's lofty selection status was merited. As a college freshman he finished third in voting for the Heisman Trophy, and even though he only played one additional year he demonstrated a rare combination of arm strength, running speed, and superior leadership ability. Vick rewarded the Falcons' trust with his performance on the field. In six seasons with the team, he was selected to three Pro Bowls and, more importantly, led the Falcons to the playoffs twice. He was a star, a celebrity, and a hero to many youths, especially young black males.

Vick's life unraveled in 2007, when he was linked to a dogfighting ring that had operated for five years on property that he owned. He initially denied any knowledge of or involvement in the illegal enterprise, but recanted after three co-offenders pleaded guilty and began cooperating with the government's prosecutors. In August, Vick also pleaded guilty. He admitted providing money for bets on the fights but claimed he never shared in any winnings. Henry E. Hudson, the presiding judge, set December 10, 2007, as the sentencing date. Hours after his plea, the NFL suspended Vick indefinitely without pay. NFL Commissioner Roger Goodell said that Vick had violated the league's player conduct policy by engaging in behavior that was "not only illegal, but also cruel and reprehensible."

Goodell's assessment of Vick's actions was accurate. Vick's farm housed and trained dozens of dogs—animals that were shackled by huge chains, starved, and forced to fight other abused dogs. Those dogs who would not—or could not—fight were killed in cruel ways, including hangings, electrocutions, and by drowning. In at least one instance, a dog was slammed to the ground until it died. Judge Hudson sentenced Vick to twenty-three months in prison to be followed by two months in home confinement. Vick was also ordered to pay nearly $1 million in restitution charges.

Race matters in the United States, so it is not surprising that the Michael Vick case touched the country's racial divide. Most of Vick's supporters were black people. Whoopi Goldberg, for example, claimed that Vick was simply participating in a longtime southern practice. Many African Americans wrote letters to Judge Hudson on Vick's behalf, including George Foreman, baseball Hall of Famer Hank Aaron, and the Honorable Shirley Franklin, mayor of Atlanta.[43] Animal rights groups made Vick a poster boy for cruelty to animals. People for the Ethical Treatment of Animals (PETA) characterized Vick as a sociopathic monster unfit for civil society.[44] Black people noticed that animal rights groups have few if any black members. Most of Vicks critics, especially the harshest critics, are whites. Susan Estrich, a white journalist, referred to Vick as "scum."[45] Tucker Carlson, a white cable news host, said, "I think personally he should have been executed."[46] His sentiments were similar to the fans on America Online's Fanhouse message board who ranted for Vick to "hang from a tree."[47] Melissa Harris-Perry believes that Carlson's comments (and similar ones) not only demonize Vick but that they are, at their core, about race:

> Despite agreeing that Vick's acts were horrendous, somehow Carlson's moral outrage seemed misplaced. It also seemed profoundly racialized. For example, Carlson did not call for the execution of BP executives despite their culpability in the devastation of Gulf wildlife. He did not denounce the Supreme Court for their decision in U.S. v. Stevens (April 2010) which overturned a portion of the 1999 Act Punishing Depictions of Animal Cruelty. After all with this "crush" decision the Court seems to have validated a marketplace for exactly the kinds of crimes Vick was convicted of committing. For many observers, the decision to demonize Vick seems motivated by something more pernicious than concern for animal welfare. It seems to be about race.[48]

Vick emerged from prison without a team and without his former wealth. His old team, the Atlanta Falcons, tried to trade him but found

no takers, so he was released. Vick suffered financially—he lost his NFL salary and many commercial endorsements. He signed with the Philadelphia Eagles in 2009. Vick had a brief renaissance. In 2010, he became the team's starting quarterback and led them to a division championship. He was named the 2010 Comeback Player of the Year. He lost his starting job with the Eagles, and became a backup for the New York Jets before assuming a backup role with the Pittsburgh Steelers in 2015. At every stop he was confronted by protesters angry about his role in the cruel dog-fighting operation—and angry about him getting additional opportunities to ply his trade. In his autobiography, *Finally Free*, Vick details his regrets and his search for forgiveness.[49] Some of his book signings have been cancelled because of death threats.

Blacks, Dogs, and Other Popular Culture Expressions

Relative to several other racial tropes, for example, blacks with watermelons or fried chicken, there are comparatively few images of blacks and dogs in the Jim Crow Museum. The museum owns a sign that reads, "No Dogs Negroes Mexicans." There are postcards and trade cards that show black dogs. Beneath them the caption reads, "Nigger Dogs" or "Niggers." In the not-so-distant past it was common for pet owners to use the racial slur as a name for their dark-hued dogs. Today, black dogs are less likely to be adopted than lighter-colored dogs and more likely to be euthanized.[50] One of the most famous dogs named Nigger was a black Labrador, who was

This is an early twentieth-century souvenir object. **187**

Riots, Natl

©

41.6 x 21.6

IN SOUTH BEND, Ind., policemen, with the aid of dogs, force Negroes off the street and into a building. Police cleared the streets when violence erupted on the West Side of city. Several persons were shot. (AP Photo)

PIX P6

FRI.

JUL 28 1967

the companion of Gus Gibson, an English pilot who led a bomber raid on three German dams during World War II. Nigger often accompanied Gibson on training flights and became a mascot for the whole squadron. The story of Gibson and his dog was portrayed in *The Dam Busters* (1955), a British film starring Michael Redgrave and Richard Todd.[51] The dog's name was mentioned at least twelve times in the movie.

Toys are pernicious ways to spread racist propaganda. Playing with racist toys, whites and others learn to embrace antiblack racist tropes, and they learn to laugh at pain inflicted on black people. Windup toys from the early 1900s are illustrative. The "Hey-Hey Chicken Snatcher" toy, made by Louis Marx, copyrighted 1926, has a figure of a black man with a dead chicken (neck wrung?) in one hand, while a small dog nips at his backside. When the toy is activated, his face moves, showing different expressions. A similar depiction is found in "Poor Pete" windup toys, made in Japan in the 1930s and sold in the United States that same decade. There are two versions, and both show a black child eating watermelon while a dog bites his butt.

The museum also has a copy of the film *Sounder* (1972), which is a coming-of-age story about the oldest son (about eleven years old) of a family of sharecroppers living in Louisiana during the Great Depression.[52] They are black, poor, and hungry, and the father steals a ham to feed his family. He is caught and sent to a prison work camp. The boy hungers for his father. He hungers for an education. And when his dog Sounder goes missing, he hungers for the dog. *Sounder* is the rare American film showing a black family that loves a dog.

A Personal Story

I carry a cane when I go on walks. There is nothing wrong with my legs. I carry the cane because I do not trust some of the dogs that I encounter—well, more accurately, I do not trust their owners. I am not afraid of dogs or their owners, but I am vigilant regarding both. In recent years, dogs, aggressively growling with bared teeth, have come within a few yards of me before their owners intervened.

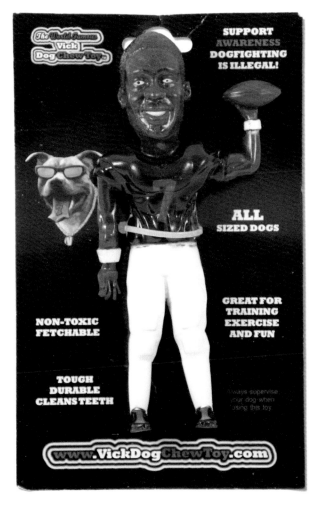

ABOVE: This chew toy for a dog was distributed in 2009. **LEFT:** Police Dogs. South Bend July 28, 1967.

If you ask my neighbors, they will tell you that we live in a racially diverse neighborhood. One of my neighbors adopted a child born in China. My family accounts for the rest of the diversity. My neighbors are living the dream: fancy homes and cars, well-fed and well-dressed children playing tag, and dogs—mostly small prissy ones wearing dog clothes— being walked around the circle that surrounds our neighborhood.

Most of the dogs are friendly. One exception is a larger dog that lives in a home behind us. Years ago he chased my son Jamie and bit him on the rear. Jamie came home crying. I was furious and considered asking for the dog to be put down. I talked to his owner and he explained that the dog was old and losing his mind. My neighbor also told me something that I already knew: the recent death of his wife had devastated their two children. Killing the dog would cause them more hurt. I agreed. He installed an invisible fence around his yard. Now, when I walk by the dog barks and runs toward me, but he stops.

My family has a little dog, Scout, who is loving and intelligent. When she was a puppy I made the mistake of intentionally dropping a small piece of human food near my bed so that she could eat it. A couple of years have gone by but each time—and I do mean each time—she comes into my room she goes to the spot where the food was dropped. When Peg, my wife, is away, Scout sits on the top of a sofa and looks through the window that shows the street. She will sit there for hours. As soon as Scout sees Peg's car, she sprints to the door, jumping up and down. I also carry the cane when I walk because I want to protect her.

We all carry racial baggage. I'd like to think that my caution when I see a white person with a dog—especially a large dog not on leash—is not amplified because of the owner's race. But I am not sure. Is my cautiousness thoughtful prudence or something deeper? It is possible these encounters tap into my familiarity with and understanding of stories of black people being chased, cornered, and bitten by dogs. Do we ever transcend the stories of our youth . . . or the images that accompanied them? I don't know. I do know that I carry a cane when I walk, even when I walk in my neighborhood.

CHAPTER SEVEN

Black People and Niggers

> "When people act like niggers, no matter who they are the only
> thing to do is treat them like a nigger."
>
> —William Faulkner, *The Sound and the Fury*[1]

In 1996, Chris Rock, an African American comedian, performed an HBO stand-up comedy special, *Bring the Pain*.[2] He drew huge laughs from the mostly black audience with his bit about the difference between black people and niggers. Rock said: "Who's more racist? Black people or white people? Black people. You know why? Because we hate black people too! Everything white people don't like about black people, black people *really* don't like about black people. There's some shit going on with black people right now. There's like a civil war going on with black people, and there's two sides. There's black people and there's niggas. The niggas have got to go."[3] Rock is an intelligent man, well versed in the history lessons of this country. He knows that the word "nigger" embodies all the venom and opprobrium that this nation has directed against black people. He also knows that many contemporary Americans, blacks and whites, accept a tired racial trope: there are good black people and there are niggers, who are bad black people.[4]

Origins

There is a direct and strong link between the word "nigger" and antiblack caricatures.[5] Although "nigger" has been used to refer to any person of known African ancestry,[6] it is usually directed against black people who supposedly have certain negative characteristics. The coon caricature portrays black men as lazy, ignorant, and obsessively self-indulgent—traits also historically represented by the word "nigger." The brute caricature depicts black men as angry, physically strong, animalistic, and prone to wanton violence. This depiction is also implied in the word "nigger." The Tom and mammy caricatures are portrayed as kind, loving friends of whites, but they are also presented as intellectually childlike, physically unattractive, and neglectful of their biological families. These latter traits have been associated with blacks, generally, and are implied in the word "nigger," which is a shorthand way of saying that blacks possess the physical, intellectual, moral, and behavioral characteristics of the coon, brute, Tom, mammy, and other racial caricatures. Like the caricatures it encompasses and implies, "nigger" belittles black people, and rationalizes their mistreatment.

The etymology of "nigger" is often traced to the Latin *niger*, meaning black. The Latin *niger* became the noun "negro" (black person) in English, and simply the color black in Spanish and Portuguese. In Early Modern French *niger* became *negre*, and later "negress" (black woman) was clearly a part of lexical history. One can compare to *negre* the derogatory *nigger*—and earlier English variants such as *negar*, *neegar*, *neger*, and *niggor*—which developed into a parallel lexico-semantic reality in English. It is likely that "nigger" is a phonetic spelling of the white Southern mispronunciation of Negro. Whatever its origins, by the early 1800s it was firmly established as a denigrative epithet. Almost two centuries later, it remains a chief symbol of white racism.

Social scientists refer to words like "nigger," "kike," "spic," and "wetback" as ethnophaulisms. Such terms are the language of prejudice—verbal pictures of negative stereotypes. Howard J. Ehrlich, a sociologist, argued that ethnophaulisms are of three types: disparaging nicknames like "nigger"; explicit group devaluations (e.g., "Jew him down," or "niggering the land"); and irrelevant ethnic names used as a mild disparagement (e.g., "jewbird" for cuckoos having prominent beaks or "Irish confetti" for bricks thrown in a fight).[7] Erdman Palmore, another sociologist, observed that the number of ethnophaulisms used correlates positively with the amount of out-group prejudice and that ethnophaulisms express and support negative stereotypes about the most visible racial and cultural differences.[8]

All racial and ethnic groups have been victimized by slurs, but no American group has suffered as many racial epithets as have black people: Tom, Sambo, coon, savage, picaninny, mammy, buck, jigaboo, and buckwheat are typical.[9] Many of these slurs double as fully developed pseudoscientific, literary, cinematic, and everyday caricatures of African Americans. These caricatures, whether spoken, written, or reproduced in material objects, reflect the extent of the vast network of antiblack prejudice. The word "nigger" has historically been one expression of that prejudice.

Nigger: Before There Was the N-Word

The word "nigger" carries with it much of the hatred and repulsion directed toward Africans and African Americans. Historically, it defined, limited, and mocked African Americans. It was a term of exclusion, a verbal justification for discrimination. Whether used as a noun, verb, or adjective, it reinforced the stereotype of the lazy, stupid, dirty, worthless parasite. No other American ethnophaulism carried so much purposeful venom, as the following representative list suggests:

> nigger, v. To wear out, spoil or destroy.
> nigger-flicker, n. A small knife or razor with one side heavily taped to preserve the user's fingers.
> nigger heaven, n. A designated place, usually the balcony, where blacks were forced to sit, for example, in an integrated movie theater or church.
> nigger in the woodpile, n. A concealed motive or unknown factor affecting a situation in an adverse way.
> niggerish, adj. Acting in an indolent and irresponsible manner.
> nigger knocker, n. Axe handle or weapon made from an axe handle.
> niggerlipping, v. Wetting the end of a cigarette while smoking it.
> nigger lover, n. Derogatory term aimed at whites lacking in the necessary loathing of blacks.
> nigger luck, n. Exceptionally good luck, emphasis on undeserved.
> nigger rich, adj. Deeply in debt but ostentatious.
> nigger shooter, n. A slingshot.
> nigger steak, n. A slice of liver or a cheap piece of meat.
> nigger stick, n. Police officer's baton.
> nigger tip, n. Leaving a small tip or no tip in a restaurant.
> nigger work, n. Demeaning, menial tasks.[10]

"Nigger" has been used to describe a dark shade of color (nigger-brown, nigger-black), the status of whites who interacted with blacks (nigger-breaker, -dealer, -driver, -killer, -stealer, -worshipper, and -looking), and anything belonging to or associated with African Americans (nigger-baby, -boy, -girl, -mouth, -feet, -preacher, -job, -love, -culture, -college, -music, and so forth).[11] Nigger is the ultimate American insult. It is even used to insult other ethnic groups, as when Jews are called "white niggers," Arabs "sand niggers," or Japanese "yellow niggers."

The more than three-century historical relationship between European Americans and African Americans was shaped by a racial

hierarchy, with whites at the top and blacks at the bottom. Antiblack attitudes, values, and behavior were normative. The hierarchy was undergirded by an ideology that justified the use of deceit, manipulation, coercion, and violence to oppress black people. Every major societal institution offered legitimacy to the racial hierarchy. Ministers preached that God had condemned blacks to be servants. Scientists measured black people's heads, brains, faces, and genitalia, seeking to prove that whites were genetically superior to blacks. White teachers, teaching only white students, taught that blacks were less evolved cognitively, psychologically, and socially. The entertainment media, from vaudeville to television, portrayed blacks as docile servants, happy-go-lucky idiots, and dangerous thugs. The criminal justice system sanctioned a double standard of justice, including tacit approval of mob violence against blacks. Historically, "nigger," more than any other word, captured the individual hatred and institutionalized racism directed toward blacks.

Both American slavery and the Jim Crow caste system that followed were undergirded by antiblack images. The negative portrayals of blacks were both reflected in and shaped by everyday material objects: toys, postcards, ashtrays, detergent boxes, fishing lures, and children's books. These items, and countless others, portrayed blacks with bulging, darting eyes, fire-red and oversized lips, and jet-black skin, who were either naked or poorly clothed. The majority of these objects did not use the word "nigger," but more than a few did. In 1874, the McLoughlin Brothers of New York manufactured a puzzle game called "Chopped Up Niggers." Beginning in 1878, the B. Leidersdory Company of Milwaukee, Wisconsin, produced Nigger Hair Smoking Tobacco, changing the name to Bigger Hair Smoking Tobacco several decades later. In 1916, a magazine advertisement copyrighted by Morris & Bendien showed a black child drinking from an ink bottle. The caption read "Nigger Milk." The following year, the American Tobacco Company had a Nigger Hair redemption promotion. Nigger Hair coupons were redeemable for "cash, tobacco, S. & H. Green stamps, or presents."

The J. Millhoff Company of England produced a series of cards (circa 1930s) that were widely distributed in the United States. One of the cards shows ten small black dogs with the caption: "Ten Little Nigger Boys Went Out To Dine." This is the first line from the popular children's story "The Ten Little Niggers."

Ten Little Nigger Boys went out to dine;
One choked his little self, and then there were Nine.
Nine Little Nigger Boys sat up very late;
One overslept himself, and then there were Eight.

This stuffed bear was purchased in 2015 from a white supremacist website. **195**

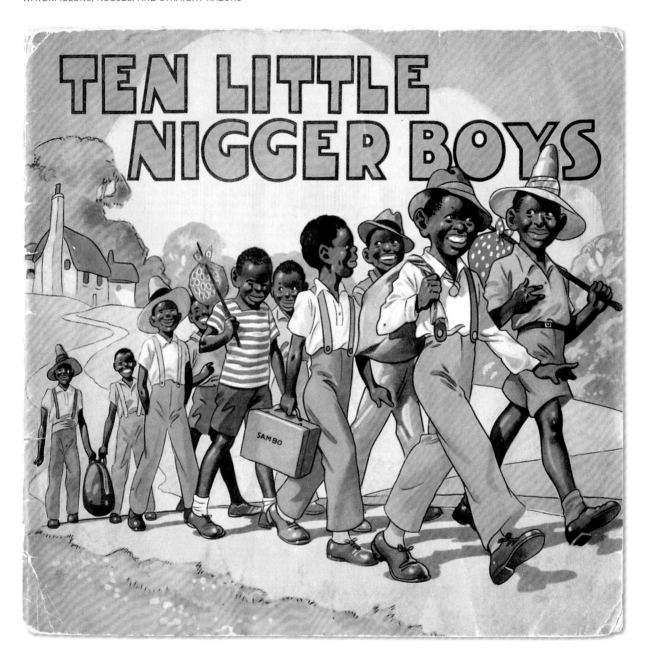

Eight Little Nigger Boys traveling in Devon;
One said he'd stay there, and then there were Seven.
Seven Little Nigger Boys chopping up sticks;
One chopped himself in halves, and then there were Six.
Six Little Nigger Boys playing with a hive;
A Bumble-Bee stung one, and then there were Five.
Five Little Nigger Boys going in for Law;
One got in Chancery, and then there were Four.

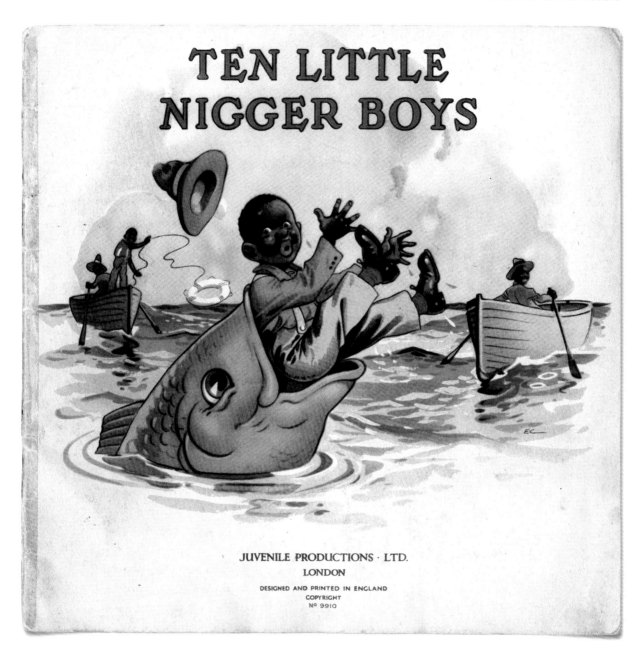

Four Little Nigger Boys going out to Sea;
A Red Herring swallowed one, and then there were Three.
Three Little Nigger Boys walking in the Zoo;
The big Bear hugged one, and then there were Two;
Two Little Nigger Boys sitting in the Sun;
One got frizzled up, and then there was One.
One Little Nigger Boy living all alone;
He got married, and then there were None.[12]

This book was published by Juvenile Productions, Ltd., London, undated.

In 1939, Agatha Christie, the popular fiction writer, published a novel called *Ten Little Niggers*. Later editions sometimes changed the name to *Ten Little Indians*, or *And Then There Were None*, but copies of the book with the original title were still being produced in 1978. It was not rare for sheet music produced in the first half of the twentieth century to use the word "nigger" on the cover. The Howley, Haviland Company of New York, produced sheet music for the songs "Hesitate Mr. Nigger, Hesitate," and "You'se Just a Little Nigger, Still You'se Mine, All Mine." The latter was billed as a children's lullaby.

Some small towns used the word in their names, for example, Nigger Run Fork, Virginia. Nigger was a common name for darkly colored pets, especially dogs, cats, and horses. So-called "Jolly Nigger Banks," first made in the 1800s, were widely distributed as late as the 1960s. Another common item, with many variants, produced on posters, postcards, and prints, is a picture of a dozen black children rushing for a swimming hole. The caption reads, "Last One In's a Nigger."

The racial hierarchy, created during slavery and extended into the Jim Crow period, was severely eroded by a civil rights movement, landmark Supreme Court decisions, a black empowerment movement, comprehensive civil rights legislation, and a general embracing of democratic principles by many American citizens. Yet the word "nigger" has not died. The relationship between the word and antiblack prejudice is symbiotic. They are interrelated and interconnected but not automatically interdependent. In other words, a racist society created the word and continues to feed and sustain it, but it no longer needs racism, at least in its brutal and obvious forms, to exist. "Nigger" now has a life of its own.

There are Americans who wax nostalgic for the old days, a time when all white people were elevated above all black people, a nation where black people were still seen as niggers. In the past the white people who held these views were the majority; today, they are dismissed as white supremacists and their views are mocked. Nevertheless, these people continue to spread their beliefs. An internet search of "nigger" locates many antiblack websites: Niggers Must Die, Hang a Nigger for America, Nigger Jokes Page, Nigger Memes, and literally hundreds of others. Visitors to these sites learn what most blacks know experientially, that "nigger" is an expression of antiblack hatred. Consider the website niggermania.com where one finds antiblack jokes, cartoons, photographs, and essays, for instance, "Of Knots and Kniggers," which gives instructions for tying a knot to be used to lynch a black person:

> This knot is also known as the Lark's Head, or Cow Hitch. It's
> an easy knot to tie and is ideal for attaching a nigger to an axle,

bumper, or other rigid automotive fixture. The knot gives you two free ends for accommodating two limbs. This is particularly useful if you'll be treating your "client" to a ride on gravel or rutted roads and you don't want ALL the big pieces to get away. Depending on your equipment (ie cable, man-made, or hemp rope), this could be a valuable knot to master.[13]

It is not surprising that the word "nigger" appears on white supremacy sites.[14] These sites portray black people in ways that are reminiscent of depictions that existed in pre–civil rights movement America, including portrayals that existed during the time when black people were enslaved in this country. White supremacists do not want to bury the word "nigger"; they want to bury black people.

Black People Calling Black People Niggers

William Moore was enslaved in Alabama just before the Civil War. He is one of many slaves who left testimonies. In one statement, he said: "Seem like niggers just got to pray; half they life is in prayin.' Some niggers just turn 'bout with nuther nigger to watch to see if Marse Tom anyways 'bout."[15] Enslaved black people sometimes had to sneak to pray. They also called each other niggers. This is not surprising. The entire society treated them as niggers, called them niggers, taught them to see themselves as niggers. Black people have never stopped calling other black people niggers.

In the late 1800s through the early 1900s, it was fairly common to hear "the better element of the negro race" refer to a poor black person as a "Jim Crow nigger."[16] In 1874, a "fashionable young lady of color" referred to apparently homeless black men as "poor Jim Crow niggers, no 'count trash."[17] This race/class epithet was used by both blacks and whites to portray impoverished blacks, especially young men, as worthless coons with "loafing habits, his crap dice, his razzer and his offensive yah-yahing in public places."[18] There were writers and speakers who used "Jim Crow nigger" as a synonym for Uncle Tom—black people kowtowing to whites and accepting their roles in the Jim Crow hierarchy—but more commonly, when used by blacks against other black people, it was used in the same way that Chris Rock would later use the word "nigger."

A hundred years after slavery, the word "nigger" was prominent in the writings of African American poets, one of the more progressive segments of black communities. Major and minor poets alike have used it, often with startling results. Amiri Baraka, a poet who often wrote about the racism of white people and the liberation of black people, uses the word in one of his angriest poems, "I Don't Love You": "and what was the

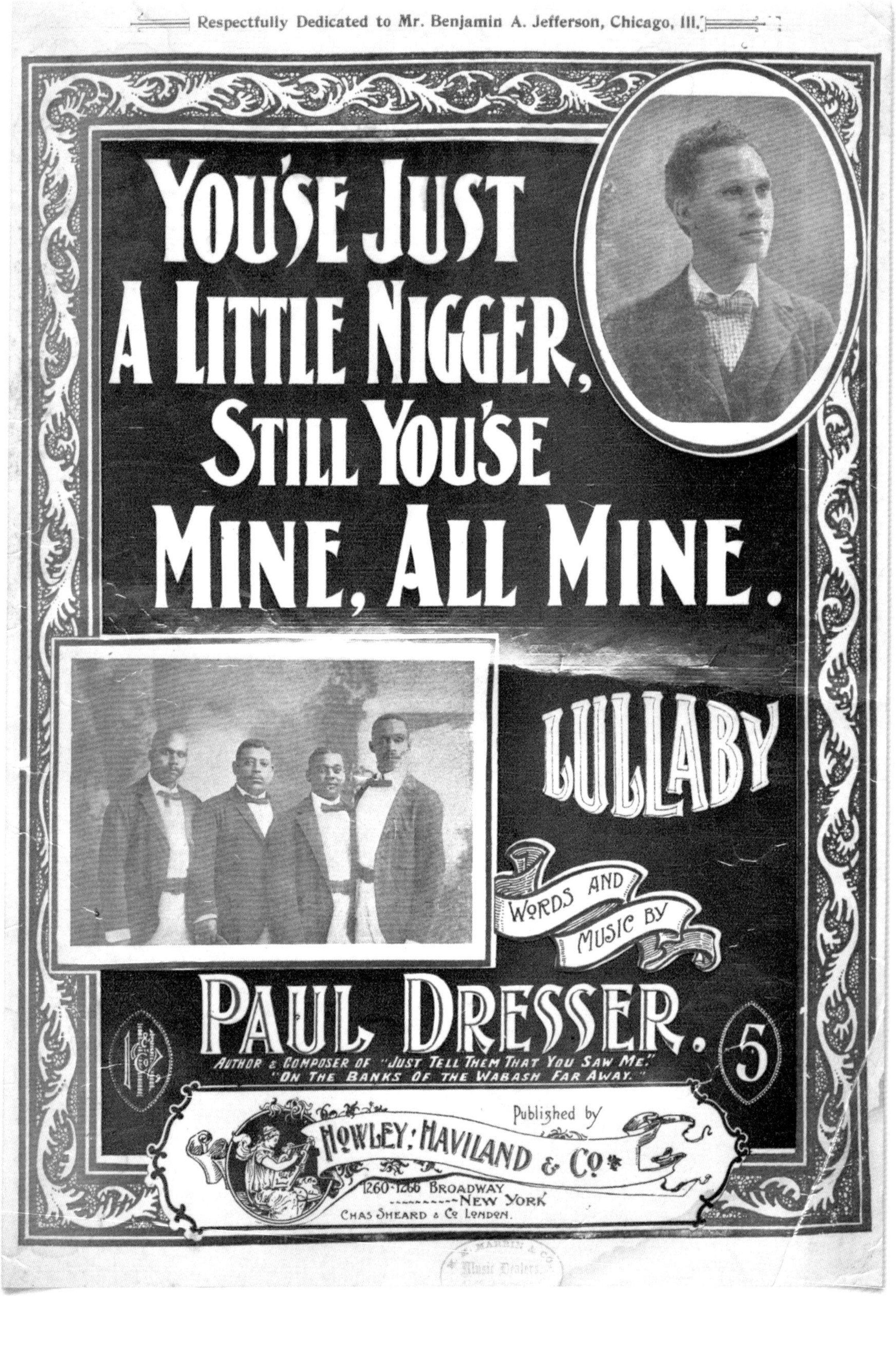
Respectfully Dedicated to Mr. Benjamin A. Jefferson, Chicago, Ill.
YOU'SE JUST A LITTLE NIGGER, STILL YOU'SE MINE, ALL MINE.
LULLABY
WORDS AND MUSIC BY
PAUL DRESSER.
AUTHOR & COMPOSER OF "JUST TELL THEM THAT YOU SAW ME."
"ON THE BANKS OF THE WABASH FAR AWAY."
5
Published by
HOWLEY, HAVILAND & CO.
1260-1266 BROADWAY
NEW YORK
CHAS SHEARD & CO LONDON.

world to the words of slick nigger fathers too depressed to explain why they could not appear to be men."[19]

One wonders: How are readers supposed to understand "nigger fathers"? Baraka's use of this imagery, regardless of his intention, reinforces the stereotype of the worthless, hedonistic coon caricature. Ted Joans's use of "nigger" in "The Nice Colored Man," however, renders Baraka's comparatively harmless and innocent. Joans tells the story about how he came to write this unusual piece. He was, he says, asked to give a reading in London because he was a "nice colored man." Infuriated by the labels "nice" and "colored," Joans set down the quintessential truculent poem. While the poem should be read in its entirety, a few lines will suffice here: "Smart Black Nigger Smart Black Nigger Smart Black Nigger Smart Black Nigger Knife Carrying Nigger Gun Toting Nigger Military Nigger Clock Watching Nigger Poisoning Nigger Disgusting Nigger Black Ass Nigger."[20]

The poem is simply adjective upon adjective attached to the word "nigger." The reality is that many of these uses can be heard in contemporary American society. Herein lies part of the problem: the word persists because it is used over and over again, even by the people it defames. Poet and novelist Devorah Major said, "It's hard for me to say what someone can or can't say, because I work with language all the time, and I don't want to be limited." Opal Palmer Adisa, a poet and professor, claims that the use of "nigger" or "nigga" is "the same as young people's obsession with cursing. A lot of their use of such language is an internalization of negativity about themselves."[21]

A century and a half removed from slavery, rap musicians, themselves poets, rap about "niggers"—or its linguistic cousin, "nigga"—sometimes before mostly white audiences, some of whom refer to one another as "my nigga."[22] Snoop Doggy Dogg, in his single, "You Thought," raps, "Wanna grab a skinny nigga like Snoop Dogg/Cause you like it tall/and work it baby doll." Tupac Shakur, one of the most talented and popular rap musicians, had a song called "Crooked Ass Nigga." The song's lyrics include, "Now I could be a crooked nigga too/When I'm rollin' with my crew/Watch what crooked niggers do/I got a nine millimeter Glock pistol/ I'm ready to get with you at the drop of a whistle/So make your move and act like you wanna flip/I fire thirteen shots and pop another clip." Rap lyrics that debase women and glamorize violence also reinforce the historical brute caricature.

Lil Jon's "Real Nigga Roll Call" (2004) featuring Ice Cube contains more than 325 profane words, including 165 instances of "nigga" being used. That song is not alone. Lil Wayne's album *I Am Not a Human Being II* (2013) has 182 uses of the word "nigga." The use of the word

"You'se Just a Little Nigger, Still You'se Mine, All Mine," words and music by Paul Dresser (New York: Howley, Haviland & Co., 1898).

reached its zenith—or nadir—with "The Nigga Song" (2013), produced by B-Money. The song uses the word more than one hundred times. According to a story in the *Washington Post*, use of the term is increasing in rap songs.

> For decades, a debate has raged within the hip-hop community about the extent to which the prevalence of the n-word among youth of all races is connected to its rise in hip-hop —and the debate has perhaps never been more relevant. When N.W.A.—short for Niggaz With Attitude—first appeared on the scene in the late 1980s, its use of the word felt revolutionary. Now, to achieve the same effect, it requires more effort—and more n-words. The 2013 hit song "My Nigga" by YG used the word a whopping 128 times.[23]

When used by black people today, nigger/nigga refers to the following: all blacks ("A nigger can't get a break."); black men ("Sisters want niggers to work all day long."); blacks who behave in a stereotypical manner ("He's a lazy, good-for-nothing nigger.");[24] things ("This piece-of-shit car is such a nigger."); foes ("I'm sick and tired of those bitch-ass niggers bothering me!"); and friends ("Me and my niggers are tight."). Black people who use "nigger" or its variants claim the following: it has to be understood contextually; continual use of the word by blacks will make it less offensive;[25] it is not really the same word because whites are saying nigger (and niggers) but blacks are saying "nigga" (and "niggaz"); and it is just a word and blacks should not be prisoners of the past or the ugly words which originated during slavery.

It is psychologically and socially meaningful for people to form in-groups—groups with emotional bonds. It is common in the United States for people to form in-groups along racial or ethnic lines. When a black person says "we" they may mean black people or a subset of black people. Once individuals identify themselves as belonging to a group, they typically perceive themselves and the other members of their group as being different from other groups. They tend to think of the world in terms of us and them. In-groups further distinguish themselves from other groups (out-groups) based on membership criteria and boundaries. For many black people, the use of "nigga" is an indicator of in-group membership, a way of saying that we are a part of the same group. It is not so much a term of endearment as it is a badge of membership. Whereas there are rap artists, most prominently JAY-Z and Kanye West, who encourage the whites at their concerts to sing the lyrics of songs that include the word "nigga," many black people argue that only black people should use the term. Other black people argue that no one, black or white, should use the term.

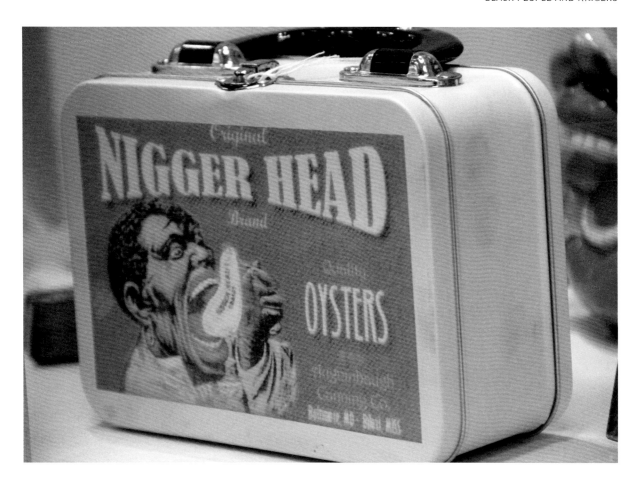

The debate in African American communities about who, if anyone, should use "nigger" or "nigga" often occurs along generational lines. Older black people are more likely to oppose its use and point out its connection with slavery and Jim Crow. Younger black people, raised in a society where the word is normative in songs and movies, are more likely to argue that some version of the word is acceptable, depending on the circumstances of its use. It is the latter who often make the claim that "nigger" is racist but "nigga" is a term of endearment. As the next section demonstrates, sometimes when black people use the word "nigger" it is not a descriptor and certainly not a term of endearment.

John Ridley's Niggers

John Ridley is a film director, novelist, and screenwriter. In 2013, he won the Best Adapted Screenplay Academy Award for the movie *12 Years a Slave*. Receiving this award made Ridley a hero to many black Americans—that is until *Esquire* reprinted an essay that he published in their magazine in 2006. That essay, "The Manifesto of Ascendancy for the Modern American Nigger," divided black people into two broad

An image from the 1930s was reproduced on a lunchbox in the early 2000s. This is a relatively common practice.

203

Congratulations on your purchase of a brand new nigger! If handled properly, your apeman will give years of valuable, if reluctant, service.

This manual is a joke and is for entertainment purposes only.

categories: loathsome niggers and hardworking, talented black people. He began that essay this way:

> Let me tell you something about niggers, the oppressed minority within our minority. Always down. Always out. Always complaining that they can't catch a break. Notoriously poor about doing for themselves. Constantly in need of a leader but unable to follow in any direction that's navigated by hard work, self-reliance. And though they spliff and drink and procreate their way onto welfare doles and WIC lines, niggers will tell you their state of being is no fault of their own. They are not responsible for their nearly 5 percent incarceration rate and their 9.2 percent unemployment rate. Not responsible for the 11.8 percent rate at which they drop out of high school. For the 69.3 percent of births they create out of wedlock.[26]

The ideas in John Ridley's *Esquire* article were provocative, but they were not fresh. For decades, upper- and middle-class African Americans have been highlighting the pathologies of the black underclass as a way to both distance themselves from such behavior and to blame poor blacks for their poverty. These successful African Americans accept the false dichotomy between "good blacks" and "niggers." Nigger, for them, is a class-based slur, a way of saying, "You are not my brother. You are less than I am. You are contemptible, raggedy, and ghetto, a victim of your own immorality and ineptitude, blaming whites for what ails you. I am not one of you. I am better than you. You don't educate your children or pay your bills. You don't have a job. You are ill bred. You are a walking crime spree. You are a nightmare. You give decent black people a bad name. Look at me: I read, speak in a monotone, make a steady paycheck, talk intelligently, and act civilly. I have dreams. White people are right to despise you. I'm tired of your poor, ignorant, thuggish ass." Ridley placed those ideas in a national magazine.

Ridley's essay demonstrates that the problem with the word "nigger" is not simply that Americans, including blacks, routinely use it but rather that many African Americans believe that niggers really exist. The question, "How do we stop Americans from treating us as niggers?" is replaced by "How do I keep from becoming a nigger?" Ridley is, in effect, saying, "The best thing black people can do for niggers is not to become one."

Who is Ridley calling a nigger? For much of his essay his scorn appears to be directed toward the black underclass, yet he gives statistics that are reflective of the entire black American population. For example, he says that niggers are responsible for their 9.2 percent unemployment rate, but that rate looks a lot like the rate of unemployment for all blacks.

This was published by Tightrope Records and sold to the museum in 2014.

The recession of 2001 raised the unemployment rate for whites from 3.5 percent in 2000 to 5.2 percent by 2003. During that same period the unemployment rate for African Americans jumped to 10.8 percent. Was Ridley suggesting that all unemployed blacks are niggers? What about unemployed whites? In 2007—data relevant when Ridley wrote his essay—the official unemployment rate for blacks was 8.3 percent. That figure exceeded the pre-recession low and was more than twice the unemployment rate for whites. When Ridley used national unemployment data for all blacks (and not data specific to the black underclass) he implied that any black person who is unemployed is a lazy nigger.

Again, who are Ridley's niggers? While discussing Condoleezza Rice and her accomplishments, Ridley mocks her critics as "Niggers and old-school shines," specifically criticizing Julian Bond. Next, Ridley, in his defense of Colin Powell, said:

> Predictably, niggers immediately abandoned him. How could any self-respecting black man want to run from the Liberal Plantation? Never mind that he was a self-made modern American hero who openly espoused the value of affirmative action. Old-schoolers tagged Powell with the usual left-wing racist jabber. Powell was a sellout. A Tom. In a particularly ugly rant, Harry Belafonte infamously alluded to Powell as being a house nigger.[27]

Ridley says that African American critics of Rice and Powell are niggers. Does "nigger" mean liberal? Calling liberal blacks niggers is the flip side of calling conservative blacks Toms. Julian Bond and Harry Belafonte are not the imagined niggers that Ridley derides in the beginning and conclusion of his essay. They are thinkers and activists whose policy recommendations offend Ridley. So, even though they are hardworking and accomplished they become niggers by association, "courtesy niggers," if you will.

Ridley's essay suggests another question: If there are real niggers what should happen to them? Ridley talks about "the deal forced upon the entrenched white social, political, and legal establishment when my parents' generation won the struggle for civil rights. The Deal: We (blacks) take what is rightfully ours and you (the afore-described establishment) get citizens who will invest the same energy and dedication into raising families and working hard and being all around good people as was invested in snapping the neck of Jim Crow."

In other words, if you stop discriminating against us, we will stop being niggers. We will assimilate: walk like, talk like, vote like the dominant group—flatter whites with our imitation of their lives. Ridley claims that poor blacks and their liberal enablers have reneged on the Deal, and their punishment should be swift, certain, and harsh: successful blacks should abandon so-called niggers, treat them like outcasts. In Ridley's words: "It's time for ascended blacks to wish niggers good luck. Just as whites may be concerned with the good of all citizens but don't travel their days worrying specifically about the well-being of hillbillies from Appalachia, we need to send niggers on their way. We need to start extolling the most virtuous of ourselves."[28]

"Nigger" is a social construct and an ugly one at that. It is a venomous insult. But, more than that, it is a way of saying that some people—in Ridley's world, mostly poor black people—are worthless. When Dr. Martin Luther King Jr. was assassinated at the Lorraine Motel in Memphis, Tennessee, he was not in Memphis to represent "ascended blacks." He was working on behalf of garbage workers, most of them black, who complained that they worked too hard for too little money in unsafe conditions. Dr. King cared deeply for the poor and his compassion grew out of his religious convictions. He did not employ shunning as a way to influence, encourage, or coerce normative behaviors. He did not exalt the "most virtuous of ourselves" to embarrass and shame the "worst of us." He did not treat black people, any black people, as niggers. Ridley's approach to the poor is different. Ridley has the right to call for shunning, avoidance, Meidung, or as he puts it, "send niggers on their way"—but he does not have the right to link his ideas to Dr. King and the civil rights movement and expect to not be challenged.

Burying and Banning

The roster of black comedians who used the word "nigger" as a synonym for black people or as a pejorative epithet is impressive, including, but not limited to, Redd Foxx, Richard Pryor, Paul Mooney, Eddie Griffith, Chris Rock, and Katt Williams. These comedians used "blue comedy"—risqué, indecent, and profane humor. "Nigger" was one of many profanities in their comedic bits.

While some criticized their use of the word, these men escaped national condemnation, in part because they were black comedians performing before black audiences. Michael Richards, a white comedian best known for his portrayal of the character Kramer on the television show *Seinfeld*, was not so lucky. On November 18, 2006, while performing a standup routine at the Laugh Factory club in West Hollywood, Richards was heckled by several black people in the audience. He became annoyed. The text below recounts his angry outburst.

RICHARDS: Shut up! Fifty years ago we'd have you upside-down with a fucking fork up your ass! You can talk, you can talk, you can talk! You're brave now, motherfucker. Throw his ass out. He's a nigger! He's a nigger! He's a nigger! A nigger, look, there's a nigger! Oooo! Ooo. . . . All right, you see? It shocks you, it shocks you, to see what's buried beneath, you stupid motherfuckers!

AUDIENCE MEMBER: That was uncalled-for.

RICHARDS: What was uncalled-for? It's uncalled-for you to interrupt my ass, you cheap motherfucker. You guys have been talking and talking and talking. I don't know. I don't know. I don't know. What's the matter? Is this too much for you to handle? They're going to arrest me for calling a black man a nigger?

Wait a minute, where's he going?

BLACK AUDIENCE MEMBER, LEAVING: That was uncalled-for, you fucking cracker-ass motherfucker.

RICHARDS: Cracker-ass? Are you calling me cracker-ass, nigger?

AUDIENCE MEMBER: Fucking white boy.

RICHARDS: Are you threatening me?

AUDIENCE MEMBER: We'll see what's up?

RICHARDS: Oh, it's a big threat. That's how you get back at the man.

AUDIENCE MEMBER: That was real uncalled-for.

RICHARDS: Wait a minute. He's not going is he?

AUDIENCE MEMBER: It's not funny. That's why you're a reject, never had no shows, never had no movies. *Seinfeld*, that's it.

RICHARDS: Oh, I guess you got me there. You're absolutely right. I'm just a washup. . . . Gotta stand on the stage.

AUDIENCE MEMBER: That's un-fucking-called-for. That ain't necessary.

RICHARDS: Well, you interrupted me, pal. That's what happens when you interrupt the white man, don't you know?

AUDIENCE MEMBER: That was uncalled-for.

RICHARDS: You see? You see? There's still those words, those words, those words.[29]

After the three-minute rant, the majority of the audience members left. Frazier Smith, the Laugh Factory's host, apologized to those who remained. Richards's "performance" was captured on a phone, and it soon appeared on television and internet sites. He became a national villain, the 2006 face of racism. It was not simply that he had repeatedly used the word "nigger" or that he had expressed the words in an angry tirade. Richards had used the language of lynching. He had evoked images of black men killed in public spectacles for insulting "the white man." He would claim in later interviews that he did not know where in his psyche those words had originated . . . did not know that those ideas were inside

COPYRIGHT, 1907, J. ROYSTER.   PUBLISHED, DIXIE W. LEACH.

"THIS QUESTION 'BOUT THE NIGGER RACE--
IT SUTTINLY AM NO BLUFF;
BUT DER'S ONE THING YOU CAN'T DENY,
WE'S ALWAYS UP TO SNUFF."

him. To salvage his career—and maybe to begin personal healing—he appeared on several television and radio shows to tell anyone listening that he was "all busted up" and sorry for the harm that he had caused. The Laugh Factory soon afterward banned the word "nigger," meaning that any performer, black or white, who used the word on their stage would no longer be invited to perform at the club.

Reverberations from Richards's rant were felt nationwide. Several months after the outburst, the New York City Council voted 49–0 to ban the word. The resolution carried no penalties. It was a symbolic act encouraging New Yorkers to stop saying the word "nigger" and to learn its racist provenance. Leroy Comrie, an African American and a member of the City Council, sponsored the resolution in the hope of starting a national movement. The well-intentioned resolution was dismissed by some African Americans, including Chris Rock. When asked about how the resolution would impact his act, Rock joked, "What? Is there a fine? Do judges say, '10 years, nigger!'?"[30] The resolution was also criticized by Robert Richards, a representative from the Pennsylvania Center for the First Amendment, who said it "seemed a waste of government resources to pass resolutions that have no impact. It's just a feel-good move for the New York city council."[31]

On July 9, 2007, a funeral was held in Detroit, Michigan. It was held outdoors. The deceased lay in a wooden coffin drawn by white horses. Thousands of people, some in business suits, others in casual clothes, and still others in African attire, braved the summer heat to attend the burial. In many ways it was not a typical procession. There was laughing, singing, dancing, drum playing, and speech giving. No tears were shed for the deceased. As Julian Bond, the chairman of the NAACP, noted: "This is the first funeral I've been to where people are happy to be here, happy to see him go. This is a happy occasion."[32]

The mourners had come to denounce the deceased. They hated him, hated what he represented, hated that he had become part of the black community. Speakers referred to him as unacceptable, ugly, and dirty, the offspring of language and hate. They spoke of his long life, a life fueled by and mired in disgust and revulsion. Most were in agreement that the world would have been better had he not been born. "This was the greatest child that racism ever birthed," the Rev. Otis Moss III, assistant pastor at Trinity United Church of Christ in Chicago, said in his eulogy. The child referred to by Moss was not a person, it was a word: "nigger."

The burial was organized by the NAACP as part of its annual convention. Most of those in attendance were African Americans. Many of them had at some time used the word in jest and in anger. More than a few of them said that Richards's racist rant opened their eyes. The funeral was

This postcard was copyrighted in 1907.

a public affirmation that they, individually and collectively, would no longer call black people niggers, and it was also a plea to others—especially black comedians, movie makers, and rap musicians—to stop using the word.

The NAACP's burial of the word "nigger" was a symbolic act, as was its banning by the New York City Council. But, in 2014, the National Football League (NFL) took action to aggressively enforce one of their existing rules that barred the use of racial slurs on the playing field, with a specific emphasis on the word "nigger." Players or coaches heard using the word would receive a fifteen-yard penalty. If they used it a second time they would be thrown out of the game. This attempt to remove "nigger" from the NFL playing field was sparked, in no small part, by two incidents. In 2013, Riley Cooper, a wide receiver for the Philadelphia Eagles, had a confrontation with a black security guard at a Kenny Chesney concert. A video shows an irate Cooper, who is white, saying, "I will jump that fence and fight every nigger here!" After the video went viral, Cooper apologized to his teammates, many of whom are African Americans. Michael Vick, an African American teammate, said, "We all make mistakes. . . . As a teammate I forgave him."[33] That same year, details emerged regarding the actions of Richie Incognito, a Miami Dolphins offensive lineman who harassed a mixed-race teammate, Jonathan Martin, including calling him a "half-nigger piece of shit."

The NFL's attempt to remove the word "nigger" from its playing fields was met by resistance from a number of players, mostly African Americans. That is not surprising, as most of the players in the NFL are black and most of the players who use the word "nigger" or "nigga" are black. Richard Sherman, a black cornerback for the Seattle Seahawks, said of the ban, "It is an atrocious idea. It's almost racist, to me. Why wouldn't all curse words be banned then?"[34]

Mock funerals, city council resolutions, and bans on athletic fields are goodhearted attempts to get rid of the word "nigger," but, alas, they are doomed to fail. The only way that a word—any word—is truly buried in this country is to have it fall into disuse. From the 1880s to 1920s it was common for Americans to refer to Irish immigrants as "Paddies." It is rare today to hear someone refer to an Irish immigrant or Irish American as a Paddy. During that same period, Jewish immigrants and Jewish Americans were sometimes insulted with the slur "hebe." This epithet has fallen into disuse, though "kike," a harsher anti-Jewish slur, remains. "Rastus" is a black slur that has fallen into disfavor. But there is something different about the word "nigger" or "nigga." It has a constituency, a constituency made up of two segments: white racists and some black people who are wedded to the word. Neither segment is willing to stop using it.

This is a tobacco tin used by the American Tobacco Company of Wisconsin to sell its product from the late 1870s through the mid-1920s. In 1926, the company changed the name from Nigger Hair to Bigger Hair. **211**

A Personal Story

Years ago, I facilitated a workshop in Virginia; almost all the participants were African Americans with advanced university degrees. We discussed a shirt that I brought from the Jim Crow Museum that had young black men depicted in stereotypical ways: pants sagging, carrying music boxes, looking threatening—and one fellow urinating on the street. When I asked the workshop participants to tell me what they saw, several said "niggers." For the next hour we discussed what that word meant to them. I can summarize their statements this way: niggers are real; they can be men or women, but the scary ones are usually young men since the women mostly hurt themselves with drug use and unwanted pregnancies; most niggers are poor, lazy, and ignorant; niggers are no-good, trifling victims who constantly complain; Washington, DC, is full of them; and, finally, none of the participants in the room were niggers (though one person quipped with unintentional irony that I had obvious sympathies).

It is a struggle for me, but I try to be objective when I facilitate workshops, and near the conclusion of this session I felt compelled to preach:

Who told you that some of us are niggers? Were the four little girls bombed in a Birmingham church niggers? Were they? Were the brothers and sisters who suffered in the civil rights movement niggers? Do you remember them—beaten with batons, kicked, bitten by police dogs, stomped, knocked against walls by power

These pinbacks were purchased in the 1990s.

hoses, jailed, kidnapped, raped, thrown in rivers, eulogized before crying neighbors. Was Rosa Parks a nigger? No, then neither is the young sister with the baby on her hip.

When I finished someone asked if I had ever lived in a large city. And when I answered no, the looks on their faces said, "Ah, then you don't really know what you are talking about." Seeing other black people as niggers is more than the residue of slavery and Jim Crow, it is part of the legacies of these oppressive periods. We were taught to see ourselves as niggers. Some of us rejected that teaching by shifting the nigger label to others. The black professionals in that room accepted the belief of Chris Rock and John Ridley that some black people, people who look like us but are not really like us, are indeed niggers.

I have told this story many times, to many audiences. I will confess that I liked the story (and the telling of it) because it made me seem rational, well-informed, a man living his principles. I was, in my mind, better than the people at the workshop. I was an African American who only used the word "nigger" as a teaching tool in much the same way I used a lynching postcard.

An honest version of me would have told the workshop participants that I too had referred to black people as niggers—though it had been a long time ago—and even then I rarely used it as a synonym for poor black people. But I had used it—not often, but sometimes—at Mattie T. Blount High School and Jarvis Christian College, where most of the teachers and all of the students were blacks. And I had used it with my black friends at the mostly white Ohio State University. In all those places, it was, most of the time, a slightly profane in-group marker. But there were other times when brown fists found brown faces and "nigger" meant to us what it meant to whites.

And then I stopped—stopped calling myself a nigger, stopped calling my friends niggers, stopped letting them call me a nigger. There was no epiphany, no Saul on the road to Damascus moment, no "Boy, who told you that some of us are niggers?" rebuke. It was inevitable. Surround yourself with postcards of naked black children calling one another nigger. Haggle with flea market dealers selling Jolly Nigger Banks or packages of Nigger Boy Licorice. Read newspaper accounts of white mobs spewing racial taunts, lynching black boys falsely accused of raping white women. And see old footage that shows black people, everyday people, people whose names are lost to history—maids, teachers, dockworkers, shoe shiners—get brutalized yet keep marching. How can one experience these things and still call his brothers and sisters niggers. So for more than two decades I did not once use the word "nigger" in jest or anger.

This journey—this racial ride—is not a straight line. Several months ago I got into an argument with a family member. Like many such arguments it grew from resentments that had built, grown, festered. I walked away, returned, walked away, and like a fool who needs to make a point, returned. It devolved. And then I said, "I am tired of you disrespecting me, tired of you treating me like a nigger. Keep it up and I will show you how a real nigger from Highway 45 in Prichard acts."

Crushed is too strong a word, but I was disappointed in myself. Why had my frustration and anger come out that way? "A real nigger from Highway 45"—that is the language of my youth, a time when you either fought or acquiesced to being mistreated. Those words scream, "Don't mess with me!" But why those words? I do, after all, know many words. My words surprised those who heard them. They had heard the word "nigger" before, but not from me . . . the man who conducts workshops on racial epithets, who tells young black people that calling ourselves niggers is an expression of self- and group-loathing. There is a hypocrite in all of us; mine reared his head that day.

I don't know if we ever totally transcend the circumstances of our upbringing—my hunch is that we do not. It took me a while to come to grips with that argument, with my words, and to apologize to others and myself. Now when I facilitate discussions about the word "nigger" I don't just tell the story of the black professionals in Virginia who divided African Americans into two categories: good black people and niggers. I also tell the story of the man who has spent his adult life combating the word but in an angry moment used it. I have work to do, more than I previously thought.

CHAPTER EIGHT

Final Words

Writing any book is difficult; writing one about the oppression of black people is especially hard. Only a heartless ideologue can read about Claude Neal and not be moved to disgust. To read about Neal's torture— and the torture of thousands of other black people—is to come to know the facts. To write about it is to imagine their hell, to visualize the faces of people who, knives and razors in hand, amputated toes and fingers to keep as souvenirs. Reading about racial atrocities insults the soul. Writing about them destroys a part of the writer.

Knowledge for the sake of knowledge is a waste of knowledge—and a waste of time. This book only has value if it helps, in some small way, to improve race relations in this country. I am unapologetically an activist. My activism is grounded in my experiences as a person of color in a society that mistreated people who were not white and by my education as a sociologist trained to view society objectively but critically. There is no inherent conflict between evenhanded research and a commitment to activism.

In the mid-1970s, I was a student at Jarvis Christian College. I had very little money. The summer between my junior and senior years, I went home to Prichard, Alabama, to look for work. Most of the available jobs were low-paying, menial work, like mopping floors in Jac's Seafood Wheel House Restaurant, where you were lucky to make three cents a minute. I complained to one of my neighbors, whom I'll call Mr. Pettaway. Although it has been more than three decades, I can remember his words. "College boy, there is good money to be made, but you have to do a man's work." Don't let those words fool you. Mr. Pettaway was proud that I was

a college student, and he knew that I could do hard work. He liked teasing me. So, I awoke early the next day to do "man's work," loading and unloading crates at the Alabama State Docks.

At first, I sat with the men at the docks, joking and playing dominoes. But then the joking stopped and all the men rushed to a makeshift stage just as a foreman appeared. The men started pushing, shoving, and working their way to the front, trying to get the foreman's attention. They shouted and begged, "Please, Mister, let me work. Let me work for you. Please, Sir, I will work hard. Get outta my way. I'm a hard worker, Sir, please give me a chance. Over here. Move over. He's gonna pick me. You know me, Boss, you know I will work hard. I got a family. Pick me. Don't stand in front of me. Pick me. Over here, Boss. I won't let you down. Move. Please, please, pick me." Imagine hundreds of men—all ages, all poor, most of them with black or brown skin—bumping, jostling, elbowing, begging, and cussing anyone who kept the foreman from seeing them. The foreman pointed to the men he wanted: "You, yeah you. No, not you. That one with the red shirt." A dozen or so men were selected and they joined the foreman on stage and then, together, they exited the stage. The unlucky majority, many cussing, went back to playing dominoes and telling bawdy stories as they waited for the next ship to dock.

Mr. Pettaway had gone to the docks for more than twenty years. Each morning he left home not knowing if he would be picked for work. He was a good and proud man, but he had to push, shove, and beg for a chance to work—each day of his adult life. This was a demeaning pattern, steeped in tradition. When that first boat came in, I watched him beg his way onto the stage, and when he was on the stage our eyes met. He was a big man, well over six feet tall with the body of a defensive end, but, and I say this with no disrespect intended, on the stage he seemed smaller, not metaphorically but physically smaller.

I share this story because I believe that there are times in life when anger is a logical and reasonable response. There was a matter-of-fact anger in many of the workers that seemed to me to be both sane and inevitable. The system was oppressive and dehumanizing. Men begged for the opportunity to do backbreaking, mind-numbing work. As soon as a foreman left the stage the men cussed like, well, longshoremen. Being treated as inferiors made the men angry, but they lacked the resources and opportunities to channel their anger into constructive social action. They were angry and their anger, like dirty water, had to drain somewhere. Poor, uneducated men rarely raise their fists against systems. More likely, they drink cheap wine and hit one another, their wives, and their children.

Funneling anger is risky business. Anger is a powerful fuel, and one could argue that much social change has resulted in no small part

This is a replica of a sign used in the 1960s by African American activists.

because of angry voices. In my half century of living, however, I have seen too many activists become frustrated and worn out—made callous by failed attempts to make change, with their idealistic passion devolving into seething anger, or worse, thick hatred, which brings me to another story.

When I was in graduate school I discovered the writings of J.A. Rogers, the mostly self-taught historian and journalist. I was fascinated by this maverick scholar who challenged prevailing theories of white intellectual supremacy. Although he was not formally trained as a sociologist, Rogers's critique of American race relations was solidly sociological. For example, in his book *Nature Knows No Color-Line*, self-published in 1952, Rogers argued that racial (color) prejudice was not an inherent trait in humans, but rather a rationalization for domination, subjugation, and warfare. Dominant groups created racial myths and stereotypes to protect and promote their interests at the expense of less powerful groups. This belief is accepted today as a sociological axiom, but in his day it was considered a radical notion.

One of my Ohio State University professors saw me reading a copy of Rogers's first book, *From Superman to Man* (self-published in 1917), and recommended that I talk to a scholar who lived in town. I will call the scholar Doc, and like Rogers, he was mainly self-educated. Though Doc had a few years of formal higher education from a historically black college somewhere in the South, he never spoke of it in specific terms.

Doc lived in a tiny apartment made smaller by chest-high stacks of books and newspapers. I remember thinking that he owned every small-run, out-of-print book about this country's race problem. I spent many days in that tiny apartment listening to Doc talk about Rogers's single-minded work to prove that people with "African blood" had made significant contributions to the arts, science, and philosophy. He quoted Rogers's books the way some people quote the Bible, meaning, with a strange combination of familiarity and awe. Doc's only regret, he joked, was that Rogers had not been darker.

There is knowledge that comes from being an eyewitness. Our initial conversations were about Rogers, but soon we were talking about the freedom marchers, civil rights leaders, and what might be called the gossip of the movement: character flaws, petty rivalries, intimate relations. Doc had walked in the second Selma to Montgomery march, not the Bloody Sunday march of March 7, 1965. He told me that he wished he had been at the first march, though he doubted whether he would have remained nonviolent. He helped register poor black voters in the Deep South. He participated in sit-ins. Doc had an album with newspaper clippings, one of which included a photograph of him being arrested.

Growing up black in the 1950s and 1960s had deeply scarred Doc. His hurt and anger led him to participate in the civil rights movement, but he was better suited for the Black Power movement. He never accepted Dr. King's belief that all men are brothers. Moreover, he thought that Dr. King's belief about seeking to defeat evil, not people, was silliness born of Christian naiveté. The gains won by the civil rights workers increased Doc's frustration. With each court victory came greater expectations, and when those expectations were not met—or met too slowly—Doc's conviction that the "whole system is corrupt" was, in his mind, validated. "No black man," he said, "could ever get a fair shake in this country." He argued that every major societal institution including government, education, religion, criminal justice, and mass media were all set up to benefit whites, and that this would never change. And he added, "Any black man who doesn't see this is a token and a fool." By the time I met Doc, he was no longer active in politics. His time was spent, as best I could tell, reading and doing odd jobs. It is hard to believe that a quarter century has passed since I last saw Doc.

Recently, I saw a YouTube video of a visit that Jesse Jackson made to Ferguson, Missouri, on the first anniversary of the killing of Michael

Visitors to the museum view cartoons from the 1930s to the early twenty-first century. Many of the cartoons depict Africans and African Americans in racially stereotypical ways. **219**

HEROES

Rosa Parks

1913–
Civil Rights Activist

When Rosa Parks refused to give up her seat on a racially segregated bus in Montgomery, Alabama, on December 1, 1955, she became a symbol of courageous resistance in the civil rights movement. "Tired of giving in," Parks's act of bravery led to a boycott and to important changes in the law within the decade. In 1999, she was awarded the Congressional Gold Medal, the nation's highest civilian honor.

"When people made up their minds that they wanted to be free and took action, then there was a change."

Brown by local police officers. Before, during, and after his visit, hundreds of protesters were demonstrating against police violence. Jackson, sitting, window rolled down, in the passenger seat of a slowly moving car, is confronted by several local black residents. They ask him why he has not been marching with them. They ask if he plans to pay the bonds of arrested protesters. They did not get the answers they wanted. Within minutes, Jackson is called a sellout and told, "This is real. We're activists out here, brother. We don't want you here. You're not a leader. . . . Matter of fact, you're not a brother." I tell this story not to embarrass Jackson, but to demonstrate what Doc and other activists—including Jackson—have always known: activism is often fueled by anger.

I know what it is like to be angry, to scream, "I am sick of this crap!" Is there a sane person of color in this country who has not experienced the anger that accompanies being treated as an outsider, an inferior, a member of Them? I have said before and I will say again that anger is a necessary leg on this racial journey but it cannot be the destination. I have tried to replace anger with focused passion and a zeal to address injustice. When that failed, I tried, not always successfully, to focus my anger against societal systems that promote injustice, not individuals. At all costs, I have tried to avoid the anger that simmers, paralyzes, and morphs into hatred.

I have a great deal of respect for people who take their activism to the streets; I often join them, but I know that there are many ways to confront injustice. We built the Jim Crow Museum as a tool to fight racial injustice. Meaningful and sustained dialogues about race, race relations, and racism occur daily in that small facility. At the risk of sounding like a cliché, I believe in the triumph of dialogue. Some of this dialogue must occur at the macro level. I will go to my grave believing that the United States should have a national Truth and Reconciliation Commission to address the lynchings and mob riots that occurred in this country, but dialogue about racism should also occur among and between small groups of people.

The mind holds some stories and releases others. Years ago I read a story told by Audre Lorde, a gifted writer and passionate civil rights activist. I have told that story many times because in it is valuable insight into the many and varied ways that race has mattered and continues to matter in the United States. It was a single paragraph, but it shook me. Here is her telling:

> I wheel my two-year-old daughter in a shopping cart through a supermarket in Eastchester in 1967, and a little white girl riding past in her mother's cart calls out excitedly, "Oh look, Mommy, a

On July 2, 1964, President Lyndon B. Johnson signed the Civil Rights Act, which prohibited discrimination in public places on the basis of race, color, religion, sex, or national origin, provided for the integration of schools and other public facilities, and made employment discrimination illegal. This visitor to the museum is looking at one of the pens that President Johnson used to sign the act. **221**

baby maid!" And your mother shushes you, but does not correct you, and so fifteen years later, at a conference on racism, you can still find that story humorous. But I hear your laughter is full of terror and dis-ease.[1]

Bothered by the child, saddened by the child's mother, and disappointed by liberal colleagues, Lorde's frustration was understandable—indeed, to be expected. What black woman wants to hear her child, her baby, maybe the person she loves most in this world, referred to as a baby maid? And Audre Lorde was not a typical black woman, or typical woman, or typical American. She was a poet—her first poem written in the eighth grade—an essayist, antiwar activist, lesbian, and one of the leading voices for radically inclusive feminism in the United States. She had a master's degree in library science from Columbia University and worked as a librarian at Mount Vernon Public Library in New York. Lorde was an intelligent, deeply reflective scholar, and the words of the white child and the laughter of colleagues hurt her terribly.

I hope the white child was young, too young to understand race and class. Sometimes children, especially very young ones, make comments that seem racial or racist but are simply uncritical observations. Children notice differences. Children are curious. "Mommy, that woman has black skin." The child is not offering a value judgment, and deeper meanings, racial or otherwise, come into play only when the adults intervene. This is the case, almost always, even when the language is a bit cruder: "Mommy, that woman has dirty skin," or "Mommy, that woman's skin is ugly," or "Oh look, Mommy, a baby maid." I understand these things. Nevertheless, had the black child been my daughter I would have been hurt and angry. I would have wondered if—no, I would have assumed that—the mother had avoided the subject of race with her child. Lorde, her feelings injured, mentions that the white mother "shushes you, but does not correct you." Yes, that would have bothered me. Shushing the child made the white mother's life easier, but quieting the child really yelled: "Race is not something we talk about." When we ignore discussions of race we also ignore discussions of discrimination, prejudice, and stereotyping. You should not talk about race without talking about racism. I wish I knew the age of the child. Was she four? Seven? Twelve? It matters. When it comes to race relations we all, meaning all, stand in need of correction, and we can start with the white woman whose child implied that black skin is a synonym for servitude, Lorde's colleagues, or ourselves.

Rexburg is a city in rural Eastern Idaho. There are just over twenty-five thousand residents in the small town—94 percent of them are white and Mormon. It is home to the Brigham Young University–Idaho, a

On March 7, 1965, hundreds of civil rights demonstrators trying to gain voting rights for African Americans were cruelly beaten by Alabama state troopers and Selma police. The nation watched televised images of the protesters being hit with billy clubs, shocked by cattle prods, trampled by horses, and choked by tear gas. The day is remembered as Bloody Sunday. On March 21, another march was held, this one with federal protection for the demonstrators. The accompanying photographs were taken by one of the demonstrators at the March 21 march.

223

private institution operated by the Church of Jesus Christ of Latter-day Saints (LDS). The LDS Church exercises an almost monolithic influence on Rexburg residents—influencing behavior on everything from proper dress to political affiliation. The area is so staunchly conservative and Republican that *Salon* referred to Rexburg and the surrounding Madison County as "the rosiest place in all of red America."[2]

The day following the 2008 presidential election, Rexburg made national news. On the bus ride home from an elementary school, second and third graders chanted, "Assassinate Obama! Assassinate Obama!" The report of Rexburg children chanting those words shocked and saddened many Americans. The election of a multiracial black-identified man as president of the United States was met by many nasty incidents. Crosses were burned in the yards of Obama supporters in Hardwick, New Jersey, and Apolacon Township, Pennsylvania. In the Pittsburgh suburb of Forest Hills, a black man found a note with the threat "now that you voted for Obama, just watch out for your house." Marsha L. Houston, a professor at the University of Alabama, had a poster of the Obama family removed from her office door. A replacement poster was defaced with a death threat and a racial slur. Racist graffiti was found in many places, including Long Island, New York, where two dozen cars were spray painted, Kilgore, Texas, where the local high school and skate park were defaced, and the Los Angeles area, where swastikas, racial slurs, and "Go Back to Africa" were spray painted on sidewalks, houses, and cars. At Standish, Maine, a sign inside the Oak Hill General Store read: "Osama Obama Shotgun Pool." Customers bet one dollar on a date when Obama would be killed. "Stabbing, shooting, roadside bombs, they all count," the sign said. At the bottom of the marker board were these words, "Let's hope someone wins."[3] In California's San Jacinto Valley and on Staten Island in New York there were instances of whites physically attacking black people in response to Obama winning the election.[4]

Among the many racist responses to Obama's election—including representations of him hanged in effigy—the Rexburg children chanting "Assassinate Obama! Assassinate Obama!" seemed especially unsettling. These were not middle-aged ideologues angry that their candidate lost the election or college fraternity boys showing off for one another. These were children—seven to nine years old—practically babes, and from their mouths came an ugliness generally associated with adults.

Children that young have only a vague idea of what it means to assassinate someone. It is likely they were parroting the words of older relatives. I wonder which words they heard. In the "rosiest of all red states," which stories were these children taught about Obama—about people with black skin, about those who are not in your We. I was not in their

homes, but I know there was a story told by many American families in 2008. Here is one version of that story.

In the last several decades we have been a nation in decline—and it is getting worse. There is an erosion of national identity and purpose. We don't know who we are or where we are going. Our forefathers—armed with an unwavering belief in God—built this country; no one gave them anything. They built a great nation. Today, large-scale immigration from non-European countries, much of it illegal, is changing the character and morals of the nation. Our schools are a disaster, with too much emphasis on multiculturalism and diversity. The more we give to minorities the more they want. The American family is under attack. We are bound by no common faith or culture. Our once great nation has been robbed, ruined from within. Our grandparents and parents could work their way into the middle class. Now, the benefits of hard work are not realized because there are fewer good jobs. And those with jobs are living paycheck to paycheck. We are no longer a great nation. There is a growing contempt for us around the world.

The museum was created to facilitate difficult dialogues about race, race relations, and racism.

Our leaders are inept and undeserving of our trust or respect. The decline in America made it possible for Obama to be elected— and his presidency will hasten the nation's decay. His wife hates America and he is not one of us.

My reaction to Senator Obama's election was different. On the night of the election my wife and I held each other and cried with joy. But there were other people crying for different reasons. Some of them told stories about him being the Antichrist—or paving the way for the Antichrist. He was portrayed as a racist, in part because of his relationship with the Reverend Jeremiah Wright, pastor emeritus of Trinity United Church of Christ in Chicago, where Obama was a member. There was an unfounded rumor that Michelle Obama had been videotaped expressing hatred for "whitey." Had the Rexburg children heard these stories? Obama was portrayed as a Muslim, a terrorist, a pimp, a sexual deviant, a witchdoctor. Had the children heard these stories? It matters. Rod Dreher, a blogger, said it well, "The stories we live by—the literature, of course, but also the stories we tell ourselves and our children to explain the world—have consequences both private and public."[5] We won't change America until we change the stories we tell our children—and ourselves.

Because of my work with the museum I am sometimes afforded the opportunity to lecture at colleges and universities. I relish these opportunities. In my talks I do not tell people what to believe, but I do tell them what I believe. Americans like "happy history," but much of what I discuss is not happy, especially not for the victims or their descendants. I discuss these things not to induce guilt, but to give an accurate portrayal of this nation's journey. I encourage the listeners to push back, and they do. In the process we create dialogue. I sometimes end a lecture by reading one of my essays. It seems somehow fitting to end this book with a personal essay called "Brothers," updated to include recent events.

I have a brother who lives as a white man. He is the principal of Cedar Brook Elementary School in Bakersfield, California. He has a wife, a son, and a daughter. I have not met them; I have not met him. If my brother were here today, he would politely deny our kinship. I understand. It takes two men to make a brother.

I have a brother serving five years in Atmore State Penitentiary. Even as a child he took things that didn't belong to him. He is scheduled for release on January 21, 2024. No one will be there to welcome him. He is a thief, a career criminal, and I, despite a log in my eye, can see the speck in his.

I have a brother who was the pastor of Mount Olive Baptist Church in Pittsburgh, the second-largest black church in Pennsylvania. He was the most powerful public speaker I've heard. It was like listening to Moses. His voice booming, arms flailing, he would preach until his shirt was drenched with sweat, but before the shirt was dry he would have some young sister spinning in the backseat of his BMW. One day he left that big church and started a ministry for the homeless and those afflicted with AIDS. A newspaper reporter asked him why he'd left Mount Olive and he answered, "I got saved." Today, he lives, as much as is humanly possible, a life devoid of any hint of hypocrisy.

A year ago a thought came into my head—and took residence. Forgive the likely hyperbole, but this thought tortured me, ripped me. It was not an original thought, nor was it especially profound. It wouldn't go away. It wouldn't leave me alone. I tried to not think the thought, which, of course, cemented it in my mind—this thought that tortured me. Five words. Five simple words. It seems so melodramatic, so silly to say that one was tortured by a thought. But I was.

I remember when the thought came. I was delivering a lecture at a conference in Indiana, and I said something—the thought—and the audience applauded. I am a professor, meaning I like applause and rarely get it, so I said it again; this time the audience stood, clapped, some even

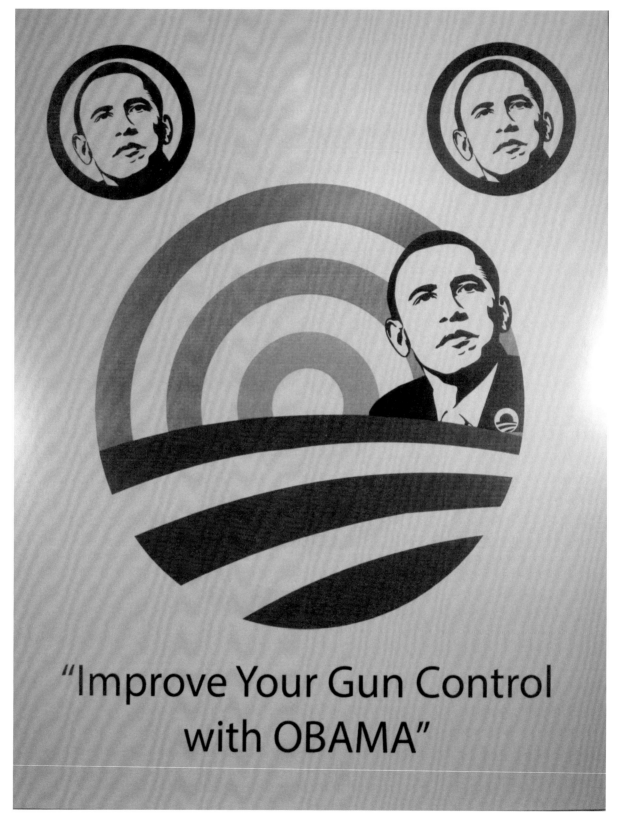

cheered. On the return drive to Michigan those five words came back to me and I, like my brother, felt like a charlatan.

The five words were these: every man is my brother.

I've never believed that, and, again, I don't know why I said it that first time. Why does anyone say anything? I have certainly lied before, white ones, black ones, big ones, ones not so big. It was a lie because I didn't believe it, yet I had said it, twice. I thought: What's the big deal, people say things, orators say things, it sounded good, it worked, what's the harm, no one will remember, why did I say that, maybe I didn't really say that, people misspeak, there is a hypocrite hugging my children, professors say things, it sounded good, what's the harm . . . But it did matter, and later, it mattered more.

It's so corny to say, "Every man is my brother." It sounds like something you'd read in *Mother Jones* magazine, or maybe even *Reader's Digest*.

I have always felt a kinship with men of color, especially brown ones. I like it when we say, "Yo, what's up, brother?" or "What's happening, brother?" or "True that, brother." A shared history of oppression will make you call a stranger brother, or brotha. But even in these cases it was purely symbolic. I didn't think we were actually brothers.

Weeks and months passed and I couldn't get the thought out of my head. One day I was in the Jim Crow Museum and I saw a postcard with a black man being publicly whipped. I've seen that postcard many times; after all, I bought it, I put it in the cabinet, and it's in my PowerPoint presentations. I looked at that man being beaten and I thought my brother was being beaten, publicly, naked to the waist, beaten like a dog, worse than a dog. At that moment I felt in a way that I can't describe that he was indeed my brother, not my symbolic brother, no, a real brother. I wanted to run to him, rip him from the post, and beat his tormentors. I wanted to hold him, hold his head to my chest and tell him that his brother, this brother, cared for him and had come to rescue him. My God, he really was my brother. Later, I tried to talk to some people about it, but most people won't go with you when you're trippin'.

Sometimes when I went to the museum I would not look at that postcard; sometimes it was all I looked at. One day I looked and in the postcard I saw a little white boy, he was standing near my beaten brother, and that little boy, he was not laughing, not protesting either, just standing there, near the white man with the whip, and I looked at that child, and it hit me, like a heel to the face, that little boy was also my brother. I thought: "No, no, I don't want this. He hates me before he knows the fifth grade. I want to cuss him and the woman who made him. His brother is the white man with the whip; my brother is the black man being beaten. How can that child be my brother? I don't want this."

This shooting target was distributed in 2015.

Then I understood the thought that tortured me.

It wasn't only, or even primarily, that I had said something in a public lecture that I didn't believe. I've done that too many times for that to torture me. No, the real torture was the realization that maybe, just maybe, all men are my brothers. And I didn't want that. I tried to dismiss those five words as a hollow religious slogan, liberal tripe, mawkish muck from the mouths of idealistic zealots. Why? Because if that little boy was my brother, then so was the white man with the whip. My heart said: "He's not my brother. He's a monster. I don't hate the whip. I hate him. I don't hate what he stands for. I hate him. I want to make him feel that whip. Strip him naked, beat him till my arm is tired, and beat him like he is not a child of God. Put his naked white back on a postcard. If he's my brother then so was every slaveholder who raped a girl or boy. I don't want that. That's too much. Every overseer. Every lyncher. Every foot on a neck. I don't want this. Every man is my brother. It changes nothing. And from that deepest place came one last yowl: No! No! No!"

My Uncle Sonny looks like the black man who was being beaten, and that little white boy who stood and watched looks like my son Jamie.

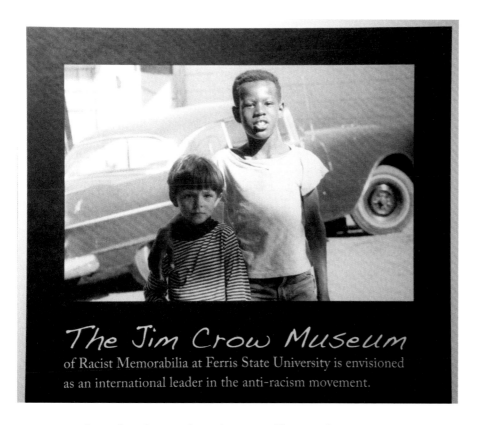

The Jim Crow Museum of Racist Memorabilia at Ferris State University is envisioned as an international leader in the anti-racism movement.

Every man is my brother. It doesn't matter if I want it or not. In a moment, the idle thought became a truth, a matter-of-fact truth, absolute. I am the only male born from my mother's womb but every man is my brother: white elementary school principals who deny me, prisoners who rob, preachers who leave big churches to help the helpless, every man. This kinship is not based on shared wombs, common ancestors, similar skin, communal beliefs, or brotherly love. We are brothers because we spring from the same fountain, and that water flows one way.

I can hate a man, but he is still my brother. I admired Dr. King and I detested James Earl Ray, but they were both my brothers. We don't choose our brothers. George Bush is my brother, and so is the person who made his breakfast this morning; and Stevie Wonder who cannot see and David Duke who chooses not to, along with Leonard Peltier and Mumia Abu-Jamal and the men they killed or didn't kill; and Reverend Pat Robertson and his white sons, and Minister Farrakhan and his black sons, and Bill Gates, who has more money than the Devil, and Eminem, always bitter, and brothers who cry and brothers who need to, and the men who crashed airplanes into the Twin Towers were my brothers—and they killed my brothers; and pimps are my brothers too, and date rapists, and punks, and brothers slinging dope, and Dylann Roof, a young man robbed of the truth, and Donald Trump, who believes he

Renowned photographer Johnny Simmons donated a print to the museum, reproduced here.

is the truth, and moonshiners and revenuers, and Jerry Springer, who
brings me down, and Stephen Hawking, who lifts me, and brothers who
live as white men, and brothers who live as black men, and brothers
who live as red men, and brothers who don't want to live, but none are
niggers, kikes, crackers, wops, chinks, or fags, because God didn't make
any of those; and the men in the Abu Ghraib photographs are my brothers and so are the men who behead the helpless; and Jared Fogle is my
brother and so is Bill Cosby; and Cain, and Abel, and hawks, and doves,
and those who sleep in urine-stained hallways, and malicious talkers,
and Jon Stewart and Bill O'Reilly and those who carry their bags; and
capitalists and communists, and some are beautiful, and some disfig-
ured, some run, some sit always in iron chairs, and villagers too, some
are strangers but none are alien; and brothers with tender hearts, and
wicked brothers, and weak ones like me; O.J. Simpson is my brother
and so is the father of Nicole Simpson; I've got brothers I want to hit
and brothers I want to hold; and some who hate me, and some who hate
you; and some of my brothers are old, some poor, some ugly, some with
whips and strong right arms. Every day is a family reunion because
every man—every good man and every bad one—every man born of

a woman is my brother and to know this changes nothing—changes everything.

My son is Eustace Jamison Pilgrim. After his fifth birthday I asked him, "How do you like being five?" He said he liked being five because the number five was cute. He is my son; he is my little brother. One day he said to me, "I don't love you." He saw my frown. He smiled and said, "Dad, it's Opposite Day." I said, "Oh, then I don't love you either." My son is my brother and that changes everything. A reshuffling of the cards and he is the man with the whip, or the man being beaten, either way, my brother, my little brother. Today, I will hold his head to my chest. He is my son, he is my brother, and I am his keeper.

A new thought has entered my head and taken residence. It is not an original thought nor is it especially profound. I will not let it torture me. It is a simple thought and it is this: every woman is my sister. Soon I will talk to you about that.

About the Museum

The Jim Crow Museum, located at Ferris State University, is the nation's largest publicly accessible collection of racist artifacts, primarily but not exclusively segregation-related memorabilia. These objects are used as tools to facilitate a deeper understanding of historical and contemporary patterns and expressions of racism. The museum is a resource for scholars, students, civil rights activists, and media, including the *New York Times*, Associated Press, British Broadcasting Corporation, National Public Radio, and many others. To learn more about the museum, visit www.ferris.edu/jimcrow.

About the Author

Dr. David Pilgrim is a public speaker and one of this country's leading experts on issues relating to multiculturalism, diversity, and race relations. He is best known as the founder and curator of the Jim Crow Museum. Dr. Pilgrim is a recipient of Ferris State University's Distinguished Teacher Award and has delivered public lectures at dozens of institutions, among them Stanford University, Colby College, the University of Michigan, Smith College, and the University of North Carolina. He is an applied sociologist who challenges audiences to think deeply about diversity and race relations. His goal is to get people talking about diversity and race relations in meaningful ways, and then to go and do something positive.

Notes

CHAPTER ONE

1   Stevie Wonder, "Jesus Children of America" (Motown Records, 1973).

2   *Lynching in America: Confronting the Legacy of Racial Terror* (Montgomery, AL: Equal Justice Initiative, 2015), 14.

3   Ibid., 14.

4   In an interview with Timothy B. Tyson, the author of *The Blood of Emmett Till*, Carolyn Donham, the woman at the center of case, recanted her claim that Till had verbally and physically assaulted her. See Hillel Italie, "Key Till Witness Gave False Testimony, Historian Says," *Clarion-Ledger* (Jackson, MS), January 29, 2017, A4.

5   "A Quiet Lynching: Business Men Hang Criminals to Prevent Rioting," *The Caucasian* (Clinton, NC), October 11, 1906.

6   "Negro's Body Found Hanging Head Down," *Odessa American*, September 22, 1968.

7   Helen Bannerman, *The Story of Little Black Sambo* (London: Grant Richards, 1899; New York: Harper & Row, 1923); Helen Bannerman and Christopher Bing, *The Story of Little Black Sambo* (New York: Handprint Books, 2003).

8   Thomas Dixon, *The Clansman: An Historical Romance of the Ku Klux Klan* (New York: Grosset & Dunlap, 1905); D.W. Griffith, *The Birth of a Nation* (David W. Griffith Corp., 1915).

9   Dick Lehr, *The Birth of a Nation: How a Legendary Filmmaker and a Crusading Editor Reignited America's Civil War* (New York: Public Affairs, 2014), 122.

10 Ibid., 127.

11 Richard Wormser, "D.W. Griffith's *The Birth of a Nation* (1915)," PBS, http://www.pbs.org/wnet/jimcrow/stories_events_birth.html, accessed June 7, 2017.

12 John Milton Cooper, *Woodrow Wilson: A Biography* (New York: Alfred A. Knopf, 2009), 272.

13 Ibid.

14 Samuel Cartwright, "Diseases and Peculiarities of the Negro Race," *DeBow's Review*, http://www.pbs.org/wgbh/aia/part4/4h3106t.html, accessed June 3, 2017.

15 "Outrages in Texas Other Than Indian," *New York Times*, January 12, 1855.

16 F. Gary Gray, *Friday* (New Line Cinema, 1995).

17 *Coontown Suffragettes* (Lubin Manufacturing Company, 1914).

18 Victor Fleming, *Gone with the Wind* (Selznick International Pictures, 1939).

19 John M. Stahl, *Imitation of Life* (Universal Pictures, 1934).

20 Gerald Nachman, *Raised on Radio: In Quest of the Lone Ranger* (Berkeley: University of California Press, 2000).

21 It aired on ABC Television from 1950 to 1952.

22 O.U. Schweinickle, *The Book of a Thousand Laughs* (n.p., 1928), 58.

23 *Roots* (David L. Wolper Productions, 1977).

24 Gualtiero Jacopetti and Franco Prosperi, *Goodbye Uncle Tom* (Euro International Film, 1971).

25 Gualtiero Jacopetti and Franco Prosperi, *Africa Addio* (Cineriz, 1966).

26 Melvin Van Peebles, *Sweet Sweetback's Baadasssss Song* (Yeah, 1971); Gordon Parks, *Shaft* (Metro-Goldwyn-Mayer, 1971).

27 Roger Ebert, "Farewell Uncle Tom," November 14, 1972, http://www.rogerebert.com/reviews/farewell-uncle-tom-1972, accessed June 9, 2017.

28 William Styron, *The Confessions of Nat Turner* (New York: Random House, 1965).

29 "Lawn Jockeys," *Jim Crow Museum of Racist Memorabilia*, July 2008, http://www.ferris.edu/htmls/news/jimcrow/question/july08/index.htm, accessed June 8, 2017.

30 Anna Ditkoff, "Jockeying for Respect: With His New Children's Book, Waymon LeFall Wants to Change the Way People Think about Lawn Jockeys," *City Paper*, May 31, 2008.

31 "Frequently Asked Questions: Lawn Jockeys," http://www.horseinfo.com/info/misc/jockeyinfo.html, accessed June 8, 2017.

32 Kenneth W. Goings, *Mammy and Uncle Mose: Black Collectibles and American Stereotyping* (Bloomington: Indiana University Press, 1994).

33 James Robert Saunders and Monica Renae Saunders, *Black Winning Jockeys in the Kentucky Derby* (Jefferson, NC: McFarland, 2003), 6.

34 "Uncle Thomas: Lawn Jockey for the Far Right," *Emerge* (November, 1996).

35 "Empty Chair 'Lynchings': Anti-Obama Protests Gone Too Far?" *NBC News*, September 20, 2012, http://usnews.nbcnews.com/_news/2012/09/20/13989510-empty-chair-lynchings-anti-obama-protests-gone-too-far?lite, accessed June 9, 2017.

CHAPTER TWO

1 H.L. Mencken, "The Aframerican: New Style," review of *The New Negro*, by Alain Locke, *American Mercury* 31 (February 1926): 255.

2 Michael Apted, *Gorillas in the Mist* (Universal Pictures, 1988).

3 Thomas Jefferson and Richard Holland, *The Writings of Thomas Jefferson*, vols. 1–2 (Thomas Jefferson Memorial Association of the United States, 1905), 193.

4 Gustav Jahoda, *Images of Savages: Ancient Roots of Modern Prejudice in Western Culture* (New York: Routledge, 1999), 82.

5 John H. Van Evrie, *Negroes and Negro "Slavery": The First an Inferior Race; the Latter Its Normal Condition* (New York: Van Evrie, Horton & Co., 1861).

6 Jahoda, *Images of Savages*, 83.

7 Ibid., 83.

8 Benjamin H. Isaac, *The Invention of Racism in Classical Antiquity* (Princeton: Princeton University Press, 2004), 150.

9 "Ethnology," *Sydney Morning Herald* (Sydney, Australia), January 14, 1851.

10 Adam Dewbury, *The American School and Scientific Racism in Early American Anthropology.* vol. 3, in *Histories of Anthropology Annual*, eds. Regna Darnell and Frederic W. Gleach (Lincoln: University of Nebraska Press, 2007), 142.

11 Eric Sakyi Nketiah, *Distance Forum A Multidisciplinary Book of Scholarly Articles*, vol. 1 (Bloomington, IN: AuthorHouse, 2011), 21.

12 Ariel, *The Negro: What Is His Ethnological Status?* (Cincinnati: Published for the Proprietor, 1867), 30, https://archive.org/details/negrowhatishiset00payn, accessed June 8, 2017.

13   Paul Harvey, *Freedom's Coming: Religious Culture and the Shaping of the South from the Civil War through the Civil Rights Era* (Chapel Hill: University of North Carolina Press, 2005), 43.

14   S. Plous and Tyrone Williams, "Racial Stereotypes from the Days of American Slavery: A Continuing Legacy," *Journal of Applied Social Psychology* 25 (1995): 795–817.

15   "Police Court," *Louisville Daily Courier*, October 25, 1856.

16   *Pee Dee Herald* (Wadesboro, NC), September 6, 1876.

17   "Man Caught Here May Be 'Masked Burglar,'" *New York Times*, May 13, 1904, 3.

18   "Andrew Jackson Executed Friday," *Lincoln County News* (Lincolnton, NC), November 8, 1920.

19   "Jail Gorilla Man," *Pittsburgh Press*, March 6, 1927, 1.

20   "Negro 'Ape Man' Slayer of Women Held in New York," *Lincoln Star* (Lincoln, NE), July 26, 1935, 2.

21   Claire Jean Kim, *Dangerous Crossings: Race, Species, and Nature in a Multicultural Age* (Cambridge: Cambridge University Press, 2015).

22   Colin Kidd, *The Forging of Races: Race and Scripture in the Protestant Atlantic World, 1600–2000* (Cambridge: Cambridge University Press, 2006), 150; George M. Fredrickson, *The Black Image in the White Mind: The Debate on Afro-American Character and Destiny, 1817–1914* (New York: Harper & Row. 1971), 277.

23   Kenneth Smith, *True Origin of Man* (iUniverse.com, 2013).

24   To read the complaint, see https://ecf.wvnd.uscourts.gov/cgi-bin/show_public_doc?2011cv0048-35, accessed September 14, 2015, available via Archive.org at https://web.archive.org/web/20161216203158/https://ecf.wvnd.uscourts.gov/cgi-bin/show_public_doc?2011cv0048-35.

25   Phillips V. Bradford and Harvey Blume, *Ota Benga: The Pygmy in the Zoo* (New York: St. Martin's Press, 1992), 185.

26   In a 1903 memoir about pygmies, Verner asked, "Are they men, or the highest of apes?"; Jeannette E. Jones and Patrick B. Sharp, *Darwin in Atlantic Cultures: Evolutionary Visions of Race, Gender, and Sexuality* (New York: Routledge, 2010), 139.

27   Madison Grant, *The Passing of the Great Race; or, The Racial Basis of European History* (New York: Charles Scribner's Sons, 1916).

28   Jonathan P. Spiro, *Defending the Master Race: Conservation, Eugenics, and the Legacy of Madison Grant* (Burlington: University of Vermont Press, 2009), 48.

29   Jones and Sharp, *Darwin in Atlantic Cultures*, 138.

30   Columbus Salley, *The Black 100: A Ranking of the Most Influential African-Americans, Past and Present* (New York: Citadel Press, 1999), 82.

31   Marcus Garvey and Amy J. Garvey, *The Philosophy and Opinions of Marcus Garvey; or, Africa for the Africans,* vol. 1. (Dover, MA: Majority Press, 1986), 310.

32   Christopher R. Reed, *The Chicago NAACP and the Rise of Black Professional Leadership, 1910–1966* (Bloomington: Indiana University Press, 1997), 219.

33   William Nack, *My Turf: Horses, Boxers, Blood Money, and the Sporting Life* (Cambridge, MA: Da Capo Press, 2004), 117.

34   Thomas Hauser, *Muhammad Ali: His Life and Times* (New York: Simon & Schuster, 2006), 325.

35   John Wiebusch, "Mail Fails to Slow Rod Carew," *Courier-Journal* (Louisville, KY), May 24, 1970.

36   Dikembe Mutombo, another Georgetown player, was also slurred as a gorilla and an ape.

37   Jennifer H. Lansbury, *A Spectacular Leap: Black Women Athletes in Twentieth-Century America* (Fayetteville: University of Arkansas Press, 2014), 222.

38   Karen Crouse, "Struggle for Serena," *Palm Beach Post*, August 28, 2001.

39   Colin Marshall, "Veith Apologizes for Williams 'Ape' Comments," *NZ Herald*, September 5, 2005, http://www.nzherald.co.nz/nz/news/article.cfm?c_id=1&objectid=10344087, accessed March 8, 2016, inactive June 9, 2017.

40 Tiffany Drayton, "On Serena Williams & the Racism Experienced by Black Women Athletes," *Frisky*, September 9, 2014, http://www.thefrisky.com/2014-09-09/on-serena-williams-the-racism-experienced-by-black-women-athletes/, accessed June 9, 2017.

41 Joe Lapointe, "Cosell 'Monkey' Remark Draws Complaints," *Detroit Free Press*, September 15, 1983, 1D.

42 Bill Collison, "Palmer Wants PGA to Park Carts," *Detroit Free Press*, September 15, 1983, 2D.

43 Lauren J. Nile, *Race: My Story and Humanity's Bottom Line* (Bloomington, IN: iUniverse, 2014).

44 Merian C. Cooper (uncredited) and Ernest B. Schoedsack (uncredited), *King Kong* (RKO Radio Pictures, 1933).

45 Jeff Pearlman, "Rocker Spews Hate in This Week's SI," *Sports Illustrated,* December 23, 1999, https://web.archive.org/web/20000817193712/http://sportsillustrated.cnn.com/features/cover/news/1999/12/22/rocker/, accessed June 9, 2017.

46 Cecil Harris, *Breaking the Ice: The Black Experience in Professional Hockey* (Toronto: Insomniac Press, 2003), 60.

47 "Worrell Can't Believe His Luck at being in NHL," *Palm Beach Post*, December 15, 1998.

48 John MacKinnon, "Racism in Hockey Happens Too Often," *National Post*, September 24, 2011, http://news.nationalpost.com/sports/nhl/racism-in-hockey-all-too-often, accessed June 9, 2017.

49 David Boroff, "Red Wings Fan Who Tosses Banana at Black NHL Player Wayne Simmonds Is Hit with $200 Fine," *Daily News*, January 10, 2012, http://www.nydailynews.com/sports/hockey/red-wings-fan-tossed-banana-black-nhl-player-wayne-simmonds-hit-200-fine-article-1.1003712, accessed June 9, 2017.

50 Errin Haines, "Obama/Curious George T-shirt Draws Protests," *Washington Post*, May 15, 2008, http://www.washingtonpost.com/wp-dyn/content/article/2008/05/14/AR2008051403613.html, accessed June 9, 2017.

51 "Obama Sock Monkey," *Herald and Review* (Decatur, IL), June 15, 2008, 3.

52 Morrill Majority, *More Racism at a Palin Rally in PA*, YouTube, October 11, 2008, https://www.youtube.com/watch?v=bKUovpF9LWU, accessed June 9, 2017.

53 Jaime Fuller, "Ferguson Releases Copies of Racist Emails," *New York Magazine*, April 3, 2015, http://nymag.com/daily/intelligencer/2015/04/ferguson-departments-emails-shocking.html, accessed June 9, 2017.

54 Dan Amira, "GOP Official Who E-mailed an Obama Monkey Photo Won't Resign," *New York Magazine*, April 20, 2011, http://nymag.com/daily/intelligencer/2011/04/gop_official_wont_resign_over.html#, accessed June 9, 2017.

55 "Conservatives Call Out Ann Coulter over Obama 'Monkey' Comment," *Reddingnewsreview,* September 10, 2013, http://www.reddingnewsreview.com/newspages/2013newspages/conservatives_call_out_ann_coult_13_1000060.htm, accessed June 9, 2017.

56 National Center for Public Policy Research, "Press Release: Conservatives Call Out Ann Coulter," September 10, 2013, http://www.nationalcenter.org/PR-Coulter_091013.html, accessed June 9, 2017.

57 Evan Goldberg and Seth Rogen, *The Interview* (Columbia Pictures, 2014).

58 Aamer Madhani, "N. Korea Has Another Internet Outage," *Jackson Sun* (Jackson, MS), December 28, 2014, A9.

59 Sophia Tesfaye, "'Gorilla Face Michelle' Obama Only Attractive to 'Monkey Man Barack': WA Mayor Refuses to Resign after Racist Facebook Rant," *Salon,* July 17, 2015, http://www.salon.com/2015/07/17/gorilla_face_michelle_obama_only_attractive_to_monkey_man_barack_wa_mayor_refuses_to_resign_after_racist_facebook_rant/, accessed June 9, 2017.

60 David McCormack, "Univision Sacks Emmy-Winning Host after He Says Michelle Obama 'Looks Like She's Part of the Cast of Planet of the Apes,'" *Daily Mail,* March 12, 2015, http://www.dailymail.co.uk/news/article-2992012/Univision-sacks-Emmy-

winning-host-says-Michelle-Obama-looks-like-s-cast-Planet-Apes.html, accessed June 9, 2017.

61   Philip Sherwell, "New York Post Apologises over 'Racist' Barack Obama Cartoon," *Telegraph,* February 20, 2009, http://www.telegraph.co.uk/news/worldnews/barackobama/4724866/New-York-Post-apologises-over-racist-Barack-Obama-cartoon.html, accessed June 9, 2017.

62   Sam Stein, "New York Post Chimp Cartoon Compares Stimulus Author to Dead Primate," *Huffington Post*, March 21, 2009, http://www.huffingtonpost.com/2009/02/18/new-york-post-chimp-carto_n_167841.html, accessed June 9, 2017.

63   "NYU Settles EEOC Race and National Origin Harassment and Retaliation Lawsuit," *U.S. Equal Employment Opportunity Commission*, August 16, 2011, https://www.eeoc.gov/eeoc/newsroom/release/8-16-11a.cfm, accessed June 9, 2017.

64   Latifa Muhammad, "ESPN Columnist Jemele Hill Called a 'Thick-Lipped Gorilla' in Racist (Handwritten) Letter," *HipHopWired*, January 4, 2013, http://hiphopwired.com/206169/espn-columnist-jemele-hill-called-a-thick-lipped-gorilla-in-racist-hand-written-letter-photo/, accessed June 9, 2017.

65   Katy Reckdahl, "Tulane Police Department Administrator Refers to African-American Lieutenant as 'Gorilla,'" *Advocate*, July 15, 2015, http://theadvocate.com/news/neworleans/neworleansnews/12922104-65/source-tulane-police-department-administrator, accessed June 9, 2017.

66   The research team included Jennifer Eberhardt, associate professor of psychology at Stanford University, and Matthew C. Jackson and Melissa J. Williams, graduate students at Pennsylvania State University and University of California Berkeley.

67   This paragraph draws heavily from the research summation found at Phys.org, see: "Subconscious Mental Connection between Blacks, Apes May Reinforce Subtle Discrimination," *Medical Xpress,* March 5, 2008, https://medicalxpress.com/news/2008-03-subconscious-mental-blacks-apes-subtle.html, accessed June 9, 2017.

68   Martin Luther King Jr., *Why We Can't Wait* (Boston: Beacon Press, 2011).

CHAPTER THREE

1   Carl Sandburg, *Cornhuskers* (New York: H. Holt and Company, 1918).

2   Verne O. Graham, *The Great Turkey-Stealing Case of Watermelon County* (Chicago: Beckley-Cardy Co., 1917).

3   Ibid., 19.

4   Gary Lucier and Biing-Hwan Lin, "Factors Affecting Watermelon Consumption in the United States," *Vegetables and Specialties: Situation and Outlook,* November 2001, available at http://fliphtml5.com/ofmd/vfrh, accessed June 9, 2017. This study uses the most recent data available, from the U.S. Department of Agriculture, 1994–1996.

5   Watermelon seeds that date from the eighth century or earlier were recovered in archaeological excavations from the Inyanga ruins in Africa. See T. Shaw, "Early Crops in Africa: A Review of the Evidence," in *Origins of African Plant Domestication*, eds. Jack R. Harlan, Jan M.J. De Wet, and Ann B.L. Stemler (Chicago: Aldine Publishing Company, 1976), 107–53.

6   Leonard W. Blake, "Early Acceptance of Watermelon by Indians of the Upper States," *Journal of Ethnobiology* 1, no. 2 (1981): 193–99.

7   Volney H. Jones, "Notes on Some Organic Remains from Abó Mission," in *The Mission of San Gregorio de Abó: A Report on the Excavation and Repair of a Seventeenth-Century New Mexico Mission*, ed. Joseph H. Toulouse (Albuquerque: University of New Mexico Press, 1949), Appendix 2, 29–32.

8   Herbert C. Covey and Dwight Eisnach, *What the Slaves Ate: Recollections of African American Foods and Foodways from the Slave Narrative* (Santa Barbara: Greenwood Press/ABC-CLIO, 2009), 178.

9   William Black, "How Watermelons Became a Racist Trope," *Atlantic*, December 8, 2014, https://www.theatlantic.com/national/archive/2014/12/how-watermelons-became-a-racist-trope/383529/, accessed June 9, 2017.

10   Keith Woods, "Talking Race over a Slice of Watermelon," *Poynter*, July 28, 2003, http://www.poynter.org/2003/talking-race-over-a-slice-of-watermelon/14065/, accessed June 9, 2017.

11   *True Democrat* (Wilkes-Barre, PA), August 3, 1853.

12   Black, "How Watermelons Became a Racist Trope."

13   Ibid.

14   *Galveston Daily News* (Galveston, TX), October 12, 1895.

15   The zenith of the professional minstrel shows was between 1850 and 1870. Amateur minstrel shows lasted until the 1950s. These latter shows were often fundraisers by groups like Rotary clubs and churches.

16   Carl F. Wittke, *Tambo and Bones: A History of the American Minstrel Stage* (New York: Greenwood Press, 1968), 10.

17   This is the way Graupner introduced himself. The word "gay" was used to mean "happy."

18   Wittke, *Tambo and Bones*, 20.

19   Ibid., 24. Some observers claim that the black man's name was Jim Crow. "Negro Minstrelsy," *Allentown Leader* (Allentown, PA), January 16, 1901, 7.

20   Wittke, *Tambo and Bones,* 34.

21   *Ogden Standard-Examiner* (Ogden, UT), July 1, 1947.

22   Wittke, *Tambo and Bones*, 8–9.

23   John Strausbaugh, *Black Like You: Blackface, Whiteface, Insult & Imitation in American Popular Culture* (New York: Jeremy P. Tarcher/Penguin, 2006), 118.

24   Frederick Douglass, "The Hutchinson Family—Hunkerism," *North Star*, October 27, 1848.

25   James M. Dorman, "Shaping the Popular Image of Post-Reconstruction American Blacks: The 'Coon Song' Phenomenon of the Gilded Age," *American Quarterly* 40 (1988): 455.

26   Seymour Stark, *Men in Blackface: True Stories of the Minstrel Show* (Bloomington, IN: Xlibris, 2000).

27   Ibid.

28   This is the description used in the Mutoscope film catalog, and it is also the description used today on the IMBD website, see http://www.imdb.com/title/tt0000135/, accessed June 10, 2017.

29   James H. White, *The Watermelon Contest* (Edison Manufacturing Company, 1896); James H. White, *Watermelon Contest* (Edison Manufacturing Company, 1900); William K. L. Dickson, *A Watermelon Feast* (American Mutoscope Company, 1896); *Eating Watermelon for a Prize* (S. Lubin, 1903); *Who Said Watermelon* (Selig Polyscope Company, 1903).

30   Wallace McCutcheon and Edwin S. Porter, *The Watermelon Patch* (Edison Manufacturing Company, 1905).

31   Stephen Bourne, *Butterfly McQueen Remembered* (Lanham, MD: Scarecrow Press, 2008), 99.

32   Dave Fleischer, *Making Stars* (Fleischer Studios, 1935).

33   Walter Lantz (uncredited), *Scrub Me Mama with a Boogie Beat* (Universal Pictures, 1941).

34   Tex Avery, *Half-Pint Pygmy* (Metro-Goldwyn-Mayer, 1948).

35   Paul Feig, *The Heat* (Twentieth Century Fox Film Corporation, 2013).

36   "Gregory Travels 4,000 Miles Daily for Rights Protests," *Jet* 28, no. 14 (July 15, 1965). 62.

37   Doris Witt, *Black Hunger: Food and the Politics of U.S. Identity* (New York: Oxford University Press, 1999).

38   Melvin Van Peebles, *Watermelon Man* (Columbia Pictures, 1970).

39   Cheryl Dunye, *The Watermelon Woman* (Dancing Girl, 1996).

40   Julia Duin, "Black Lesbian Film Likely to Rekindle Arts-Funding Furor," *Washington Times*, June 14, 1996.

41   Brian Cronin, "The Abandoned An' Forsaked—Whitewashing Whitewash Jones," *CBR,* March 30, 2013, http://www.cbr.com/the-abandoned-an-forsaked-whitewashing-whitewash-jones/, accessed June 10, 2017.

42   On October 16, 1867, the Pennsylvania State Convention of Baseball in Harrisburg denied admission to the "colored" Pythian Baseball Club. This represented the formal start of banning black players.

43   Charles A. Gallagher and Cameron D. Lippard, *Race and Racism in the United States: An Encyclopedia of the American Mosaic* (Santa Barbara: Greenwood, 2014), 595.

44   Ashley Killough, "Boston Herald Apologizes for Obama Cartoon after Backlash," *CNN,* October 1, 2014, http://www.cnn.com/2014/10/01/politics/boston-herald-cartoon/, accessed June 10, 2017..

45   Casey Gane-McCalla, "Man Fired for Calling Watermelon 'Obama Fruit,'" *Newsone,* July 10, 2010, http://newsone.com/605595/man-fired-for-calling-watermelon-obama-fruit/, accessed June 10, 2017.

46   Tony Norman, "Paging AG Holder: Can We Talk?" *Pittsburgh Post-Gazette*, February 27, 2009, 2.

47   Jason Howerton, "Racist? Kentucky Man Under Fire for Effigy of Obama Eating Watermelon," *Blaze,* December 27, 2012, http://www.theblaze.com/stories/2012/12/27/racist-kentucky-man-under-fire-for-effigy-of-obama-eating-watermelon/, accessed June 10, 2017.

48   *Columbia Herald* (Columbia, TN), March 11, 1870.

49   At the 1993 Friars Club roast of Whoopi Goldberg, Ted Danson, her former boyfriend, gave a nigger-laced performance in blackface in front of three thousand people. At one point he ate a watermelon.

50   Reddit, /r/Jokes subreddit, https://www.reddit.com/r/Jokes/comments/5zuojx/a_redneck_is_driving_down_the_road_one_day/, accessed June 10, 2017.

51   http://www.tightrope.cc/jokes4.htm, accessed June 10, 2017.

52   David Yamane, *Student Movements for Multiculturalism: Challenging the Curricular Color Line in Higher Education* (Baltimore: Johns Hopkins University Press, 2002), 30.

53   Craig L. Torbenson and Gregory Parks, *Brothers and Sisters: Diversity in College Fraternities and Sororities* (Madison, NJ: Fairleigh Dickinson University Press, 2009).

54   Black, "How Watermelons Became a Racist Trope."

55   Jonathan Rieder, *The Word of the Lord Is Upon Me: The Righteous Performance of Martin Luther King, Jr.* (Cambridge: Harvard University Press, 2008), 24.

56   Abdul Salaam, *Is the White Man Still the Devil?* (Victoria, BC: FriesenPress, 2013), 235.

57   James Baldwin, Fred L. Standley, and Louis H. Pratt, *Conversations with James Baldwin* (Jackson: University of Mississippi Press, 1989), 4.

CHAPTER FOUR

1   Charles Waddell Chesnutt, *Tales of Conjure and the Color Line: 10 Stories* (Mineola, NY: Dover Books, 2012), 115.

2   Thomas Gabor, *Everybody Does It! Crime by the Public* (Toronto: University of Toronto Press, 1994), 37.

3   Marlon Riggs, "Ethnic Notions Transcript," *California Newsreel* (1987), http://www.newsreel.org/transcripts/ethnicno.htm, accessed June 10, 2017.

4   The first explicitly coon-themed song was "The Dandy Coon's Parade" by J.P. Skelley, published in 1880.

5   James M. Dorman, "Shaping the Popular Image of Post-Reconstruction American Blacks: The 'Coon Song' Phenomenon of the Gilded Age," *American Quarterly* 40 (1988): 455.

6   C. Vann Woodward, *The Strange Career of Jim Crow* (New York: Oxford University Press, 1974).

7   Seymour Stark, *Men in Blackface: True Stories of the Minstrel Show* (Xlibris Corp., 2000).

8   "The Coon's Trade Mark, Baylor University: Frances G. Spencer Collection of American Popular Sheet Music, http://digitalcollections.baylor.edu/cdm/ref/collection/fa-spnc/id/5635, accessed June 13, 2017.

9   "Coon Dat Carried De Razor," Duke University Libraries: Digital Collections, http://library.duke.edu/digitalcollections/songsheets_bsvg200731/, accessed June 14, 2017.

10   "'Coon' Songs Denounced by a Negro Education," *Elwood Daily* (Elwood, IN), January 10, 1905, 2.

11   Azizi Powell, ed., "Two Songs & Comments about the Name 'Leroy,'" *pancocojams*, May 2, 2014, http://pancocojams.blogspot.ca/2014/05/jimmy-castor-bunch-hey-leroy-your-mama.html, accessed June 14, 2017.

12   "Negro Attacks Chinese Cook with a Razor; Small Sized Riot Occurs in the Kitchen of the Hotel Hollywood, Special to *The Herald*," *Los Angeles Herald*, August, 1905.

13   "Negro Slashed with Razor—Wounds Serious," *High Point Enterprise* (High Point, NC), February 9, 1914, 1.

14   Paul Kirchner, "Fighting with the Straight Razor," *bowieknifefightsfighters*, February 26, 2011, http://bowieknifefightsfighters.blogspot.com/2011/02/razor-black-mans-bowie-knife.html, accessed June 10, 2017.

15   "Mrs. Lehman Loeb Cut by Negro Thief," Daily Arkansas Gazette (Little Rock, Arkansas), October 1, 1905, 1.

16   "Negro Burglar Attacks White Man with Razor," *Eugene Guard* (Eugene, OR), October 24, 1922, 7.

17   C.H. Smith, "Have Negroes Too Much Liberty?" *Forum* 16 (1893): 181.

18   It is true that whites suspected of raping women and children were sometimes hanged—and sometimes referred to as white brutes in newspapers. However, their hangings were not typically accompanied by castration, burnings, and other forms of torture.

19   George M. Fredrickson, *The Black Image in the White Mind: The Debate on Afro-American Character and Destiny, 1817–1914* (Middletown, CT: Wesleyan University Press, 1987), 273.

20   John D'Emilio and Estelle B. Freedman, *Intimate Matters: A History of Sexuality in America* (New York: Harper & Row, 1988), 217.

21   "Letters from the People," *Monroe News-Star* (Monroe, LA), June 2, 1919, 14.

22   D'Emilio and Freedman, *Intimate Matters,* 105.

23   Ron Wolfe and Guy Lancaster, *Arkansas in Ink: Gunslingers, Ghosts, and Other Graphic Tales* (Little Rock: Butler Center Books, 2014), 72.

24   Ibid.

25   "At the Stake: Ed Coy, a Negro, Burned to Death by a Band of Avengers," *Atchison Daily Champion* (Atchison, KS), February 21, 1892.

26   Carole Merritt, *Something So Horrible: The Springfield Race Riot of 1908* (Springfield, IL: Abraham Lincoln Presidential Library Foundation, 2008), 11–12.

27   Quentin Tarantino, *Django Unchained* (Weinstein Company, 2012).

28   Hunter Oatman-Stanford, "Straight Razors and Social Justice: The Empowering Evolution of Black Barbershops," *Collectors Weekly*, May 30, 2014, http://www.collectorsweekly.com/articles/the-empowering-evolution-of-black-barbershops/, accessed June 10, 2017.

29   Thomas R. Eddlem, "The Racist Origin of America's Gun Control Laws," *New American*, September 9, 2014, https://www.thenewamerican.com/usnews/politics/item/19083-the-racist-origin-of-america-s-gun-control-laws, accessed June 10, 2017.

30   Ibid.

31   "Timeline: 'Laws Designed to Disarm Slaves, Freedmen, and African-Americans,'" *GachiYellow*, May 6, 2015, https://gachiyellow.wordpress.com/2015/05/06/timeline-laws-designed-to-disarm-slaves-freedmen-and-african-americans/, accessed June 10, 2017.

32   Kirchner, "Fighting with the Straight Razor."

33   Leroy G. Schultz, "Why the Negro Carries Weapons," *Journal of Criminal Law and Criminology* 53 (1962): 476.

34   Ibid., 482.

35   *Pokes and Jabbs* (Wizard Film Company, 1915).

36   Anthony Balducci, "The Black Brute," *Anthony Balducci's Journal*, April 2, 2015, http://anthonybalducci.blogspot.com/2015/04/the-black-brute.html, accessed June 13, 2017

37   William Hanna and Joseph Barbera, *The Lonesome Mouse* (Metro-Goldwyn-Meyer, 1943); George Pal, *Puppetoons*.

38   Karl F. Cohen, *Forbidden Animation: Censored Cartoons and Blacklisted Animators in America* (Jefferson, NC: McFarland, 2004), 58.

39   Louis King (as Luis King), *Charlie Chan in Egypt* (Fox Film Corporation, 1935); Elia Kazan and John Ford (uncredited), *Pinky* (Twentieth Century Fox Film Corporation, 1949).

40   Viktor Pickard, *America's Battle for Media Democracy: The Triumph of Corporate Libertarianism and the Future of Media Reform,* (Cambridge: Cambridge University Press, 2014), 20.

41   Sidney J. Furie, *Lady Sings the Blues* (Jobete Productions, 1972); Arthur Marks, *J.D.'s Revenge* (American International Pictures, 1976); John Badham, *The Bingo Long Traveling All-Stars & Motor Kings* (Motown Productions, 1976); Steven Spielberg, *The Color Purple* (Amblin Entertainment, 1985); Eddie Murphy, *Harlem Nights* (Eddie Murphy Productions, 1989); Bill Duke, *Hoodlum* (United Artists Pictures, 1997).

42   Larry Cohen, *Black Caesar* (American International Pictures, 1973); Jack Hill, *Coffy* (American International Pictures, 1973).

43   Alan Parker, *Angel Heart* (Carolco International N.V., 1987); Alan Parker, *Mississippi Burning* (Orion Pictures, 1988); Jamaa Fanaka (as Jamaa Fanaka), *Welcome Home Brother Charles* aka *Jamaa Fanaka's Soul Vengeance* (Bob-Bea Productions, 1975).

44   Norman Thomas et al., *The World Tomorrow* (World Tomorrow, Inc., 1921), 74.

45   Neil Lanctot, *Negro League Baseball: The Rise and Ruin of a Black Institution* (Philadelphia: University of Pennsylvania Press, 2008), 108.

46   Michelle Shocked and Bart Bull, "L.A. Riots: Cartoons vs. Reality: Gangster Rappers Preserve White Myths," *Billboard*, June 20, 1992, 6.

47   Roxanne Shanté, "Straight Razor," *Genius*, https://genius.com/7913276, accessed June 14, 2017.

48   Cancerslug, "Straight Razor Rape," *LyricsFreak*, http://www.lyricsfreak.com/c/cancerslug/straight+razor+rape_20591487.html, accessed June 14, 2017.

49   "Cash Disguised as Negro," *Harrisburg Daily Independent* (Harrisburg, PA), March 24, 1885, 1.

50   "Christmas Carol," *Evening Bulletin* (Maysville, KY), December 28, 1894, 1.

51   "Disguised as a Negro," *Portsmouth Herald* (Portsmouth, NH), April 24, 1902, 1.

52   "Killed by Robbers," *Hamilton Daily Republican* (Hamilton, OH), August 25, 1894, 1.

53   "Clever Robbers Seek Disguise," *Los Angeles Herald*, January 12. 1906, 6.

54   "Manhunt for Gardner Continues: Mail Bandit Leaves Posse No Clew," *Oakland Tribune*, September 6, 1921, 1.

55   "Farmer Walks into Bank and Shoots Teller: Tyrone Man, Disguised as Negro, Fires Bullet into Curwensville Employee," *Pittsburgh Daily Post*, June 10, 1916, 1.

56   "Real Jolly Hold-Up Men," *Barton County Democrat* (Great Bend, KS), October 27, 1915, 1.

57   *Cayton's Weekly* (Seattle, WA) January 3, 1920, 2.

58   "Two Women Robbed in Bold Highway Holdup Near Odd: Warrant Sworn Out for Man Disguised as Negro," *Raleigh Register,* August 4, 1935, 1.

59   "Disguised as Negro Woman," *Tennessean* (Nashville, TN), May 2, 1909, 1.

60   "Beat Off Her Assailant: Young Woman in Desperate Struggle at Canton, Georgia," *Washington Post*, February 7, 1906, 1.

61 "Black Face Disguise for Criminals," *St. Louis Post-Dispatch*, May 4, 1927, 24.

62 "Brands Affinity as Dayton Slayer: Woman Says Intimate Admitted Brutal Murder That Stirred Town to Frenzy," *Chicago Daily Tribune*, April 26, 1909, 5.

63 "Injustice," *Pittsburgh Courier*, October 8, 1927, 20.

64 "Views and Reviews," *New York Age*, March 17, 1923, 4.

65 "The White Robber Who Carried Out Six Raids Disguised as a Black Man (and Very Nearly Got Away with It)," *Daily Mail*, December 11, 2000.

CHAPTER FIVE

1 From the film *Mandingo* (Paramount Pictures, 1975).

2 Jack Shuler, "The Ominous Symbolism of the Noose," *Los Angeles Times*, October 27, 2014, http://www.latimes.com/opinion/op-ed/la-oe-shuler-noose-hate-crimes-20141028-story.html, accessed June 10, 2017.

3 Equal Justice Initiative, *Lynching in America: Confronting the Legacy of Racial Terror* (Montgomery, AL: Equal Justice Initiative, 2015), 40.

4 Walter White asserted that "lynching is much more an expression of Southern fear of Negro progress than Negro crime." See Walter White, *Rope and Faggot: A Biography of Judge Lynch* (Notre Dame, IN: University of Notre Dame Press, 2002), 11.

5 Leon F. Litwack, *Been in the Storm So Long: The Aftermath of Slavery* (New York: Knopf, 1979), 276–77.

6 Equal Justice Initiative, *Lynching in America*, 28.

7 Amy L. Wood, *Lynching and Spectacle: Witnessing Racial Violence in America, 1890–1940* (Chapel Hill: University of North Carolina Press, 2011), 7.

8 David B. Parker, "Rebecca Latimer Felton (1835–1930)," *New Georgia Encyclopedia*, May 14, 2003, http://www.georgiaencyclopedia.org/articles/history-archaeology/rebecca-latimer-felton-1835-1930, accessed June 11, 2017.

9 "Human Torch," *El Paso Herald* (El Paso, TX), August 21, 1901, 1.

10 Robert W. Thurston, *Lynching: American Mob Murder in Global Perspective* (Burlington, VT: Ashgate, 2011), 108.

11 "Lynched in Dorchester," *Charleston, South Carolina News and Courier,* January 16, 1904.

12 Equal Justice Initiative, *Lynching in America*, 31.

13 Maria De Longoria, "'Stranger Fruit': The Lynching of Black Women: The Cases of Rosa Jefferson and Marie Scott" (PhD dissertation, University of Mississippi-Columbia, 2006), 1, 77, 142, https://mospace.umsystem.edu/xmlui/bitstream/handle/10355/4447/research.pdf?sequence=3&isAllowed=y, accessed June 11, 2017.

14 Philip Dray, *At the Hands of Persons Unknown: The Lynching of Black America* (New York: Random House, 2002), 81–82.

15 Ibid. Dray's book is a well-written social history of lynching.

16 Another narrative is that the word "picnic" is derived from the term "pick-a-nig," a festive gathering for slave traders and their families—after a day of successful slave trading. There is no evidence to support this claim.

17 The French *piquer* may have referred to a leisurely style of eating ("pick at your food") or it may simply have meant "pick" (pic). The nique was probably a silly rhyming compound (as in English words like hoity-toity) but may have referred to an obsolete word meaning "a trifle."

18 The information in this paragraph was drawn from several sources. See Frederick C. Mish, ed., *Merriam-Webster's Collegiate Dictionary*, 11th ed. (Springfield, MA: Merriam-Webster, 2003); Stuart B. Flexner, ed., *The Random House Dictionary of the English Language* (New York: Random House, 1963); Philip B. Gove, ed., *Webster's Third New International Dictionary* (Springfield, MA: Merriam-Webster, 1993).

19 Stephan Thernstrom and Abigail M. Thernstrom, *America in Black and White: One Nation, Indivisible* (New York: Simon & Schuster, 1997).

20 Dray, *At the Hands of Persons Unknown*, 81.

21 Ibid., 77–78.

22 McKay Jenkins, *The South in Black and White: Race, Sex, and Literature in the 1940s* (Chapel Hill: University of North Carolina Press, 1999), 49.

23 Ben Montgomery, "Spectacle: The Lynching of Claude Neal," *Tampa Bay Times*, October 20, 2011, http://www.tampabay.com/features/humaninterest/spectacle-the-lynching-of-claude-neal/1197360, accessed June 13, 2017.

24 Neil R. McMillen, *Dark Journey: Black Mississippians in the Age of Jim Crow* (Urbana: University of Illinois Press, 1990), 98.

25 Dominic J. Capeci, *The Lynching of Cleo Wright* (Lexington: University Press of Kentucky, 1998), 181.

26 "An Innocent Negro Lynched," *Leavenworth Times* (Leavenworth, KS), August 26, 1891, 1.

27 "An Innocent Negro Lynched," *Salt Lake Tribune*, November 22, 1895, 1.

28 "Innocent Negro Lynched for Murder," *Reno Gazette-Journal*, December 21, 1900, 4.

29 "Innocent Negro Lynched," *Arizona Republic* (Phoenix, AZ), August 1, 1903, 6.

30 "Innocent Negro Lynched," *Leavenworth Post* (Leavenworth, KS), September 7, 1912, 5.

31 "Innocent Negro Lynched by Mob in Mississippi," *Concord Times* (Concord, NC), January 25, 1915, 1.

32 "What Louisiana Worships," *Chicago Defender*, November 23, 1933, p. 4.

33 Ibid., 4.

34 "The Lynching of Fred Moore and the Escape of Norman Thibodaux," Civil Rights and Restorative Justice Project, http://nuweb9.nev.edu, accessed September 19, 2017.

35 A third man, James Cameron, barely escaped being lynched and later founded the Black Holocaust Museum in Milwaukee, Wisconsin.

36 "The Lynching of Thomas Shipp and Abram Smith, 1930," *Rare Historical Photos,* March 16, 2014, http://rarehistoricalphotos.com/lynching-thomas-shipp-abram-smith-1930/, accessed June 13, 2017.

37 Meg Greene, *Billie Holiday: A Biography* (Westport, CT: Greenwood Publishing Group, 2007), 60.

38 Mari Crabtree, "Elegy and Effigy," *Appendix*, May 22, 2014, http://theappendix.net/issues/2014/4/elegy-and-effigy, accessed June 11, 2017.

39 Ibid.

40 "Ole Miss Marks Integration Anniversary," *Washington Post*, October 1, 2006, http://www.washingtonpost.com/wp-dyn/content/article/2006/10/01/AR2006100100804.html, accessed June 11, 2017.

41 Crabtree, "Elegy and Effigy."

42 "Negro Pupils' Presence Evokes Demonstration," *News-Review* (Roseburg, OR), March 18, 1947, 1.

43 "Texas Police Quiet Mob at Negro's Home," *Chicago Tribune*, September 3, 1956, 2, http://archives.chicagotribune.com/1956/09/03/page/2/article/texas-police-quiet-mob-at-negros-home, accessed June 11, 2017.

44 Equal Justice Initiative, "Resistance to School De-segregation," http://eji.org/history-racial-injustice resistance-to-school-desegregation, accessed June 11, 2017.

45 "Angry Whites Revolt; Police Use Tear Gas," *Anniston Star* (Anniston, AL), September 14, 1967, 1.

46 Jeremy Pelofsky, "Bush Calls Nooses and Lynch Threats Deeply Offensive," *Reuters*, February 12, 2008, http://www.reuters.com/article/us-bush-race-idUSN1227217020080212, accessed June 11, 2017.

47 Jack Shuler. "The Ominous Symbolism of the Noose," *Los Angeles Times*, October 27, 2014, http://www.latimes.com/opinion/op-ed/la-oe-shuler-noose-hate-crimes-20141028-story.html.

48 Julia Glum, "Duke University Noose Incident Seen as 'Tipping Point' for Black Students Feeling Marginalized," *International Business Times*, April 2, 2015, http://www.ibtimes.com/duke-university-noose-incident-seen-tipping-point-black-students-feeling-marginalized-1868426, accessed June 11, 2017.

49   Linda Loyd, "2 Charged in Noose 'Prank.' The Pair Put a Rope around a Black Co-worker's Neck. They Said It Was 'in Good Fun,'" *Philadelphia Inquirer*, February 10, 1999, http://articles.philly.com/1999-02-10/news/25503973_1_noose-criminal-complaint-truck-driver, accessed August 9, 2015.

50   Keegan Hamilton, "Is the Noose an Inherently Racist Object?" *Riverfront Times*. September 10, 2000, http://www.riverfronttimes.com/newsblog/2010/09/10/is-the-noose-an-inherently-racist-object, accessed June 14, 2017.

51   Steven H. Foskett Jr., "Postal Officials Echo Concern about Noose in Worcester Branch," *Telegram* (Worcester, MA), November 12, 2014, http://www.telegram.com/article/20141113/NEWS/311139816, accessed June 13, 2017.

52   U.S. Equal Employment Opportunity Commission E-RACE (Eradicating Racism & Colorism from Employment), *Significant EEOC Race/Color Cases,* Government Report (Washington: U.S. Equal Employment Opportunity Commission), http://www.eeoc.gov/eeoc/initiatives/e-race/caselist.cfm#hostile, accessed June 13, 2017.

53   "Plead with Pleasant for Suppression of Lynching," *Times* (Shreveport, LA), April 29, 1918, 6.

54   "Accused Governor: Blease Has Made Many Enemies," *Houston Post,* July 19, 1912, 7.

55   "A Negro Burned in Kentucky," *Times-Picayune* (New Orleans, LA), December 7, 1899, 8.

56   "Lynching In Indiana," *Scranton Republican* (Scranton, PA), February 27, 1901, 1.

57   "The Murderer Hose at Bay," *Wilmington Messenger* (Wilmington, NC), April 15, 1899, 4.

58   Christopher Waldrep, ed., *Lynching in America: A History in Documents* (New York: New York University Press, 1999), 147.

59   Jacqueline M. Moore, *Booker T. Washington, W.E.B. Du Bois, and the Struggle for Racial Uplift* (Lanham, MD: Rowman & Littlefield, 2003), 194.

60   Diana Ramey Berry, *The Price of Their Pound of Flesh: The Value of the Enslaved from Womb to Grave in the Building of a Nation* (Boston: Beacon Press, 2017), 101.

61   Kenneth S. Greenberg, *Nat Turner: A Slave Rebellion in History and Memory* (New York: Oxford University Press, 2004), 20.

62   "Old Nat Turner Skinned," *Richmond Dispatch* (Richmond, VA), February 16, 1902.

63   "Down East Yankee Tanned Negro's Hide," *Tennessean* (Nashville, TN), March 3, 1907, 35.

64   "A Tewksbury Tale," *Semi-Weekly Citizen* (Asheville, NC), November 22, 1883, 1.

65   "Our Correspondents," *Times* (Clay Center, Kansas), November 1, 1883, 8.

66   *Bismarck Tribune* (Bismarck, ND), May 4, 1883, 7.

67   "A Tewksbury Tale," *Semi-Weekly Citizen* (Asheville, NC), November 22, 1883, 1.

68   "Tanned Human Skin," *Saint Paul Globe* (Saint Paul, MN), July 10, 1887, 21.

69   Ibid.

70   "Leather From Human Skin," *Oskaloosa Independent* (Oskaloosa, KS), October 29, 1887, 1.

71   "Shoes of Negroes' Skin," *Richmond Climax*, December 9, 1896.

72   "Negro Skin Wallet," *Union Republican* (Winston-Salem, NC), November 1, 1900, 1.

73   "Alton Woman to Have Rug of Setter's Hide," *St. Louis Post Dispatch*, December 15, 1912, 29.

CHAPTER SIX

1   Abel C. Thomas, *The Gospel of Slavery: A Primer of Freedom* (New York: T.W. Strong, 1864).

2   Esther Y. Lee, "Los Angeles Police Dogs Only Bit Blacks and Latinos in the First Six Months of 2013," *ThinkProgress*, October 10, 2013, https://thinkprogress.org/los-angeles-police-dogs-only-bit-blacks-and-latinos-in-the-first-six-months-of-2013-f70c01a349fd, accessed June 11, 2017.

3   Jennifer B. Pickens, *Pets at the White House: 50 Years of Presidents and Their Pets* (Dallas: Fife & Drum Press, 2012).

4   Roger Spottiswoode, *Turner & Hooch* (Touchstone Pictures, 1989); Matthew Robbins, *Bingo* (TriStar Pictures, 1991); Brian Levant, *Beethoven* (Universal Pictures, 1992); Stephen Harek, *101 Dalmatians* (Walt Disney Pictures, 1996); Brian Levant, *Snow Dogs* (Walt Disney Pictures, 2002); Wayne Wang, *Because of Winn-Dixie* (Twentieth Century Fox Film Corporation, 2005); Robert Vince, *Air Buddies* (Keystone Family Pictures, 2006); David Frankel, *Marley & Me* (Fox 2000 Pictures, 2008); Lasse Hallstrom, *Hachi: A Dog's Tale* (Stage 6 Films, 2009); Tom Dey, *Marmaduke* (Twentieth Century Fox Film Corporation, 2010); and Boaz Yakin, *Max* (Metro-Goldwyn-Mayer, 2015).

5   Spencer R. Crew et al., *Slave Culture: A Documentary Collection of the Slave Narratives from the Federal Writers' Project* (Santa Barbara: Greenwood, 2014), 971.

6   David Doddington, "Slavery and Dogs in the Antebellum South," *Sniffing the Past*, February 23, 2012, https://sniffingthepast.wordpress.com/2012/02/23/slavery-and-dogs-in-the-antebellum-south/, accessed June 11, 2017.

7   John H. Franklin and Loren Schweninger, *Runaway Slaves: Rebels on the Plantation* (New York: Oxford University Press, 1999), 164.

8   Frederick L. Olmsted, "A Journey in the Seaboard Slave State; with Remarks on their Economy," *Documenting the American South* (Chapel Hill: University of North Carolina, 2001, orig. 1856), 160–61, http://docsouth.unc.edu/nc/olmsted/olmsted.html#p160, accessed June 11, 2017.

9   Ibid., 161.

10   The Cuban bloodhound is presumed to be extinct. Information about the dog is difficult to find.

11   Franklin and Schweninger, *Runaway Slaves*, 161.

12   Sally E. Hadden, *Slave Patrols: Law and Violence in Virginia and the Carolinas* (Cambridge, MA: Harvard University Press, 2001).

13   Fergus M. Bordewich, *Bound for Canaan: The Underground Railroad and the War for the Soul of America* (New York: Amistad, 2005), 109–10.

14   Franklin and Schweninger, *Runaway Slaves*, 163.

15   "The Bloodhounds of Slavery," *Liberator* (Boston), March 23, 1855, 4.

16   Eric Foner, "Slavery in the Modern World: David Brion Davis's Pathbreaking Study of the Problem of Slavery," *Nation*, February 17, 2014, https://www.thenation.com/article/slavery-modern-world/, accessed June 11, 2017.

17   Carl N. Degler, *Neither Black nor White: Slavery and Race Relations in Brazil and the United States* (Madison: University of Wisconsin Press, 1971), 73.

18   Claude H. Nolen, *African American Southerners in Slavery, Civil War, and Reconstruction* (Jefferson, NC: McFarland, 1971), 81.

19   "Interview with Fountain Hughes, Baltimore, Maryland, June 11, 1949 (Transcription)," *Voices from the Days of Slavery*, June 11, 1949, http://hdl.loc.gov/loc.afc/afc9999001.t9990a, accessed June 11, 2017.

20   "From the WPA Slave Narratives: Charlie Moses Age 84," *Mississippi Slave Narratives from the WPA Records,* http://msgw.org/slaves/moses-xslave.htm, accessed June 11, 2017.

21   Arnold Arluke and Robert Bogdan, *Beauty and the Beast: Human-Animal Relations as Revealed in Real Photo Postcards, 1905–1935* (Syracuse: Syracuse University Press, 2010), 14.

22   "Horrors of the Peonage System," *Washington Times* (Washington, DC), March 20, 1904.

23   "An Open Letter from the Hon. Jay A. Hubbell," *Bismarck Tribune* (Bismarck, ND), November 5, 1880.

24   "A Breeder of 'Nigger Dogs,'" *St. Louis Post-Dispatch*, May 5, 1901, 21.

25   "The Nigger Dog: What an Atlanta, Ga., Man Says Regarding It. Runs Down Criminals," *Sedalia Weekly Democrat* (Sedalia, MO), May 10, 1901, 2.

26   "A Breeder of 'Nigger Dogs,'" *St. Louis Post-Dispatch*. May 5, 1901, 21.

27   "Most Exciting Hunt in Georgia Is the Man Hunt," *Tacoma Times*, March 28, 1910, 5.

28   "How Bloodhounds Are Trained at Prison," *Tennessean* (Nashville, TN), January 20, 1908, 3.

29   "Events at Hearne: Subscription for Buying 'Nigger Dogs,'" *Houston Post*, February 8, 1904, 7.

30   "Miscellaneous," *Houston Post*, November 11, 1910, 13.

31   Pamela S. King, "The Awful Legacy of Jim Crow," *Weld for Birmingham*, August 15, 2012, http://weldbham.com/blog/2012/08/15/the-awful-legacy-of-jim-crow/, accessed June 11, 2017.

32   "Police Helped by Dogs Halt Negro March," *Daily Telegram* (Eau Claire, WI), April 8, 1963, 1.

33   Joshunda Sanders, "Healing Fraught History of African Americans and Dogs," *The Bark,* http://thebark.com/content/healing-fraught-history-african-americans-and-dogs, accessed June 11, 2017.

34   Jack Hitt, "Police Dog Bites Black Man," *New Yorker*, March 18, 2015, http://www.newyorker.com/news/news-desk/police-dog-bites-black-man, accessed June 11, 2017.

35   Wallace McCutcheon and Edwin S. Porter, *The Watermelon Patch* (Edison Manufacturing Company, 1905); *The Slave, a Story of the South Before the War* aka *The Slave Hunt* (Vitagraph Company of America, 1907); Laurence Trimble, *Chased by Bloodhounds* (Vitagraph Company of America, 1912), Edgar Lewis, *The Nigger* (Fox Film Corporation, 1915); D.W. Griffith, *The Birth of a Nation* (David W. Griffith Corp, 1915); Harry A. Pollard, *Uncle Tom's Cabin* (Universal Pictures, 1927).

36   Melvin Van Peebles, *Sweet Sweetback's Baadasssss Song* (Yeah, 1971); Ivan Dixon, *The Spook Who Sat by the Door* (Bokari, 1973); Leon Gast, *When We Were Kings* (Das Films, 1996).

37   Samuel Fuller, *White Dog* (Paramount Pictures, 1982).

38   Charles Taylor, "White Dog 1982," *New York Times*, November 2, 2008, MT16.

39   Slarek, "The Dogs of Race War," *Cine Outsider*, April 13, 2014, http://www.cineoutsider.com/reviews/bluray/w/white_dog_br.html, accessed June 11, 2017.

40   Robert Mulligan, *To Kill a Mockingbird* (Universal International Pictures, 1962).

41   Josh Jones, "Albert Einstein Called Racism 'A Disease of White People' in His Little-Known Fight for Civil Rights," *Open Culture*, August 28, 2013, http://www.openculture.com/2013/08/albert-einstein-civil-rights-activist.html, accessed June 11, 2017.

42   These data are from the Mintel report (2011) as quoted in: Brent Toellner, "US Pet Ownership Statistical Breakdown," *KC Dog Blog*, November 12, 2012, http://btoellner.typepad.com/kcdogblog/2012/11/us-pet-ownership-statistical-breakdown.html, accessed June 11, 2017. Toellner also notes that black households are less likely to have cats: 36 percent for whites, 34 percent for Hispanics, and 14 percent for blacks.

43   Kenneth N. Robinson, *From Vick-Tim to Vick-Tory: The Fall and Rise of Michael Vick* (Houston: Strategic Book Publishing, 2013), 13.

44   D. Shannon, "Is Michael Vick a Clinically Diagnosable Psychopath or a Reformed Dogfighter?" *PETA Files*.

45   Susan Estrich, "In Defense of Speech You Hate" *Star-Democrat* (Easton, MD), March 15, 2013, 8.

46   Philip Caulfield, "Tucker Carlson: Michael Vick 'Should Have Been Executed' for Running Dogfighting Ring," *Daily News*, December 29, 2009, http://www.nydailynews.com/news/politics/tucker-carlson-michael-vick-executed-running-dogfighting-ring-video-article-1.469583, accessed June 13, 2017.

47   Dave Zirin, "Who Let the Dogs Out on Michael Vick?" *Nation*, July 19, 2007, http://www.thenation.com/article/who-let-dogs-out-michael-vick/, accessed June 13, 2017.

48   Melissa Harris-Perry, "Michael Vick, Racial History and Animal Rights," *Nation*, December 30, 2010, http://www.thenation.com/article/michael-vick-racial-history-and-animal-rights/, accessed June 12, 2017.

49 Michael Vick, *Finally Free: An Autobiography* (Brentworth, TN: Worthy Publishing, 2012).

50 Katy Waldman, "Black Dog Syndrome," *Slate*, http://www.slate.com/articles/health_and_science/science/2014/06/black_dog_syndrome_are_people_racist_against_black_pets.html, accessed June 12, 2017

51 Michael Anderson, *The Dam Busters* (Associated British Picture Corporation, 1955).

52 Martin Ritt, *Sounder* (Radnitz/Mattel Productions, 1972).

CHAPTER SEVEN

1 Taylor Hagood, *Faulkner's Imperialism: Space, Place, and the Materiality of Myth* (Baton Rouge: Louisiana State University Press), 140.

2 Keith Truesdell, *Chris Rock: Bring the Pain* (CR Enterprises, 1996).

3 Chris Rock, "Niggas vs. Black People," *Genius*, http://genius.com/Chris-rock-niggas-vs-black-people-annotated, accessed June 12, 2017.

4 Leonard Pitts Jr., an African American writer for the *Miami Herald*, was so frustrated with Chris Rock's persistent in-your-face use of the word "nigger" that he compared Rock's thinking to that of a slave and referred to Rock as a "mind maimer." Leonard Pitts Jr., "Chris Rock Is a Mind Maimer," *Democrat and Chronicle* (Rochester, NY), October 9, 2008, 10.

5 The first portion of this chapter is an updated version of an earlier paper. See David Pilgrim and Phillip Middleton, "Purposeful Venom Revisited," in *The Implications of Race and Racism*, ed. Gerald Matthews (New York: Farber, 1999), 91–93.

6 Dictionaries historically defined "nigger" as a synonym for Negro, black, or dark-skinned people. See, for example, Howard Wentworth, *American Dialect Dictionary* (New York: Thomas Y. Crowell Co., 1944). Recent dictionaries are more likely to mention that "nigger" is a term of contempt. See C.M. Williams, "Nigger," in *Kim Pearson's Dictionary of Slurs*, by Kim Pearson (2001), http://web.archive.org/web/20090223185954/http://kpearson.faculty.tcnj.edu/Dictionary/nigger.htm, accessed June 12, 2017; Richard T. Schaefer, *Racial and Ethnic Groups*, 8th edition (Upper Saddle River: Prentice Hall, 2000), 44.

7 Howard J. Ehrlich, *The Social Psychology of Prejudice: A Systematic Theoretical Review and Propositional Inventory of the American Social Psychological Study of Prejudice* (New York: Wiley, 1973), 22.

8 E. Palmore, "Ethnophaulisms and Ethnocentrism," *American Journal of Sociology* 67 (1962): 442–45.

9 Even innocent words—"boy," "girl," and "uncle"—took on racist meanings when applied to blacks.

10 Jonathon Green, *The Dictionary of Contemporary Slang* (New York: Stein and Day, 1984).

11 For a brief analysis of these terms see John A. Simpson and Edmund S. C. Weiner, *The Oxford English Dictionary*, 2nd edition (Oxford: Oxford University Press, 1989), 401–5.

12 *Mother Goose, Her Rhymes* (Akron, OH: Saalfield Publishing Company, 1915), 135.

13 Pik, "Of Knots and Kniggers," *niggermania.com*, http://niggermania.com/raptorman/essays/essay16.htm, accessed June 12, 2017.

14 Among the most popular white supremacy sites are tightrope.cc, vnnforum.com, and chimpout.wordpress.com, all accessed June 17, 2017.

15 Dwight N. Hopkins and George C.L. Cummings, *Cut Loose Your Stammering Tongue: Black Theology in the Slave Narratives*, 2nd edition (Louisville, KY: Westminster John Knox Press, 2003).

16 "Will Avert Race War," *Logan Republican* (Logan, UT), July 18, 1903.

17 "Alabama: Nigger Day in a Country Town," *New York Times*, November 30, 1874.

18 *Oakland Tribune*, September 25 1906.

19 Amiri Baraka, *Black Magic: Sabotage, Target Study, Black Art; Collected Poetry, 1961–1967* (Indianapolis: Bobbs-Merrill, 1969), 55.

20 Stephen E. Henderson, *Understanding the New Black Poetry: Black Speech and Black Music as Poetic References* (New York: William Morrow and Company, 1972), 223–25.

21 J. Douglas Allen-Taylor, "New Word Order," *Metro*, April 9–15, 1998, http://www.metroactive.com/papers/metro/04.09.98/cover/nigger-9814.html accessed June 11, 2017.

22 H. Lewis Smith, the author of *Bury That Sucka! A Scandalous Love Affair with the N-Word* (Baltimore: PublishAmerica, 2004), noted, "replacing the 'er' with an 'a' changes nothing other than the pronunciation."

23 Dave Sheinin and Krissah Thompson, "Redefining the Word: Examining a Racist Slur Entrenched in American Vernacular That Is More Prevalent Than Ever," *Washington Post*, November 9, 2014, 2015, http://www.washingtonpost.com/sf/national/2014/11/09/the-n-word-an-entrenched-racial-slur-now-more-prevalent-than-ever/, accessed June 12, 2017.

24 The false dichotomy between blacks or African Americans (respectable and middle-class) and niggers (disrespectable and lower class) is discussed in the section of this chapter that deals with the views of John Ridley.

25 If continued use of the word lessened its sting, then "nigger" would by now have no sting.

26 John Ridley, "The Manifesto of Ascendancy for the Modern American Nigger," *Esquire*, December, 2006.

27 Ibid.

28 Ibid.

29 "Michael Richards Spews Racial Hate—Kramer Racist Rant," *YouTube*, July 14, 2012, 2015, https://www.youtube.com/watch?v=BoLPLsQbdt0, accessed June 12, 2017.

30 Tom Leonard, "New York Bans the Word 'Nigger,'" *Telegraph*, March 2, 2007, http://www.telegraph.co.uk/news/worldnews/1544390/New-York-bans-the-word-nigger.html, accessed June 12, 2017.

31 Ed Pilkington, "New York City Council Bans Use of the N-Word," *Guardian*, March 1, 2007, http://www.theguardian.com/world/2007/mar/01/usa.edpilkington, accessed June 12, 2017.

32 "NAACP Funeral of the N-Word," *YouTube*, July 12, 2007, https://www.youtube.com/watch?v=reU0PXr7-Pk, accessed June 12, 2017.

33 "Skip & Stephen A on Riley Cooper Saying 'Nigger,'" *YouTube,* August 3, 2013, https://www.youtube.com/watch?v=yuCyXrqPuvY, accessed June 12, 2017.

34 Peter King, "Legislating Language: Will the NFL Ban the N-Word?" *Monday Morning Quarterback*, March 3, 2014, http://mmqb.si.com/2014/03/03/nfl-n-word-ban-monday-morning-quarterback, accessed October 27, 2015.

CHAPTER EIGHT

1 Audre Lorde, "The Uses of Anger" in *Sister Outsider: Essays and Speeches* (Freedom, CA: Crossing Press, 1984), 126.

2 Tim Grieve, "The Reddest Place in America," *Salon*, October 24, 2006, www.salon.com/2006/10/24/reddest_state/, accessed June 13, 2017.

3 "Post-Racial USA? Not So Fast," *CBS News*, November 15, 2008, http://www.cbsnews.com/news/post-racial-usa-not-so-fast/, accessed June 13, 2017.

4 Mark Ledwidge, Kavern Verney, and Inderjeet Parmar, *Barack Obama and the Myth of a Post-Racial America* (New York: Routledge, 2013), 85.

5 Rod Dreher, "The Crap Stories We Tell Our Kids," February 3, 2014, http://www.theamericanconservative.com/dreher/the-crap-stories-we-tell-our-kids/, accessed June 13, 2017.

Index

Page numbers in *italic* refer to illustrations. "Passim" (literally "scattered") indicates intermittent discussion of a topic over a cluster of pages.

torture, 127, 130, 133–34, 156–57, 161, 168, 173
toys, *65, 68,* 189. *See also* stuffed animals
trade cards, *22, 86, 96, 173*
The True Order of Man (Smith), 43, 45
T-shirts, *13, 58,* 59, 88, *93, 117, 146, 153*
Tucker, Darcy, 56
Tulane University, 63
Turner, Felton, *160*
Turner, Nat, 158–59

"Uncle Tom" (term), 32–33, 49, 199, 205
Uncle Tom caricature. *See* Tom caricature
Uncle Tom's Cabin (Stowe): adaptations, 178, *179*
Underground Railroad, 30
unemployment, 204–5
United Negro Improvement Association (UNIA), 48
Universal Pictures, 80
University of Alabama, 12–13, 224
University of California, San Diego, 90
University of Mississippi, 140, 142
University of Oklahoma, 89
University of Wisconsin, 90
U.S. Equal Employment Opportunity Commission, 63, 153, 155
U.S. Supreme Court, 49, 95, 144, 186, 198

valentines, *180*
Van Evrie, John H., 40–41
Van Peebles, Melvin: *Sweet Sweetback's Baadasssss Song,* 23, 178, 181; *Watermelon Man,* 83–84
Veitch, Tony, 52
Verner, Samuel Phillips, 46
Vick, Michael, 185–87, 211
video evidence, 35, 36, 37
violent black man (caricature). *See* brute caricature; razor-toting coon caricature
Virginia, 48, 113, 166, 170, 185, 198
Virginia Minstrels, 74
Vogt, Karl, 40
voting, 98, 108, 127, 142, 144, *157,* 224

Walker, George: "The Coon's Trade Mark," 98
Walker, Wyatt Tee, 177
Watermelon Man (Van Peebles) 83–84
watermelons, 19, 67–94, 98, 99, *167,* 178, 189, 242n49
Watermelon Woman (Dunye), 84
websites, xi, *153,* 198–99, 250n14
Weekes, Kevin, 56
Wells, Ida B., 130
West, Kanye, 202
West Virginia, 43, 45, 135
When We Were Kings, 181
whipping and beating. *See* corporal punishment
White, Phillip, 178
White, Walter, 245n4
White Dog (Gary): film adaptations, 181–84
whites disguised as blacks. *See* blackface
"white trash" (label), 5
Wilkins, Roy, 151
Williams, Bert, *83;* "The Coon's Trade Mark," 98
Williams, Serena, 52, 54
Williams, Venus, 52
Wilson, Darren, 178
Wilson, Woodrow, 9
Wisconsin, 155
Wittke, Carl, 74
Woods, Keith M., 69–70
World's Fair, Chicago, 1893. *See* Chicago World's Fair, 1893
World War II, *47*
Wormser, Richard, 8–9
Worrell, Peter, 56
Wright, Jeremiah, 226

X, Malcolm. *See* Malcolm X

Zip Coon, 73, 97, 103
zoo exhibits, Africans in. *See* Africans in zoo exhibits
Zulu Cannibal Giants, 118, 120

ABOUT PM PRESS

PM Press was founded at the end of 2007 by a small collection of folks with decades of publishing, media, and organizing experience. PM Press co-conspirators have published and distributed hundreds of books, pamphlets, CDs, and DVDs. Members of PM have founded enduring book fairs, spearheaded victorious tenant organizing campaigns, and worked closely with bookstores, academic conferences, and even rock bands to deliver political and challenging ideas to all walks of life. We're old enough to know what we're doing and young enough to know what's at stake.

We seek to create radical and stimulating fiction and non-fiction books, pamphlets, T-shirts, visual and audio materials to entertain, educate, and inspire you. We aim to distribute these through every available channel with every available technology— whether that means you are seeing anarchist classics at our bookfair stalls, reading our latest vegan cookbook at the café, downloading geeky fiction e-books, or digging new music and timely videos from our website.

PM Press is always on the lookout for talented and skilled volunteers, artists, activists, and writers to work with. If you have a great idea for a project or can contribute in some way, please get in touch.

PM Press
PO Box 23912
Oakland, CA 94623
www.pmpress.org

FRIENDS OF PM PRESS

Friends of PM allows you to directly help impact, amplify, and revitalize the discourse and actions of radical writers, filmmakers, and artists. It provides us with a stable foundation from which we can build upon our early successes and provides a much-needed subsidy for the materials that can't necessarily pay their own way. You can help make that happen—and receive every new title automatically delivered to your door once a month—by joining as a Friend of PM Press. And, we'll throw in a free T-shirt when you sign up.

- **$30 a month** Get all books and pamphlets plus 50% discount on all webstore purchases

- **$40 a month** Get all PM Press releases (including CDs and DVDs) plus 50% discount on all webstore purchases

- **$100 a month** Superstar—Everything plus PM merchandise, free downloads, and 50% discount on all webstore purchases

For those who can't afford $30 or more a month, we're introducing **Sustainer Rates** at $15, $10 and $5. Sustainers get a free PM Press T-shirt and a 50% discount on all purchases from our website.

Your Visa or Mastercard will be billed once a month, until you tell us to stop. Or until our efforts succeed in bringing the revolution around. Or the financial meltdown of Capital makes plastic redundant. Whichever comes first.

Understanding Jim Crow:
Using Racist Memorabilia to Teach Tolerance and Promote Social Justice

David Pilgrim with a foreword by Henry Louis Gates Jr.

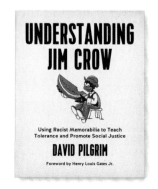

ISBN: 978-1-62963-114-1
$21.95   208 pages

For many people, especially those who came of age after landmark civil rights legislation was passed, it is difficult to understand what it was like to be an African American living under Jim Crow segregation in the United States. Most young Americans have little or no knowledge about restrictive covenants, literacy tests, poll taxes, lynchings, and other oppressive features of the Jim Crow racial hierarchy. Even those who have some familiarity with the period may initially view racist segregation and injustices as mere relics of a distant, shameful past. A proper understanding of race relations in this country must include a solid knowledge of Jim Crow—how it emerged, what it was like, how it ended, and its impact on the culture.

Understanding Jim Crow introduces readers to the Jim Crow Museum of Racist Memorabilia, a collection of more than ten thousand contemptible collectibles that are used to engage visitors in intense and intelligent discussions about race, race relations, and racism. The items are offensive. They were meant to be offensive. The items in the Jim Crow Museum served to dehumanize blacks and legitimized patterns of prejudice, discrimination, and segregation.

Using racist objects as teaching tools seems counterintuitive—and, quite frankly, needlessly risky. Many Americans are already apprehensive discussing race relations, especially in settings where their ideas are challenged. The museum and this book exist to help overcome our collective trepidation and reluctance to talk about race.

Fully illustrated, and with context provided by the museum's founder and director David Pilgrim, *Understanding Jim Crow* is both a grisly tour through America's past and an auspicious starting point for racial understanding and healing.

"One of the most important contributions to the study of American history that I have ever experienced."
—Henry Louis Gates Jr., director of the W.E.B. Du Bois Institute for African American Research

"This was a horrific time in our history, but it needs to be taught and seen and heard. This is very well done, very well done."
—Malaak Shabazz, daughter of Malcolm X and Betty Shabazz

"The museum's contents are only a small part of the damaging effects of the Jim Crow laws that were found all across America, including bright and sunny California. This history is not only an important part of understanding where America was but, in an age of states making it harder and harder for citizens to vote, it is relevant to note that we have been here before."
—Henry Rollins, host of the History Channel's *10 Things You Don't Know About*